THE PAPERS & THE PAPERS

Books by Sanford J. Ungar

THE ALMOST REVOLUTION: FRANCE—1968 *(with Allan Priaulx)*

THE PAPERS & THE PAPERS: An Account of the Legal and Political Battle Over the Pentagon Papers

FBI: An Uncensored Look Behind the Walls

AFRICA: The People and Politics of an Emerging Continent

ESTRANGEMENT: America and the World *(editor)*

The Papers & The Papers

AN ACCOUNT
OF THE LEGAL AND POLITICAL BATTLE
OVER THE PENTAGON PAPERS

BY
SANFORD J. UNGAR

COLUMBIA UNIVERSITY PRESS ★ NEW YORK

A portion of this book was published in *Esquire*.

Columbia University Press Morningside Edition 1989
Columbia University Press
New York   Guildford, Surrey
Copyright © 1972, 1989 by Sanford J. Ungar
All rights reserved

Library of Congress Cataloging-in-Publication Data

Ungar, Sanford J.
The papers & the papers
an account of the legal and political battle over the Pentagon Papers
Sanford J. Ungar.
—Columbia University Press Morningside ed.
p.   cm.
Reprint, with new pref. Originally published: Pbk. ed. New York :
Dutton, 1975, c1972. Includes index.
ISBN 0-231-06948-0 (alk. paper). —ISBN 0-231-06949-9 (pbk. : alk. paper)
1. New York Times (Firm)—Trials, litigation, etc.
2. Ellsberg, Daniel—Trials, litigation, etc.
3. Russo, Anthony J. (Anthony Joseph)—Trials, litigation, etc.
4. Freedom of the press—United States.
5. Pentagon Papers.
I. Title.   II. Title: Papers and the papers.
KF224.N39U54   1989   88-38764
323.44'5'0973—dc19   CIP

Printed in the United States of America
Casebound editions of Columbia University Press books are Smyth-sewn
and are printed on permanent and durable acid-free paper

For Beth

[PREFACE TO THE MORNINGSIDE EDITION]

Many events quite naturally fade in significance with the passage of time; but after nearly two decades, the publication of the Pentagon Papers and the epic legal struggle surrounding that journalistic decision have, in many respects, grown in importance. Looked back upon from the end of the Reagan administration in the late 1980s, the early 1970s stand out as a time when the American press was under serious and genuine threat from the American government and when, perhaps as a result, the press was uniquely willing to stand up to authority. The episode described in this book remains an emblem of that era of confrontation. Moreover, as I explain in the prologue to this edition, it is now apparent that the Watergate affair probably would not have occurred—and Richard Nixon's presidency therefore might not have ended prematurely—if it were not for the bitter conflict over the Pentagon Papers.

Those were exciting and frightening days, as anyone involved in them remembers. Many things have changed, of course—including the composition of the Supreme Court—but it is not at all clear that the media would have the stamina for a battle so bitter and on so many fronts, were it to occur today. The ease with which Ronald Reagan was able to dictate the agenda for the national media and the seemingly uncritical coverage he received have, for the most part, rendered confrontation irrelevant and unnecessary.

So it is that, for reasons that go beyond the nostalgia a reporter feels for one of his biggest stories, I am offering this book once again to the public and to students of American government and journalism. With the exception of a few minor corrections that were made for a paperback edition published in 1975, the main body of the book appears here as originally published in 1972. Several new sections, however, have been added—the prologue, the epilogue, and an appendix tracing the later paths of the people originally caught up in this drama. At a moment when the bicentennial of the United States Constitution seems to have been observed mostly on cereal boxes and at fireworks displays, the retelling of this story may make a contribution to thoughtful discussions of how to keep the First Amendment alive and vibrant. At a minimum, I hope that by reexamining the details of one landmark case, we can all be moved to remember that freedom of the press is not automatically self-preserving, but must be vigorously defended.

For his encouragement to have this book republished, I am especially grateful to James L. Baughman, a distinguished historian of American journalism. My agent, Robert Lescher, and Ann Miller of Columbia University Press have been generous with their time and energy on this project. The material for the additions comes in part from my coverage for *The Washington Post* of the criminal trial of Daniel Ellsberg and Anthony Russo (which occurred after this book was originally published), from my subsequent book about the FBI, and from my writings on related issues for a number of magazines and newspapers. But my own ongoing ruminations about the Pentagon Papers case have also benefited greatly from the insights of my students in a seminar on the news media and foreign policy at the School of Communication of American University. For some of the work in the trenches that made the new sections here possible, I particularly thank Marta Cleaveland, Erik Kopp, and John Mies.

Sanford J. Ungar

Washington
November 1988

[PREFACE]

This book is intended as a portrait of people and institutions under stress, a chronicle of what I believe to have been a period of critical importance in the relationship between the American government and the press.

My research began when the Pentagon Papers first broke on the public in *The New York Times* and when I covered the Justice Department's case against *The Washington Post* in the federal courts of the District of Columbia. I subsequently relied on available documents and transcripts, as well as personal interviews with most of the principals involved with the Pentagon Papers, their compilation, disclosure, and publication, and the litigation that followed. They, and others who gave me the benefit of their observations and insights, were often reluctant to be cited for the information they provided; some were insistent that even the fact that they had spoken with me remain confidential, at least until the dust has settled on the confrontation surrounding the Papers. On these grounds I beg indulgence where attribution has not been possible.

I am grateful to my sources for their candor and their willingness to discuss events and issues. Rather than name some, I am imposing anonymity on them all. I do want to acknowledge, however, the vital contributions of a few people to this project. The editors of *The Washington Post* have been generous, not only in granting me the time and freedom to write this book, but also in recognizing that one of their reporters has the right and the obligation to report on the newspaper for which he works as well as other institutions. Peter Shepherd has given unselfishly of his time and his knowledge from the very start. Hal Scharlatt has been a patient and helpful editor. Beverly Pollock has listened and read with enormous sensitivity and devotion. Anthony Furano's nightly stops for cognac and commiseration were a great source of strength. My wife Beth has made many and significant sacrifices for this book, with profound and delicate understanding.

Sanford J. Ungar

Washington
February 1972

THE PAPERS & THE PAPERS

[PROLOGUE]

The legal and political struggle between the government and the press detailed in this book is just one part of the uproar set off by publication in June 1971 of the Pentagon Papers, the top secret Defense Department history of the role of the United States in Southeast Asia. It was almost two years after the Papers became public (and a year after this book originally appeared) that the nation finally learned just how seriously the Nixon administration had viewed the alleged breach of security at the heart of the whole affair—seriously enough to establish an extralegal investigative unit operating out of the White House, which came to be known as "the plumbers."

Members of that unit first became famous (and went to jail) because they had burglarized the offices of the Democratic National Committee in Washington's Watergate office complex in June 1972, as part of a political espionage operation on behalf of President Richard M. Nixon's re-election campaign. But there is much we know now that we did not know then: for example, that the plumbers were actually created and put to work as a result of the unauthorized publication of the Pentagon Papers; their nickname, in fact, came from their original mission of probing and plugging just such leaks of government information.

Nixon and his close aides, it turned out, did not trust J. Edgar Hoover, the aging and aloof director of the Federal Bureau of Investigation, to conduct a thorough criminal investigation of how the Papers got into the hands of the press. Indeed, Hoover, knowing how rarely the government succeeded with such prosecutions, believed that a "leak case" of this sort should be the primary responsibility of the department where the leak had occurred; he felt it was a waste of FBI agents' precious time and expertise to pursue these matters.

But there was another wrinkle, too: once Daniel Ellsberg, formerly of the Defense Department and the Rand Corporation, had been identified as the probable source of the documents published in *The New York Times* and other newspapers, the Bureau's Domestic Intelligence Division (as it was then called) recommended that Hoover permit agents in New York to interview Ellsberg's father-in-law, millionaire toy manufacturer Louis Marx. Special permission was required, because Hoover and Marx were casual acquaintances and at Christmastime Marx often sent the bachelor director a large shipment of free toys to distribute to the children of friends and to his favorite charities. Hoover, ever more crotchety and protective of this special relationships (indeed, less than a year away from his death), officially denied the permission to interview the toy magnate — although in fact agents had already visited the politically conservative Marx, who was no great admirer of his son-in-law. When Nixon's aides got wind of Hoover's refusal, they were furious.

After the Supreme Court ruled against the administration's

effort to suspend publication of articles based on the documents, Nixon, who was convinced that there was a conspiracy at work, decided that the White House would have to conduct its own investigation parallel to what the Justice Department was doing. Especially because the case seemed to present an opportunity to discredit the New Left and to reveal its connections to possible Democratic presidential candidates, there was a high premium on obtaining personal information about Ellsberg himself—including what E. Howard Hunt, Jr., the chief of the plumbers, later described as "some rather bizarre sexual practices" and "a very unusual life style."

When Ellsberg's former psychoanalyst, Dr. Lewis Fielding of Beverly Hills, declined to be interviewed by the FBI (or, in keeping with ethical guidelines, even to acknowledge that this controversial figure had been his patient), the White House turned to the Central Intelligence Agency for a psychiatric profile of Ellsberg drawn from public sources and the limited information in government files. But the result there proved to be disappointing; while acknowledging that Ellsberg had probably been passing through a mid-life crisis and found himself "not nearly having achieved the prominence and success he expected and desired," the head of the psychiatric unit at the CIA noted that in making the Papers public Ellsberg "seemed to be responding to what he deemed a higher order of patriotism" and "saw himself as having a special mission." There was certainly nothing very sinister about that.

Dissatisfied, and feeling increasingly panicked over other leaks of national security information, the White House team supervising the plumbers (including Nixon's top adviser on domestic policy, John D. Ehrlichman) decided it was time to take more drastic steps. In the naive belief that they could obtain the truth behind Ellsberg's political and emotional motivations, and the identity of any accomplices, from his psychoanalyst's files, Hunt and G. Gordon Liddy, a former FBI agent known for his strange bravado, flew to Los Angeles in August 1971 to conduct a

[5]

"feasibility and vulnerability study" for a "bag job"—a surreptitious entry—at Fielding's office. They returned to Washington with an optimistic report and obtained permission from the White House to do the deed. They were promptly equipped by the CIA with intelligence paraphernalia and false identity cards.

A few weeks later, on September 3, 1971, accompanied by a team of Cuban exiles from Miami who were opposed to Fidel Castro and willing to do anything in the cause of anticommunism, these agents of the Nixon White House conducted a simple burglary at Fielding's office. (Actually, it was a botched burglary; they had to break in through another office when they found the door to the building locked.) Once again, the results were not very impressive. Although they took some pictures to prove they had been there, the plumbers found nothing special about Ellsberg in Fielding's files. They came back empty-handed. The White House would have to rely on ordinary channels and procedures—and a vigorous, perhaps overzealous prosecution at that—to deal with the man Nixon regarded as such a menace.

However, the plumbers' actions against Ellsberg (including their later attempt to assault him during an antiwar demonstration on the steps of the U.S. Capitol in May 1972) were not without effect. Their burglary at Fielding's office ended up destroying the government's case against Ellsberg and Anthony J. Russo, Jr., the old friend from Vietnam who had helped him photocopy the Pentagon Papers. (Russo, in fact, was the only person who ever spent any time in prison in connection with release of the Pentagon Papers—for his refusal to testify in secret before a federal grand jury in Los Angeles.)

Here is how it happened:

Ellsberg had first been indicted for violating the Espionage Act and for converting government documents to his own use on June 28, 1971—in what many observers assumed was an effort by the Justice Department to influence the Supreme Court, which was still weighing its decision in the civil case against the newspapers at the time. But a superseding indictment was returned in Los Angeles six months later, increasing the charges (and potential penalties) against Ellsberg and adding Russo as a defendant. The Justice Department still claimed that Ellsberg had violated the Espionage Act and now also accused him of stealing government property. Because of the way Russo was charged, as the recipient of stolen property, his conviction could have set a dangerous precedent for any journalist who ever accepted a leak of classified information from a government official.

It was the long, drawn-out proceedings on that indictment which provided a new round of theater surrounding the Pentagon Papers and the last great trial of the 1960s and 1970s antiwar movement. The steely government prosecutors planned to make quick work of what they claimed to believe was a cut-and-dried case, while the ideologically committed defense lawyers wanted to put the Nixon administration and the Vietnam war on trial.

After nearly six months of pretrial arguments, jury selection got underway in June 1972 (the month of the Watergate break-in) in the Los Angeles courtroom of U.S. District Judge William Matthew Byrne, Jr., himself a former federal prosecutor whose conduct of the case could profoundly affect his future career. There were weeks of public interviews and challenges of prospective jurors by the defense and the prosecution, efforts to determine whether people who worked for the military-related industries pervasive in Southern California, for example, could possibly be fair in evaluating such a controversial case.

A jury had finally been empaneled by late July and opening statements in the trial were about to begin, when the prosecutors suddenly disclosed that there had been a government "interception"—presumably in a national security-related wiretap —of a conversation by one of the defendants, their lawyers, or their consultants. Byrne refused to halt the case for a special hearing on the intercept, as did the Ninth U.S. Circuit Court of Appeals; but the Supreme Court's leading civil libertarian, Justice William O. Douglas, who had jurisdiction over emergency appeals in the Ninth Circuit, agreed to hear arguments on the issue at a courtroom in Yakima, Washington, near his summer home. The day after the arguments, Douglas decided to stop the trial altogether until the full Supreme Court could rule on the matter. When the high court members declined to convene in a special session, Byrne had to excuse the jury until October.

It was November 1972—and Nixon had been re-elected—before the full Supreme Court decided not to hear the defense's appeal of the rulings on the interception; Byrne, warned by the Ninth Circuit Court that "it would be foolish" to proceed with the same jurors, potentially tainted by publicity on the case, agreed to dismiss them and start over again. By the time the trial did resume, on January 17, 1973 (a second jury having been selected much more quickly), the Watergate burglars were themselves already on trial in Washington.

The testimony droned on for months, as the case turned into a battle of experts over whether disclosure of the Papers constituted a threat to national security. With other dramatic issues in the news (including the negotiations to end the war in Vietnam and the first release and return of American prisoners of war), the trial attracted much less public attention than had been anticipated; but it seemed to be going reasonably well for Ellsberg and Russo, with the government unable to sustain its ambitious case against them.

Then, on April 26, came the bombshell: that the Watergate prosecutors in Washington had learned eleven days earlier about the plumbers' 1971 burglary at Fielding's office. It was obviously, at the very least, an outrageous investigative tactic and a violation of various people's rights. Nonetheless, Byrne seemed at first reluctant to grant a mistrial and dismiss the charges, to throw the case out after so much time and energy had gone into it; the prosecutors, for their part, insisted that the government's misconduct had had no effect whatever on their evidence or their performance. But then, after it was further revealed that

[8]

Ellsberg himself had actually been overheard in ostensibly
gal wiretaps on government officials and reporters betv
1969 and 1971 (and that the logs of these wiretaps were missing), Byrne finally reached his limit; he dismissed the charges
entirely on May 11, 1973.*

There was yet another dramatic revelation of impropriety in
the final days of the trial, this one implicating the judge himself.
On April 30, the *Washington Star-News* reported that several
weeks earlier, on a short court day, Byrne had traveled to
Nixon's Western White House at San Clemente to discuss with
the president and Ehrlichman the possibility of becoming FBI
director; a subsequent meeting with Ehrlichman alone had taken
place on a park bench in Santa Monica, at Byrne's request, two
days later. The strong suggestion was that the administration
had been dangling in front of Byrne a job that he was known to
want, and that Byrne, at a minimum, was willing to listen.

Thus did the Pentagon Papers case ruin, or at least truncate,
another career. Byrne, a Democrat who was popular among
such Republicans as Attorney General Richard G. Kleindienst
(whom he had come to know while in Washington serving as
executive director of the Scranton Commission on Campus Unrest in 1970), had been seen as a golden boy who might well be
able to clean up the mess Hoover had left at the FBI. Byrne
had followed in his father's footsteps when he was named to the
U.S. District Court in Los Angeles, but he was not expected to
remain there long; he was ambitious for a major job that would
take him back to Washington. Byrne insisted that he had done
nothing improper and had discussed only the length and timing
of the trial with Ehrlichman. Yet after such an indiscretion, he
was never seriously considered again for another high appointment. Byrne had been on the federal trial court in Los Angeles

* An excellent account of the trial of Ellsberg and Russo and the events
surrounding it can be found in *Test of Loyalty: Daniel Ellsberg and the Rituals
of Secret Government,* by Peter Schrag (New York: Simon and Schuster,
1974).

for just a few weeks at the time the Pentagon Papers were published; there he would remain.

Ellsberg and Russo, to their dismay, were never formally acquitted of the grave charges against them. The government's misbehavior, ironically, denied them that privilege. Watergate, with its nationally televised hearings, became the main spectacle beginning in the summer of 1973.

In one of several sideshows, Ehrlichman, Liddy, and White House aides Egil Krogh, Jr. and David R. Young were indicted by a Los Angeles grand jury in September 1973 for their involvement in the Fielding burglary. In March 1974, a federal grand jury in Washington indicted Ehrlichman, Liddy, White House special counsel Charles W. Colson, and two of the Cubans on similar charges; the Los Angeles indictment was dropped, to permit a trial in Washington.

On July 12, 1974, Ehrlichman, Liddy, and the Cubans were found guilty of conspiracy to violate Fielding's civil rights. Colson pleaded guilty to obstructing justice; Krogh had already at that point served six months in prison after pleading guilty to a lesser charge of conspiracy filed in November 1973. Young was granted immunity for his testimony and became the only person connected to the plumbers to escape being prosecuted for a crime.

In August 1974, of course, in the midst of impeachment proceedings, Nixon resigned the presidency.

[CHAPTER I]

Steve Terry, on his way home to Vermont for a vacation, stopped overnight with relatives on Long Island on Saturday June 12, 1971. Getting up the next morning, he was stunned to see on the front page of *The New York Times* an extraordinary article on the war in Vietnam, the first in an extended series. An aide to Vermont Republican George D. Aiken, longest-serving member of his party in the U.S. Senate, Terry reflected for only a few minutes before realizing that "this must be it."

That weekend Katharine Graham, publisher of the *Times*'s rival, *The Washington Post*, had several guests at her farm in rural Virginia, including columnist Clayton Fritchey and Charles Bohlen, former American Ambassador to France and the Soviet Union. The Sunday edition of the *Post* carried a handsome full-color photograph of Tricia Nixon and Edward

Finch Cox at their White House wedding, and a comprehensive account of that event filled the entire upper half of the newspaper's front page. Mrs. Graham had learned a few hours in advance of publication that the *Times* would be carrying a spectacular scoop that Sunday morning, sure to distract her guests' attention from the *Post*. She sent into nearby Warrenton for ten copies of the *Times*.

There was a run on the Sunday edition of the *Times* in Cambridge, Massachusetts, which was in the customary post-exam, precommencement doldrums of a university town. Daniel Ellsberg, a senior research associate at the Massachusetts Institute of Technology's Center for International Studies, saw the big news in the copy of the *Times* delivered to his Hilliard Street apartment and hurried to Harvard Square to buy extra copies of the paper. Friends later recalled seeing him, his arms loaded down with newspapers and "a big beaming smile" on his face.

At Leslie Gelb's home off the George Washington Memorial Parkway between Alexandria and Mount Vernon, Virginia, the *Times* was slipped into an old-fashioned mailbox at the end of the driveway on the morning of June 13. Getting up at about 8 A.M., the man who had been commissioned by former Secretary of Defense Robert S. McNamara to supervise the compilation of a "History of U.S. Decision-Making Process on Vietnam Policy, 1945–1967," picked up the *Post* at his doorstep and went out to the mailbox for the *Times*. By the time he returned to the house, Gelb was gazing dumbstruck at the front page of the *Times*. He said to his wife: "My God, there it is."

"It"—eagerly anticipated for a few weeks by some, much dreaded by others—was more than six pages of news stories and documents based on the forty-seven-volume study of the Vietnam war directed by Gelb. The lead article, by *Times* reporter Neil Sheehan (whose "investigative reporting" was credited as the basis for the news break), described what would come to be known throughout the world as the Pentagon Papers and listed their conclusions: that the administration of President Harry S Truman "directly involved" the United States in Indochina by aiding France in its colonial war there; that the Eisenhower administration played a "direct role" in undermining the Geneva settlement of 1954; that President John F. Kennedy expanded American involvement into a "broad commitment"; that the Johnson administration waged a covert war and planned an overt one long before revealing it to Congress or the public; and that consistent with the forecasts of government intelligence agents the controversial American bombing of North Vietnam was utterly ineffective in relieving pressure on American and South Vietnamese troops. Sheehan focused in the first installment on the "pivotal period" leading up to the Gulf of Tonkin incidents in August 1964. He described the build-up of a secret "provocation strategy" and the drafting of a congressional resolution as a blank check for escalation to be held in reserve.

The story revealed such internal government documents as a brutally frank 1964 memorandum by John T. McNaughton, then Assistant Secretary of Defense for International Security Affairs, assessing American goals in South Vietnam as "70 pct.— To avoid a humiliating U.S. defeat . . . 20 pct.—to keep SVN [South Vietnamese] territory from Chinese hands. 10 pct.—To permit the people of SVN to enjoy a better, freer way of life. Also—To emerge from crisis without unacceptable taint from methods used. NOT—To 'help a friend,' although it would be hard to stay in if asked out."

The first Sheehan article and a companion one by *Times* reporter Hedrick Smith describing the compilation of the study—the opening round in what would become one of the most dramatic conflicts between press and government in American history—emerged in the *Times* after a process of nearly three months' duration, intended to insure that the Pentagon Papers story would be handled in what the news-

[13]

paper's reporters and editors proudly call "the *Times* way." Four reporters, three copy editors, and an arsenal of support personnel had been hidden away for most of that time on the eleventh floor of the New York Hilton Hotel under a security guard rivaling that of the Pentagon itself. They read, sorted out, filed, and analyzed some 7,000 pages of the Pentagon Papers, then fought one another and their superiors over the significance of each portion and how to organize the series based on the Papers. This arduous and agonizing process might have gone on for several weeks more had not *Times* publisher Arthur Ochs Sulzberger made plans to fly to London for a board meeting on the weekend of June 13 and then to vacation in Europe with his family; the publisher had set that weekend as a deadline for major decisions concerning the Papers. Sulzberger gave the final go-ahead only in a last-minute meeting in his office on Friday morning June 11.

Disclosure of the Pentagon Papers was by any standard a major event in journalism and publishing. Here was a study compiled within the government and available, surely, only through an unprecedented breach of security—a study that brought together more than twenty years of decision-making and revealed that the American people had been systematically misled by their elected and appointed leaders.

Steve Terry for one was not altogether surprised to read the *Times* stories. As the staff aide who helps Senator Aiken with his work as ranking minority member of the Senate Foreign Relations Committee, Terry had attended a recent hearing at which Senators J. William Fulbright (D-Ark.) and Stuart Symington (D-Mo.) had pummeled Secretary of Defense Melvin R. Laird with questions about the existence of such a study. Rumors had circulated through committee ranks that Fulbright and some of his personally faithful staff already had access to a Vietnam report that would cause an uproar if released. Terry, like others in the congressional world who follow the media carefully, had also noticed that "Sheehan's byline had disappeared from the *Times* for about three months, so something had to be going on." The Senate aide's first reaction on reading the stories that Sunday morning was that the Pentagon Papers must have been made available deliberately by a source within the government: "My assumption was that it was a Defense Department leak on behalf of this administration, which could not be hurt by the contents."

The theory that the Nixon administration had purposefully leaked the Pentagon Papers was promptly and easily discounted, however, if only because the *Times* story came as such a complete shock to much of the rest of the American journalistic community. Mrs. Graham's discovery of the publication of the Pentagon Papers stories on Saturday night (from *Times* vice president James Reston, a close friend, whose son's wedding she was attending at a nearby Virginia farm) was the first relief for the *Post*, whose editors had been trying for days to discover what was going on at the *Times*. Only a few days before the *Times* story broke, former Secretary of Defense McNamara got word to friends at the *Post* that he had heard its rival was about to publish something detrimental to him, but he did not furnish details; Stan Carter, a reporter from the New York *Daily News*, incited brief panic at the *Post* when he passed along to Chalmers M. Roberts the rumor that the *Times* was about to release something so astonishing that it "could end the war." Tipped off by another journalist friend about one possibility, Ben H. Bagdikian, assistant managing editor for national affairs at the *Post*, phoned Henry Rowen, president of the Rand Corporation in Santa Monica, California, on Saturday morning June 12 to ask whether the defense-oriented think tank had ever produced a study advising the American government against overcommitment in Vietnam. Rowen said no—but he wished Rand had done something like that—and the *Post* remained absolutely stymied.

Late Saturday night Bagdikian called the national desk at

the *Post* and received the same information that had just been confirmed to Katharine Graham. As intense competitors, the *Times* and the *Post* have a permanent arrangement with United Press International: every night, as soon as the early editions hit the street in New York and Washington, the UPI wirephoto service transmits to each newspaper an instant photograph of the other's front page. The picture that arrived at the *Post* carried an impressive two-deck headline across four columns at the top of the page—"Vietnam Archive: Pentagon Study Traces 3 Decades of Growing U.S. Involvement." Bagdikian had only one choice; he summoned the *Post's* top reporters covering the White House, the State Department, and the Pentagon into his office on Sunday morning to begin the humiliating chore of rewriting what had already appeared in the *Times* and running it a day late.

For Leslie Gelb there was no humiliation, only panic. "I was nearly paralyzed," he said later, remembering his reaction of Sunday June 13. "I knew what was in there and what could be coming, what they had available to print. My anxiety was very personal. Rather than thinking about the fate of the nation, I was thinking about the fate of Leslie Gelb. . . . During the early part of the day, I couldn't bring myself to read the documents, but I read the [news] stories over and over again." Gelb made about six phone calls that morning seeking the advice of close friends, among them Morton H. Halperin, a former colleague on the faculty at Harvard who had been instrumental in luring Gelb away from a job on Capitol Hill to a position in the Defense Department in June 1967. A lawyer friend urged Gelb not to say anything publicly about the Pentagon Papers and their disclosure, at least until the air cleared. Affecting calm and avoiding the telephone, Gelb then went bicycling with his wife and three children for several hours. But he was convinced, for that day at least, that "life wouldn't be the same for a long time to come."

Like Leslie Gelb, officials of *The New York Times* were confident that once the story of the Pentagon Papers broke, the official reaction would be immediate and overwhelming. The *Times* reporters assigned to the Papers were still burrowed away at the New York Hilton over the weekend (Sheehan had not yet completed the third installment, scheduled to appear on Tuesday June 15). Max Frankel, a long-time diplomatic correspondent who was now Washington bureau chief for the *Times,* stayed on in his office Saturday night. Frankel's wife wanted to go to a movie, but he was adamant about remaining, feeling certain that he would have to be prepared for "a quick government response." Not until he got a call from New York to say that the presses were running did Frankel break the aura of mystery among Sheehan's own colleagues in the bureau, posting a notice on the bulletin board explaining that the Pentagon Papers were the basis for the three months of intrigue in the office. Only the reporters gave Frankel the immediate vocal response he was expecting. Even on Sunday, when Frankel again manned his emergency post all day long, the *Times's* great journalistic coup was met with dead silence from the outside world. "We were just flabbergasted," Frankel admits.

Most flabbergasting of all, perhaps, was the fact that the rest of the American press—except the few newspapers that began rewriting the *Times* stories—virtually ignored the Pentagon Papers on Sunday June 13. Many of the newspaper clients of *The New York Times* news service, who were given an early exclusive start, made little of the story: the Portland *Oregonian* waited more than a week before running the articles on the Papers; the Chicago *Tribune* did not use them at all and later ran a front-page editorial questioning the disclosure of classified material. United Press International waited until Sunday afternoon to put its first item about the Papers on the wire; although a few hundred words long, the story was not included in UPI's daily "budget" of the most important news. The country's largest news organization, the Associated

Press, carried nothing at all until Monday afternoon, and not one of its 4,500 subscribers in the United States (who frequently complain if a baseball score is late on the wire) raised a protest in the meantime. *Time* and *Newsweek* magazines learned of the *Times's* scoop Saturday night just as their editions for the following week were closing, but the editors of both decided against making an expensive last-minute change. NBC featured the Pentagon Papers as the lead item on its Sunday night news, but the other television networks were silent. Senator Hubert Humphrey (D-Minn.), who had been Vice President during much of the period covered by the Papers, was not asked a single question about the *Times* articles during an appearance on ABC's "Issues and Answers." Nor was Defense Secretary Melvin Laird, a guest on CBS's "Face the Nation," although anticipating that he would be, Laird had conferred on the telephone in advance with Attorney General John N. Mitchell. CBS diplomatic correspondent Marvin Kalb, after seeing the *Times* in Washington on Sunday morning, called his office to urge that something be done on the air about the Papers; the idea was vetoed in New York.

Times officials later conceded that they had probably softened the immediate impact of disclosing the Pentagon Papers by putting a general, unspectacular lead on Sheehan's first article, but they had nonetheless expected more attention.

If anyone was surprised by the appearance of the Papers that Sunday, and disappointed by the low-key reaction, it was Daniel Ellsberg, who had worked relentlessly for almost two years to see that they were put before the public. All his work notwithstanding, he was shocked to see Sheehan's story published without prior notice to him. Although Ellsberg was not at first linked publicly to the *Times* stories, many people connected with the Papers thought of him immediately as the one person among those who had worked on compiling the forty-seven volume study with the strongest and most openly expressed views against American involvement in Southeast Asia. ("From the start, I thought it was Dan," Gelb said months later. "He had access and the disposition to do it. Dan was in that realm of the inconceivable . . . of all the people I knew who worked on Vietnam, he was far and away the most intense about it.") Ellsberg thought that the link would become obvious soon enough—too many people had been involved for it to remain a secret indefinitely—but he wanted the publicity to be on his own terms, and he was not quite ready. He sat tight for a few days, as rumors began to circulate, but by the time two *Newsweek* reporters interviewed him on Wednesday June 16 the heat was on. Ellsberg left his apartment after the *Newsweek* interview, checked into the Fenway Motor Inn along the Charles River in Cambridge under a fictitious name, and was not to surface again until he had become a national celebrity.

The Nixon administration moved more slowly than Ellsberg, Gelb, the *Times*, or anyone else expected. There was scarcely a word from the White House about the first stories in the *Times* series. Attorney General Mitchell read the articles that Sunday but did not bother summoning Robert C. Mardian, trusted chief of the Justice Department's Internal Security Division, which would later become involved, back from a trip to Southern California. The investigation—which would eventually reach around the world—could wait for the start of a regular business week.

The calm was not to last long. The disclosure of the Pentagon Papers and subsequent developments became, in the words of former Defense Secretary Clark Clifford, "an event of outstanding significance. I came to Washington to stay in the spring of 1945; I had never seen anything like it in twenty-six years."

[CHAPTER II]

"The first job I had was to go out and collect documents," Leslie Gelb explained in recounting the unusual task handed him only three weeks after he arrived at his desk in the International Security Affairs (ISA) section of the Defense Department in the summer of 1967. Then in its heyday, ISA functioned as the Defense Department's elite foreign policy think tank. In effect the personal staff of the Secretary of Defense, ISA officials focused on everything from new weapons systems to diplomatic relations with newly independent nations. It was a prestigious place to work. "All I had to do was call up and say: 'McNamara asked . . .' I would go to see people, explain the study, and say I wanted the following kinds of material"— memoranda, position papers, cables, field reports, and temporary assessments of policy and its effectiveness, all stretching back over more than twenty years. "They all said: 'Yeah, sure.'

No one ever batted an eyelash. The name of Robert McNamara struck terror in their hearts." To Gelb's knowledge few if any people even bothered to check with the Defense Department to determine what he was up to. "No one refused a thing."

As the documents poured in, it also fell to Gelb to find bodies, people who could take some time off from their regular jobs in and out of government—ninety days was the original estimate of the amount of time that would be required—to help compile, summarize, and annotate a rather informal catalogue of how American policy in Vietnam had evolved. Initially several people were taken from within the Pentagon itself, men who had a reputation for being able to step back and look at events without a knee-jerk military reaction; but in recruiting his assistants Gelb relied heavily on the "old boy" network, that loosely connected confraternity of bright young men who moved gracefully between government and the foreign-policy-oriented establishment of the nation's leading universities, pausing occasionally for brief and profitable sojourns in business or foundation work and joining often in the deliberations of the Council on Foreign Relations in New York. The network had functioned smoothly to staff the administrations of Presidents John F. Kennedy and Lyndon B. Johnson: McGeorge Bundy, once an adviser to presidential candidate Thomas E. Dewey and long the dean of Harvard's faculty of Arts and Sciences; his brother William, the son-in-law of cold war draftsman Dean Acheson and a long-time staff member of the Central Intelligence Agency; John T. McNaughton, a Harvard law professor and close friend of McNamara; Henry Cabot Lodge, the former U.S. Senator who repeatedly came out of retirement to undertake tough top-priority diplomatic missions for his country; and Edward Lansdale, the Air Force officer who helped put Ngo Dinh Diem in power in South Vietnam during a 1954 mission for the CIA. And now the newer generation of the "old boys" were, given their backgrounds, natural choices to evaluate what their predecessors had done: Richard H. Ullman, a history professor on leave from Princeton; Melvin Gurtov, a defense-oriented intellectual who had gone to the Rand Corporation in California after completing his doctorate at Columbia University and a fellowship in Taiwan; Hans Heymann, a Rand economist who had previously studied Soviet air power on an Air Force contract; Richard Moorstein, newly installed at Rand after a stint with ISA at the Pentagon; Richard Holbrooke, a young career foreign service officer who would later be a close aide to Averell Harriman at the Paris peace talks on Vietnam; Richard E. Balzhiser, a White House Fellow; William W. Kaufman, a former Rand researcher teaching at MIT and consulting with the Brookings Institution in Washington; Howard N. Margolis, researcher at the Institute for Defense Analyses and a former newsman specializing in military affairs; and Martin Bailey, a special assistant to the Secretary of Defense on Southeast Asian questions. There were military men, too: Col. Paul F. Gorman, ISA's counterinsurgency expert who later went to the Paris peace talks; Maj. Charles M. Cooke, Jr., a Vietnam assistant at ISA; Col. Robert G. Gard, military assistant to McNamara, among others.

Gelb had excellent "old boy" credentials himself. While completing his doctorate at Harvard, he had helped Henry A. Kissinger teach a course on international politics; Kissinger was then serving as foreign policy adviser to perpetual presidential aspirant Nelson Rockefeller. Gelb taught briefly at Wesleyan College in Connecticut but left there to serve for eighteen months as an executive assistant to Senator Jacob K. Javits (R-N.Y.). In the summer of 1967 he was lured away from Capitol Hill by Morton Halperin, who was serving as a deputy to McNaughton at ISA. When McNamara decided to commission a review of Vietnam policy, he looked to the brain trust in ISA; McNaughton said he could not spare Halperin, who was McNamara's first choice to head the project. Instead, McNaughton designated Gelb, a sallow-complected, soft-spoken man who did not mince his words and could put them on paper in a literate, easy-to-read-and-digest style.

Only a few people expressed a reluctance to work on the study. Harvard history professor Ernest May warned that rapidly produced history might be bad and unreliable history, but contributed his talents anyway. Even Kissinger, not yet in government at the time the Papers were started, was drawn in as a "consultant" on the study; he had dinner with Melvin Gurtov on one occasion to discuss how the project should be pursued in order to be most useful in the future.

By the summer of 1967 the prosecution of what had come increasingly to be known as "McNamara's war" was clearly troubling the Secretary of Defense. Almost from the time he left the presidency of the Ford Motor Company to assume a position in the original New Frontier Cabinet of John F. Kennedy, McNamara had played a central role in the development of American foreign and defense policy. He was an architect of the gradualist approach to the U.S. commitment in Southeast Asia, and as the American build-up in Vietnam grew in the early days of the Johnson administration, he argued forcefully and persuasively in its favor. McNamara, as much as anyone, shared the sense of the American mission to keep the world safe from communism and to establish "peace." Many an American citizen who entertained lingering doubts about the wisdom of the nation's Vietnam posture would be lulled time and again into reserving judgment by McNamara's invariably favorable progress reports on his return from visits to the battlefield. On one occasion, during testimony before the Senate Foreign Relations Committee in defense of the Saigon regime at a time of intense Buddhist protest and self-immolation in South Vietnam, McNamara received the backhanded congratulations of antiwar Senator Wayne Morse (D-Ore.) for his "brilliant and masterful support of an unsound policy." McNamara's public statements, on the bombing of North Vietnam as on other aspects of the war, encouraged popular confidence that there might indeed be light at the end of the tunnel, that the United States could do its job, neatly stopping "the flow of men and materiel" from North Vietnam to the South, and leave Southeast Asia in peace.

McNamara biographer Henry L. Trewhitt places the first stirrings of doubt in the Defense Secretary's mind about American involvement in Vietnam late in 1966; until then, according to Trewhitt's conversations with close associates of McNamara, "he did not understand the extent of casualties among the innocent in Vietnam, south and north." * What also began to be clear to McNamara at that point was the extent to which domestic antiwar dissent was growing among people whom he respected, including university intellectuals and his close friend Senator Robert F. Kennedy (D-N.Y.), brother of the late President. In November 1966 McNamara had a jarring experience: his visit to Harvard, one of the first ever arranged under the auspices of the Kennedy Institute of Politics (which he had helped to establish in memory of the slain President), turned into utter pandemonium. In a confrontation that was later noted as a turning point in the development of militant antiwar sentiment at Harvard and other universities, McNamara was swamped by a crowd of student demonstrators, challenged to debate the war, and repeatedly shouted down. During a gentler part of his Harvard visit, a meeting with several faculty members, McNamara spoke of the need for a written history of the Vietnam war. But it was not an idea that was immediately seized upon.

Early in 1967 evidence mounted both that McNamara was losing his enthusiasm about the war and that his influence in military policy-making was on the wane. Although he stated publicly that he was opposed to the bombing of densely populated areas of North Vietnam, those statements were in-

* Henry L. Trewhitt, *McNamara: His Ordeal in the Pentagon* (Harper and Row, 1971), p. 233 ff.

evitably followed before long by just such bombing raids. Distrustful of the military's ability to evaluate its actions objectively, McNamara had asked CIA director Richard Helms to set up a special unit to evaluate the effectiveness of the bombing operations, and the unit's monthly reports were consistently pessimistic. Nonetheless, McNamara was regularly overruled and the recommendations of the Joint Chiefs of Staff preferred by President Johnson. American casualties in the war were increasing, and the military kept asking for more and more troops.

It was against this background that McNamara, without fanfare and without telling President Johnson or Secretary of State Dean Rusk, launched what came to be known within the Pentagon as the "Vietnam History Task Force." Mutual friends said later that Robert Kennedy, increasingly hostile to the Johnson administration, had encouraged McNamara on that course, but the Secretary himself would later be unable to recall any conversations with Senator Kennedy on the subject. Two men who apparently did share McNamara's early thoughts about the study were John McNaughton and Deputy Secretary of Defense Cyrus Vance, with whom McNamara was especially close in the spring of 1967. So undramatic and routine was the start of work on the Pentagon Papers that McNamara later forgot exactly when the project got under way; in the letter of transmittal that eventually accompanied the finished product, however, Leslie Gelb noted for the record that McNamara launched the task force on June 17, 1967.

On November 1, 1967, McNamara's virtual turnabout on the war was clearly demonstrated in a crucial memorandum to President Johnson; he urged an unconditional halt in the bombing of North Vietnam, a fixed and permanent ceiling on the number of American troops, and an early start on turning over major responsibility for the war to the South Vietnamese (a process that would come to be known as "Vietnamization").

In the short run the only apparent effect of the memo was to increase Johnson's determination to dump McNamara in favor of someone more loyal to the President's policy.

Since the commissioning of the Pentagon Papers was accomplished merely by passing the word along at the ISA section of the Defense Department rather than by a formal written memorandum, it may never be possible to establish precisely what McNamara had in mind at the time. McNaughton probably knew better than anyone; but he, his wife, and son died a month later in a plane crash in North Carolina, a week before he was to switch over to a new job as Secretary of the Navy. Gelb's perceived instruction, as reiterated in his letter of transmittal, was to compile studies that were "encyclopedic and objective." "There was no indication," he said in an interview later, "that the Kennedy administration was to be treated any more lightly than any other." As Richard Ullman wrote in *Foreign Policy* magazine after the Pentagon Papers had been disclosed: "The purpose of the study"—as seen by those working on it at the time—"was not to get at larger questions of right and wrong . . . but to present an account of how it had come about that in the middle of the year 1967 . . . half a million Americans found themselves in South Vietnam fighting a land and air war against a dedicated and intransigent Asian enemy."

McNamara had been worried that when the time came for a full reevaluation of what the United States had done in Vietnam, some of the key documents bearing on the build-up during the 1960s might have disappeared and the question would become impossible to answer: not necessarily because people would consciously seek to destroy documents to avoid embarrassment—the advent of rapid, inexpensive photocopy machines made any such destruction a very difficult goal to achieve—but because as time goes on and administrations change, internal policy papers and the ideas expressed in them are inevitably dispersed. Government regulations concerning the "personal papers" of Cabinet members and other temporary high-level bureaucrats are so loose and uncodified as to permit some officials, such as President Johnson, to take entire truckloads with them on leaving office. (McNamara himself, on leaving the Pentagon early in 1968, failed during repeated interviews with Defense Department historians and the Archivist of the United States to obtain a satisfactory definition of what "personal papers" he was entitled to take along—whatever he cared to define as "personal," they told him. Eventually, McNamara had the entire contents of the private vault in the office of the Secretary of Defense shipped to the National Archives for storage in his name.)

In a gesture that was remarkable for an architect of a war that had torn the nation apart, McNamara ordered the collection of a set of documents that, on release, could expose his own judgment to harsh criticism and bitter attack. He wanted scholars to be able to examine the economic, political, and military bases of Vietnam policy when they eventually came to analyze how the war grew out of the inherited postulates of post-World War II American politics; he also sought to demonstrate the inadequacy of the staff work and background analysis of American war policy. As much as anything else, McNamara thought that the study would be revealing for what it did not include, for what simply was not there to be included. In his only public explanation of his original goals after disclosure of the Pentagon Papers, McNamara told British journalist Frances Cairncross of *The Observer*, that his objective "was to bequeath to scholars the raw material from which they could reexamine the events of the time. If historians are to make a careful examination, they need the raw materials. I simply asked that these be brought together, and I have no regrets for having done so."

There was an inherent risk in embarking on a study of policy that was still evolving and being implemented. "You have to be terribly careful about ordering studies," one former government official commented later in evaluating McNamara's decision. "He was honest and sincere. It was a thoroughly meritorious and unselfish idea. He probably knew that he wouldn't look good; he knew that the war out there had gotten to be a mess." But that was a risk that McNamara, deeply discouraged and already being slated for another powerful job at the World Bank, was willing to take. One factor mitigated the short-run risk. McNamara intended that the study be released "a reasonable time after the war was over"—a condition that was far from being met in the summer of 1971.

The Vietnam History Task Force—whose existence was an open secret in the upper ranks of the Pentagon—was provided with a special suite of rooms within the office of the Secretary of Defense. Although the group worked around the corner from his own office on the third floor of the side of the Pentagon that faces the Potomac River, McNamara never looked in on the project, staying away from direct supervision lest his original motive of an objective study be cast into doubt. Gelb and McNamara, in fact, never met before the latter left office; their occasional communications were channeled through Paul C. Warnke, McNaughton's successor as Assistant Secretary of Defense for International Security Affairs. McNamara had an opportunity to put the Pentagon Papers on a particular track when Warnke showed him the format at one point. But McNamara resisted stepping in, uttering a phrase to Warnke that would be passed along to Gelb and his growing team of part-time authors: "Let the chips fall where they may."

The first assumption about the project to drop by the wayside was that it could be completed by about six people within three months. Ultimately it would require six times as many people, not including secretaries and other assistants, and would take six times as long to assemble. Gelb, who supervised compilation of the Pentagon Papers while continuing with his other responsibilities in ISA, found that none of the authors could stay on for very long; they had to return to their regular jobs.

Thus Gelb spent a great deal of time recruiting replacements, many of whom had to pick up writing where someone else had left off in the middle of a specific period. The task force became, as a friend of Gelb's observed, "an albatross around his neck." After nine months he tried to give it up, but Warnke and Halperin persuaded Gelb to see it through.

One person who dropped in to contribute to the Pentagon Papers for a time was Daniel Ellsberg of the Rand Corporation, recently back from government service in Vietnam. He was assigned a section dealing with Vietnam policy during the early days of the Kennedy administration in 1961. "I don't think it came to much," another of the authors recalled later. "It was a very minor part of the thing, only some of which was actually used" in the final version of the Pentagon Papers. "It wasn't ready on time," the colleague remembered. "Dan has always had a very difficult time writing, and he finds it hard to produce things on time." Gelb confirms that report: "Very few of Ellsberg's words finally appeared. Dan just didn't do his work."

In his effort to preserve the image of objectivity, Gelb instituted a procedure whereby each section of the Pentagon Papers, after being drafted by one member of the task force, would be reviewed by another; the original author's choice of which documents to include with the narrative of policy and which to leave out was ultimately gone over by Gelb, who also wrote most of the eventual summaries and analyses.

Gelb would later assert that for an internal government study group the task force had "unprecedented access" to the raw materials of foreign policy. The CIA was especially responsive to Gelb's request for documents, and Undersecretary of State Nicholas deB. Katzenbach (without the knowledge of his boss, Dean Rusk) also made large amounts of material available from the normally supersensitive State Department. To avoid stirring up feelings within the Johnson administration, the task force avoided personal interviews. Presidential papers were not directly available. Although he asserted in his letter of transmittal that "we had no access to White House files," Gelb later explained that some material actually was provided directly from the White House. In a few instances, he said, White House advisers who knew personally of the project made their informal memoranda available; in other instances, task force members were welcomed at offices to inspect documents that had not been shipped over to the Pentagon. "From 1961 onwards," Gelb noted in the letter of transmittal that accompanied the completed Papers, "the records were bountiful, especially on the first Kennedy year in office, the Diem coup, and on the subjects of the deployment of ground forces, the decisions surrounding the bombing campaign against North Vietnam, US-GVN [South Vietnamese] relations, and attempts at negotiating a settlement of the conflict."

The circumstances under which the Pentagon Papers were drafted and assembled were not those that ordinarily pertain in the writing of serious history. Rather, in old-fashioned newspaper bullpen style, as many as eight people—including secretaries borrowed from other offices and agencies who were to quarrel frequently with one another—were crowded into one large room for research and writing. Anonymity was guaranteed the authors, who were in turn sworn to secrecy about the exact nature of the project. A special esprit de corps developed among the task force members, who felt free, as Gelb later put it, "to share their revelations with one another." The atmosphere became so spirited at times that some authors who were accustomed to calmer surroundings were forced to retreat to quiet rooms in the upper reaches of the Pentagon. By design, various points of view were represented among the authors: some, mostly career military men, were unbending supporters of American tactics in Southeast Asia; many were the "policy fixers" so characteristic of the period, who thought everything would be fine if only the United States applied the appropriate bandaids to its war effort; there was also a "handful of doves," Gelb said later, classifying himself among them. "No one was ever asked his views before being signed on," he wrote in *Life* magazine.

"We had a sense of doing something important and of the need to do it right," Gelb wrote in the letter of transmittal to Clark Clifford, McNamara's successor as Secretary of Defense. "Of course, we all had our prejudices and axes to grind and these shine through clearly at times, but we tried, we think, to suppress or compensate for them." Another member of the task force later confided that at the time the Pentagon Papers were being written there was also a sense that this was the only sure way to preserve certain aspects of the documentary record of the Vietnam war. "There was a feeling in the air," he said, "that Lyndon Johnson, for example, might make a great effort to get rid of the records" and—equally troubling— that the war history itself "might be delivered to a few people and then destroyed."

Late in February 1968, a few days before McNamara left the Pentagon, the task force was moved out of the special suite of rooms near the office of the Secretary of Defense. Clark Clifford, out of bureaucratic courtesy if nothing else, authorized the task force to complete the work originally commissioned by McNamara. He had even less to do with it than had Mc-Namara, however, and frequently expressed the view that it was a foolish exercise. Gelb would proclaim that "we are finally done" only on January 15, 1969, just five days before Clifford in turn left the Pentagon. But the bureaucratic courtesy of Melvin Laird, President Nixon's choice as Secretary of Defense, was also required for several months while sections of the Pentagon Papers were retyped and photocopied and distribution was arranged. Gelb, seeing that ISA was being converted into a more politically partisan and less influential unit under Laird, left his job at the Pentagon on April 30, 1969, three months after Nixon took office, for a research post with the alternative bureaucracy at the Brookings Institution, an independent political and economic research center in Washington. Only in June 1969, two years after it had been commissioned, was the mammoth study—running to well over 7,000 pages in forty-seven volumes—actually distributed.

For those who had closely followed political and military events in Vietnam since World War II, or throughout the 1960s, or for those who had been consistently skeptical about the course of American policy in Southeast Asia, the Pentagon Papers would reveal relatively few new facts. They would serve primarily to confirm private suspicions and publicly expressed doubts. They would make it amply clear, for example, that foreign statesmen who often criticized and sometimes vilified the United States for its war effort—from Charles de Gaulle to the National Liberation Front—had a sound basis for their accusations.

But still, for experts and nonexperts alike who might eventually have the opportunity to study the product of the Vietnam History Task Force, the Papers were impressive. There was an enormity about them, all the more striking because they had been assembled within the government, and an authenticity that could have been established only by quoting from documents that had the clear ring of the people who had transmitted them to one another. There, all of a piece, all in one place, was the *evidence* to prove that:

At the close of World War II President Truman and the State Department casually ignored appeals for U.S. support from Ho Chi Minh, leader of the Viet Minh insurgents. Even while the Geneva conference on Indochina was in session, Colonel Edward Lansdale's CIA mission was in Saigon setting up "paramilitary operations" and "political-psychological warfare" against the North. The United States undertook direct sabotage in Hanoi, including the pouring of contaminants into bus engines. President Kennedy, barely installed in the White House, ordered that American "advisers" be used to train South Vietnamese agents to take over the sabotage operations

[32]

and "light harassment" against the North. He approved of a "defensive security alliance" with the regime of Ngo Dinh Diem, although that represented a flagrant—albeit secret—violation of the Geneva Accords. Despite intelligence reports to the contrary, the American government relied upon Diem's unabashedly falsified figures on Communist infiltration. General Maxwell Taylor urged sending a large American military contingent to South Vietnam under the guise of a flood-relief task force. The United States continued to court Diem while joining with plotters of a coup to overthrow him; Ambassador Henry Cabot Lodge feigned ignorance of American policy during a phone conversation with a desperate Diem at the crucial moment of his downfall. After a program of clandestine military operations against the North had already begun, and after a Canadian diplomat had carried an American threat of "greatest devastation" to Hanoi, the Gulf of Tonkin resolution, which became the only specific authorization for U.S. fighting in Vietnam, was rushed through Congress under false pretenses. "Provocation" was repeatedly entertained as a means to develop a pretext for escalation of the war effort, and President Johnson eventually adopted the bombing strategy that was pressed upon him by advisers. When the emphasis of American military activity in Vietnam distinctly shifted and the United States became embroiled in a land war, the Johnson administration stubbornly labored to preserve the public impression that no changes were involved or even contemplated. Consistently discounting reports of the "enemy's" resilience, the American government sent thousands of young Americans to their death in a feverish war that, it became increasingly clear, would be impossible to "win." Even as dissent developed within the administration, especially from Assistant Secretary of State George Ball, the American effort in Vietnam forged ahead; the government concealed the fact that while the bombing of the North had done little damage to the Communists' own war effort, it killed tens of thousands of civilians. What was enlightening about the collected Papers was the total picture they presented of the United States planning and waging an arguably illegal and undeniably immoral war, all in the name of "peace."

Perhaps more than anything else, the Pentagon Papers compiled by Leslie Gelb's task force documented the continuity of the basic policy underlying the extraordinary and zealous American commitment in Southeast Asia, a continuity of assumptions and premises that were seldom questioned and never fundamentally reexamined: the "domino theory," which—contrary intelligence reports notwithstanding—perpetuated the belief that should South Vietnam be "lost" virtually every other nation in Asia would come tumbling down like unsteady children's playthings. The notion, born of the cold war epoch, that a Communist—any one—is just another Communist and that the Soviet Union and China, despite their own well-documented rift, were jointly controlling North Vietnam and the Viet Cong like puppets on so many strings. The Pentagon Papers betrayed the utter insensitivity of American policy makers to the forces of nationalism and self-determination. They showed that U.S. policy made proud zigs and zags through repeated series of "options," but that the "options" were all fashioned from the same ideological cloth while genuine "alternatives" were seldom considered or even offered for consideration. (In November 1964, for example, after the Viet Cong had attacked Bien Hoa airfield and when the Joint Chiefs of Staff were clamoring for a powerful response, William Bundy's interagency working group on Vietnam offered President Johnson three "options," all of which included bombing the North.)

One major surprise, at least for the less initiated, was the extent to which the Pentagon Papers vindicated the judgment and the advice of the Central Intelligence Agency, long regarded as the home of the bogeymen of the American government (a reputation which nonetheless remained intact insofar as the agency's own actions were concerned). Time and again the CIA told the policy makers not only that the domino theory was invalid but also that even if the philosophical basis of the war effort had been correct, the tactics selected to implement it simply would not work. Tucked under the CIA's cloak alongside its dagger was a measure of wisdom that, if logically extended, might have taught that the United States should get out of Vietnam. But the wisdom was persistently ignored by men who preferred to believe what they were already telling the world. Self-deception, Hannah Arendt would later observe in an essay based on the Pentagon Papers, went hand in hand with deception.

The Papers also documented a fundamental change that had evolved during the 1960s in the power relationships among the separate branches of government established in the Constitution. President Dwight D. Eisenhower, for whatever other faults he may have suffered, could be seen as the last chief executive to believe that the commitment of any substantial number of troops in Indochina required "congressional authority." The men who followed him in office and their advisers were not merely prepared to ignore the legislative branch in the area of foreign affairs; they also displayed a cynical, manipulative attitude toward Congress and frequently held it in utter contempt. Lyndon Johnson had built his power base during his years in Congress, but the executive branch's respect for and deference toward Capitol Hill reached a nadir during his administration.

The lack of advance consultation and the disrespect for Congress were dramatically emphasized in the Papers in two draft memoranda written by William Bundy during the crucial month of November 1964. In one, which dealt with "handling world and public opinion," the Assistant Secretary of State asserted that "Congress must be consulted before any major action, perhaps only by notification if we do a reprisal. . . ." The preferred format, Bundy said, would be "careful talks

[35]

with . . . key leaders," and his list of "leaders" carefully omitted anyone who displayed a stirring of dissent. But Bundy counseled that the President "should wait till his mind is moving clearly in one direction before such a consultation," and he further wondered "if it should be combined with other topics (budget?) to lessen the heat." Bundy made it clear, however, that "we probably do not need additional Congressional authority, even if we decide on very strong action. A session of this rump Congress might well be the scene of a messy Republican effort." Three weeks later, in a draft position paper discussing intensified American military action, Bundy turned to the need for "publicizing" alleged evidence of increased North Vietnamese infiltration of the South. Priority number one was "an on-the-record presentation to the press" in Washington and Saigon. Listed as number two was this item: "Available Congressional leaders will be given special briefings. (No special leadership meeting will be convened for this purpose.)" Such plans for "publicizing" were later dropped entirely from the final version of Bundy's paper.

Senator J. W. Fulbright, chairman of the Senate Foreign Relations Committee, who ultimately turned bitterly against the war in Vietnam, later reminisced about the "meetings" and "briefings" staged for Congress during the Johnson administration. "Lyndon used to bring the so-called Congressional leadership to the White House," Fulbright recalled. "Oh, you could have spoken up in a very ill-mannered way. But it would always start with the Speaker [of the House of Representatives, John W. McCormack]. He would praise the President and say that 'if there is to be an error, it ought to be on the side of strength.' By the time it got to me or [Senate Democratic leader Mike] Mansfield, everybody else had said: 'Yes, Mr. President.' If you differed, everybody looked at you like a skunk at a picnic. Unity behind the President is what was valued."

The Pentagon Papers illustrated the Orwellian vocabulary of Vietnam policy-making, a bizarre combination of frontier talk and show business jargon so common to President Johnson and his aides. Bundy wondered in one of his November 1964 memoranda, for example, "how loud we want to make this sound" about infiltration. It was when it came to talking about bombing that the euphemistic but clumsy jargon flourished most elaborately. The images were profoundly troubling to some members of the Vietnam History Task Force. As one of its members later explained: "To talk about the use of bombing as if it were an orchestral score—you know, heavy on the brass, a bit of tympany, and that sort of thing—when you're talking about the use of napalm and high explosives and terrible devices . . . was very dangerous." It looked as if it had been easier and less uncomfortable to discuss the great U.S. adventure in South Vietnam in terms of its "orchestration."

"The Pentagon Papers," Senator Mike Gravel (D-Alas.) would later write in the introduction to one edition, "tell of the purposeful withholding and distortion of facts. . . . The Pentagon Papers show that we have created, in the last quarter-century, a new culture, a national security culture, protected from the influences of American life by the shield of secrecy. . . . The Pentagon Papers reveal the inner workings of a government bureaucracy set up to defend this country, but now out of control, managing an international empire by garrisoning American troops around the world. . . . show that our leaders never understood the human commitments which underlay the nationalist movement in Vietnam, or the degree to which the Vietnamese were willing to sacrifice. . . . show that there was no concern in the decision-making process for the impact of our actions upon the Vietnamese people. . . . show that the enemy knew what we were not permitted to know."

It was an uncommon sort of history. "Not so much a documentary history," Leslie Gelb said in his letter of transmittal, "as a history based solely on documents—checked and rechecked with ant-like diligence." Gelb recognized the short-comings of the Pentagon Papers. "Writing history, especially where it blends into current events, especially where that current event is Vietnam, is a treacherous exercise," he said. "We could not go into the minds of the decision makers, we were not present at the decisions, and we often could not tell whether something happened because someone decided it, decided against it, or most likely because it unfolded from the situation."

On their release, the Papers would be sharply criticized. Since they were based only on partial access to government war policy documents, said the critics—mostly former high officials of the Kennedy and Johnson administrations whose reputations stood to be damaged, or columnists like Joseph Alsop and William S. White who had come to view the American effort in Vietnam as a modern crusade for "freedom" and "democracy"—the Papers presented an incomplete and distorted picture, conceivably twisted further by the handiwork of frustrated "doves" like Gelb. The Papers gave more credence to tentative draft statements that urged intensive escalation, it was argued, than those statements had ever been given in the development of policy. And without fuller details of the Presidents' innermost reactions and conclusions drawn from the drafts submitted to them, it was impossible to know what *really* motivated decisions. The Papers also seemed to be peculiarly void of any discussion of the impact of domestic politics on war policy; moves taken in the autumn of 1964, for example, were not seen in the perspective of a presidential campaign in which Lyndon Johnson was the "peace candidate."

Ernest May, the Harvard historian who joined the Vietnam History Task Force, observed that if the Papers were judged on the same criteria as college term papers or doctoral theses, they might draw a low grade. The authors had not made adequate use of material available in newspapers and other periodicals and had sometimes neglected relevant congressional hearings; in addition, they had failed to employ the standard historical process of proposing hypotheses and then testing them against the data. The study, May said, had all the earmarks of a "hurriedly turned out product."

But Richard Ullman, the Princeton historian who worked on the study, stoutly defended the Papers in *Foreign Policy* magazine. In his research for several histories of earlier periods and issues, such as British policy during the Russian civil war, Ullman said, he had discovered that "presidential papers" (or in this case those of British Prime Minister David Lloyd George) lent very little additional perspective. Presidents and other powerful leaders, after all, seldom put their views and ideas on paper, but rather vent them orally during meetings held at their own behest. "When historians gain access to the files of the Johnson White House," Ullman predicted, "they will find plenty of papers going in to the President. They will find few coming out, and fewer still which tell them what the President 'really' had on his mind." Indeed, even if they did not always fall neatly into conspiracy theories and other hypotheses, the available recommendations of high-level advisers may have been more essential than the thoughts of the Presidents in putting American policy in Vietnam into a short-range historical context in the compilation of the Pentagon Papers. Immediate history involves some scholarly sacrifice, but it has other advantages.

Some officials who had been involved in Vietnam policy, in fact, grudgingly conceded that far from twisting events to conform to a negative framework, the Pentagon Papers actually made things look better than they were. Frederick Nolting, former U.S. Ambassador to South Vietnam, for example, said that "if anything, the published records tend to varnish over these crucial events or make them less offensive and damaging to those actually involved."

Gelb himself found the Pentagon Papers quite useful in the development of current policy. Throughout 1968 he continued to wear two hats, supervising completion of the study while remaining at his post in the ISA section of the Defense Department. He was heavily relied upon, in the early days of the preliminary peace talks in Paris, for example, for his growing expertise about whether any particular statement from North Vietnam or the Viet Cong represented a change from previous declarations.

In June 1969, two years before their publication by *The New York Times,* the fifteen sets of the Pentagon Papers were ready for distribution. They were assigned on the basis of a list developed by Gelb and Assistant Secretary of Defense Paul Warnke before they left the Pentagon; Warnke cleared the list in a phone conversation with Robert McNamara, who was still considered to have substantial authority over who could see the Papers and work with them. The Rand Corporation was selected, Warnke explained, because it was a "Department of Defense repository. I had been sufficiently impressed by the ability of documents to get lost within the agencies, so that I felt that if Mr. McNamara's purpose was to be served, it was useful to have one in a readily identifiable place where it would not necessarily . . . get entangled in the bureaucratic process and perhaps get lost." At Rand, Warnke reasoned, people who had worked on the study and others involved in defense research or with the proper clearance would be guaranteed access when necessary.

Two sets were delivered to Rand, one for the Santa Monica office and one for the field office in Washington. Two went to the National Archives to be kept for the Kennedy and Johnson libraries. Two went to the State Department, personally designated for the use of Nicholas Katzenbach and William Bundy. One set was delivered to the Washington law office of Clark Clifford and immediately placed in a closet that had been converted into a "security storage area" by Pentagon security officers. "Set Number One" went to Robert McNamara's office at the Bank for International Reconstruction and Development. Seven copies were retained in the office of the Secretary of Defense, personally designated for use by, among others, Warnke, Cyrus Vance, and Paul H. Nitze, who had served for a time as Deputy Secretary of Defense.

Leslie Gelb had classified the Pentagon Papers top secret as "an absolutely routine decision"; the Defense Department's classification regulations dictated that any compendium of documents must bear the highest classification of any of its parts. Initially the Papers were not widely read. Gelb obtained one of Rand's copies in June 1970 in order to use the section on military pressures against North Vietnam in 1964 in preparing for a conference. Aides to President Johnson had the National Archives release his copy in 1970 for selective use in preparing his memoirs, *The Vantage Point*. Bundy, who had been provided with an office at the State Department by incoming Undersecretary of State Elliot Richardson, used his copy there in preparing a book about Vietnam.

Robert McNamara did not read the Pentagon Papers. "He couldn't bear to read them," says one of his closest friends.

[CHAPTER III]

One person—probably the only one initially other than Leslie Gelb—who read the Pentagon Papers, and read them thoroughly with meticulous attention to detail from beginning to end, was Daniel Ellsberg. The completed version of the study to which he had contributed came along at a fortuitous time for the brilliant analyst of game theory and decision-making in international affairs. Had Ellsberg's "perceptual and emotional experience" and his views on the Vietnam problem been charted in Ellsbergian fashion, it might have been found that in the summer of 1969 he was reaching the top of "a recurrent saw-tooth shape":* the first such saw tooth, reached some

* The images, somewhat truncated here, are modeled after those used by Ellsberg in "The Quagmire Myth and the Stalemate Machine," an article in the spring 1971 issue of *Public Policy,* the journal of the John F. Kennedy School of Government at Harvard University. Ellsberg presented a "fever chart of U.S. expectations" based on alternating periods of government optimism and pessimism about the war.

years earlier, represented his strength of conviction in *support* of the American war effort; the new one would measure his vehemence in *opposition* to it. He had made a total, albeit gradual—and to some who knew him well, occasionally unconvincing—transition from the compleat hawk to the compleat dove. Like a recent convert to a fundamentalist religious sect, Ellsberg became obsessed with a missionary zeal to set himself and others on the path to salvation. It had been a difficult path to find and would be a rocky one to travel.

Born in Chicago early in the Depression, Ellsberg moved with his unemployed engineer father and family first to southern Illinois and then to Detroit. At six he could recite Lincoln's Gettysburg Address. As a teenager he played the piano well enough to perform concertos with amateur orchestras. He could, in fact, learn to do almost anything—debate, play basketball, sky dive, scuba dive. "At nineteen," his father recalled proudly to a newspaper reporter, "Daniel decided to climb Long's Peak out in Colorado. He learned alpine climbing from an Alpine guide, who went with him. Anything that's tough he wants to do." The piano he gave up after his mother died in an automobile accident while he was a high school student at the Cranbrook School for Boys in Michigan.

Ellsberg went to Harvard on a generous Pepsi Cola scholarship, which covered, among other things, his train fare to and from college each year. His prep school had recommended him in glowing terms, as "a brilliant, superior student . . . inclined at times to feel superior, but no recluse," and his classmates there selected him as the graduate "most likely to make a contribution to human progress." When he entered Harvard, the university was in the process of changing from a rather elitist haven into a pluralistic community.

Daniel Ellsberg '52 was a notable success in Harvard's academic and extracurricular worlds; he became president of the *Advocate*, the undergraduate literary magazine, and was also elected to the editorial board of the *Crimson*, Harvard's daily student newspaper. His writings for the former, including a piece under a pseudonym describing a visit to his mother's grave, were emotionally vivid, and for the latter, socially and politically committed. In an all-night stand that, like others before and since, would be immortalized for a private audience in the *Crimson*'s "comment books," he once composed and edited an entire editorial page on his own. One Harvard classmate remembers that aside from his academic prowess, "Dan was ambitious; he wanted to make himself known. . . . But he was then a quiet person; he wouldn't talk about himself. He wasn't easy to know." This was an observation that many others would make in later years.

His senior honors thesis, on the then esoteric field of economic game theory, won rave reviews from the faculty and the highest possible grade. He was a natural for a Woodrow Wilson fellowship to study advanced economics at Cambridge University in England—a friend from that period remembers him as having "as good a mind as anybody . . . ever"—and after a year he returned to Harvard to complete work on his Master's degree (passing his oral examinations with the whimsically enthusiastic rating of "excellent plus").

Ellsberg could have proceeded directly into the elite status of a junior member in Harvard's Society of Fellows, one of the most luxurious ways in the world to get a doctorate, but he postponed the opportunity; giving up his draft deferment, he volunteered for two years in the Marine Corps.

In the winter of his junior year at Harvard Ellsberg had married Carol Cummings, a Radcliffe sophomore and the daughter of a Marine colonel, a widower who was then studying law across the Charles River at Boston University. Ellsberg's college contemporaries recall that the scholarly young man had argued against a formal wedding because he was worried about the potential contrast between himself and the ramrod-straight father of the bride in a full-dress military uniform;

so the ceremony was a small one in an Episcopal church, attended mostly by college friends, and the reception was held at the Signet Society, a literary club of which Ellsberg was a member.

Friends remember that Ellsberg became quite fond of his father-in-law, who would sometimes join the Ellsbergs and their friends for New England skiing weekends. They suggest that Colonel Cummings' example inspired him to join the service with something more than just a trace of curiosity about another life style. Indeed, Ellsberg extended for an extra tour on active duty after his battalion was called to sea patrol in the Middle East.

Action on the fringe of the 1956 Suez crisis provided the occasion for Ellsberg's first top-secret security clearance, one of many to come. It also seems to be the moment when he developed an authentically military approach to Amerca's international responsibilities; as a marine, he recently told a banquet meeting of antiwar federal employees, "I was just waiting to be told whom my commander in chief had decided we should fight against."

When Ellsberg returned to Harvard to take his place as a junior fellow, his academic work reflected his military orientation. He became a part-time consultant for the Rand Corporation, then at its height as a defense research center for the Air Force, and at the same time delivered economics lectures at the Boston Public Library and anonymously contributed military policy advice to the embryonic presidential efforts of Massachusetts Senator John F. Kennedy. Once he had his doctorate (or almost; he was late with his thesis), Ellsberg plunged into defense research full time, moving to California with his wife and two children in 1959 to join the "economics department" at Rand—a choice position at "a university without students." His first work there, concentrating on the much discussed "missile gap" and Soviet nuclear capability, was not entirely successful. "At Rand," he later told Frank Rich for an article in *Esquire* magazine, "we believed the Russians were probably going full blast for a capability to destroy our retaliatory capability, and intelligence estimates pointed that way." But those intelligence estimates were later found to be overdrawn, and Ellsberg, along with many others of the period, was responsible for helping to draft an overkill-type response in U.S. policy.

Ellsberg was repeatedly called into top-notch consultations for the government. Rand sent him to Washington on the night of President Kennedy's televised speech on the Cuban missile crisis; working around the clock at the State and Defense departments, he worried aloud that the United States might give Russian Premier Nikita Khrushchev the mistaken impression of weakness and indecision. A few years later Ellsberg would again race to Washington to join the staff of Assistant Defense Secretary John McNaughton at the very time of American retaliatory raids in response to alleged North Vietnamese attacks on U.S. vessels in the Gulf of Tonkin. Time and again Ellsberg exhibited single-minded intensity toward projects he considered important at the moment. As one long-time associate describes him: "He is unable to put himself in other people's positions very well, he's so convinced of his rectitude and morality. . . . He cannot conceive that that which he believes and stands for at a given moment will not triumph. . . . There is no halfway point for Dan."

In between the two Washington missions, Ellsberg found the issue of his career: Vietnam. Initially his was a consulting role in Washington during the early years of the Kennedy administration; he was one of the whiz kids who applied cold, hard academic (or business or legal) logic to the American "game" in Southeast Asia, with little or no acquaintance with —or even interest in—the character and the wishes of the people who would be so profoundly affected by each move. Ellsberg said in one early report that the situation in Vietnam was "unpromising," but as the Pentagon Papers would show, the basic premises of U.S. policy were already set, and for Ellsberg as for others it was really only a matter of how best to fix things up, to work them out in a way that would avoid disastrous domestic political consequences. Consistent with his earlier academic pursuits, Ellsberg was intrigued with "the analysis of high-level decision-making in international crises," and his studies of the Cuban missile crisis made him eager to have a hand in the actual decisions in Vietnam. He went to work for McNaughton.

"After a year, day and night, reading and responding to cables and intelligence on Vietnam," he later wrote to his Harvard classmates, "I felt maddeningly . . . that neither I nor the others around me, reading the same cables, knew, or could learn from all this traffic, any of the things that needed knowing about South Vietnam." Ellsberg's marriage had just broken up; frustrated with the view from afar but basically convinced of the rightness of U.S. policy, he pleaded successfully to be sent to Vietnam on an assignment that would combine policy-making with action.

Before leaving, however, Ellsberg performed briefly as a domestic missionary for the Defense Department. In the spring of 1965, when the "Rolling Thunder" air attacks against North Vietnam and the ground troop commitment were being planned (with Ellsberg's help), the serious dissent beginning to stir in Congress and on university campuses was of profound concern to the Pentagon. Ellsberg lobbied for the war effort on Capitol Hill, visiting among others Senator Edward M. Kennedy (D-Mass.) to insist upon the reasonableness of Johnson administration decisions. He also made the campus teach-in circuit, answering antiwar critics at Harvard and at Antioch College in Ohio, New York University, and Washington University in St. Louis; Ellsberg was trying, as he put it in the open letter to his classmates, "to communicate honestly some of the complexities, and my own uncertainties." He felt that he had been partially successful, as students came up to him afterward acknowledging that they were at least "confused," whereas before they had been downright opposed to the American role.

Ellsberg left for Vietnam in the middle of 1965, after systematically preparing himself through briefings from those who had already been there, both in and out of government. He went as a special "apprentice" to Major General Edward Lansdale, who was returning to Vietnam on an independent intelligence mission that would focus on the "pacification" program. Ellsberg plunged in as a member of the growing American subculture in Vietnam and became friendly there with a young engineer and political scientist from the Rand Corporation named Anthony Russo, who was studying the "motivation and morale" of the Viet Cong through interviews with captured prisoners and converts to the Saigon government's side. Ellsberg was also close to the growing Western journalistic community; he listened to reporters' impressions and in turn became an excellent news source for them. By then highly verbal and impressionable, Ellsberg developed strong ties with the Vietnamese people in the villages he visited. Only a few weeks after arriving he was laid up with an attack of dysentery and used his free time to record his impressions in a round-robin letter to friends back in the States; it was eventually published anonymously in *The Reporter*, a magazine that strongly supported the American war effort.

"The people [in the villages] act as if we were liberating them," Ellsberg said in the letter, which appeared as a "Vietnam Diary." He spoke of the children, "so gay, so friendly and funny," of "the prettiest whores in the world," and of the "uninvolved, not very highly motivated Americans who necessarily fill the ranks." Ellsberg described himself as "hopeful, desperately glad to be here."

Lansdale found Ellsberg "independent and brilliant but lacking in security discipline." He was a useful aide, however, especially because of the ease with which he learned the complex ins and outs of South Vietnamese domestic politics. The general worried at times that Ellsberg, absorbed in discussion during their trips into the countryside, would relax his guard and fall victim to an ambush. Later in his stay Ellsberg took on a "loosely defined post" as special assistant to Deputy American Ambassador William Porter, who had responsibility for "consolidating" the rather diverse Vietnamese field operations of the American aid program, the CIA, and others. (Porter would later become the chief American representative at the Paris peace talks.)

Ellsberg, who had become a pistol expert with both hands in the Marines, also accepted the necessity of carrying a gun. "I was one of those," he told an interviewer from *Look* magazine, "who felt that you should not give advice [on the kind of risks people should take] unless you were prepared to go out of your way to share those risks to some extent." He took risks all right, going on patrols with Army battalions and Marine units in the Mekong Delta. "I did a lot of shooting," he conceded in the frank and wide-ranging interview, which appeared in *Look* shortly before the magazine's demise late in 1971, "because in the delta we were under a lot of fire, some days every half-hour or so. I carried a weapon because the alternative was, if you didn't carry a weapon, other people would have to take care of you. I was anxious not to attract attention to myself." No one could ever accuse Ellsberg of being unaware of the nature of the ground fighting in Vietnam. "A couple of times when I was with the lead squad going through a paddy," he told *Look*, "Viet Cong rose from the paddy we had just walked through and fired at the people behind us. That kind of experience gives you a very intimate sense of the nature of this conflict and a very strong impression of the opponent we're fighting. . . . when you're being fired at, you don't worry at all about the moral dilemmas involved in firing back."

He would later have nagging doubts about just such experiences. "It was only after I got away from that situation and even from the country," he said, "that I really began to think harder about the question: After all, why were we there to be fired at? I knew why I was there. But why were *we* there? Why was our battalion there? The guerrillas we were fighting were clearly firing at foreigners to get them out of their own home yards. It was extremely hard to justify what we were doing there."

Ellsberg had equally strong doubts about the pacification program in Vietnamese villages. In 1966, as he had once done as a shipboard marine, he was again keeping track of "progress" on military charts, of the extent to which each village had proceeded through the efficient stages of clearing out hostile units, cooperating with "revolutionary development cadres," building up confidence in local leaders, and working to keep the community "secure" from the Viet Cong. The reports flowing into headquarters were inevitably optimistic about the accomplishments of the South Vietnamese army, about one village after another becoming secure enough to be "colored blue" (rather than red or an "intermediate" color) on American maps. Despite the field reports, Ellsberg later revealed, "there were no small-unit actions going on, as claimed." The villages weren't really "pacified" at all: "I was concerned about getting the truth to the President. . . . I had this feeling, 'If only the czar knew . . .'" Occasionally, Ellsberg took matters in his own hands to transmit information, violating established procedure by sending private, realistic memos back to Washington.

In December 1966 he prepared a hasty report for Wade Lathram, an official of the American Office of Civil Operations in Vietnam, who was returning for consultations in Washington; the report pointed out the delusions in believing that there had been genuine "progress" in the Vietnamese countryside and that there were genuine hopes for the future. The memo, on "The Day Loc Tien Was Pacified," later appeared in the summer 1971 issue of the *Antioch Review*. It described Ellsberg's visit to Loc Tien—one of the villages in the "regional quota" for 1966—on the morning of an official ceremony marking its graduation into the "secure" category. After ten weeks all the criteria for pacification had been met; the ceremony was cheerful, filled with flowers and orations and pretty girls dressed up for the occasion. But as Ellsberg toured with his U.S. Army guides, he quickly discovered that the celebration and Loc Tien's "blue" marking, like those for so many other villages, were an utter farce: soldiers, not villagers, had built the wall around the hamlet and other fortifications; it had taken a special clearing mission to make the approach to Loc Tien safe enough for visitors. The American guides warned Ellsberg not to veer off a carefully defined path. Villagers told of South Vietnamese soldiers stealing food from them during the pacification effort. The cadres had done little but take a census, provide doorsigns, and assign people to meaningless "organizations." The hamlet chiefs wouldn't dare risk sleeping in the village at night, at least not until they had been confirmed in their jobs by their provincial superiors so that their families could qualify for death benefits; their predecessors had been assassinated. Individual villagers had no idea how the war had started and cared not at all who won. Cadres, when pressed, admitted shamelessly that "there is no security here." Ellsberg and his guides nearly had to fight their way out of Loc Tien, and a cadre leader conceded: "Ten weeks is not enough to do anything, in an area like this. But it doesn't make any difference; ten months would not have been enough either. We worked hard, and we did the best we could; but the people do not really want to talk to us because the VC are all around and they are afraid. Maybe somewhere else we can do more. . . ."

Ellsberg retained a modicum of confidence, over the objections of some other Americans in Vietnam with growing feelings against the war. He argued bitterly, for example, with an old girlfriend, Patricia Marx, who came to Saigon to do tapes for her radio program on WNYC in New York and to help research a magazine article on the war. They were almost engaged, but their relationship broke up for a time, in part because of emotional disagreements over the prospects for U.S. policy. Ellsberg returned to the States briefly to see old friends, but then went back to Vietnam.

Were it not for a siege of hepatitis in 1967, Ellsberg might have stayed on there indefinitely. He was working with men whom he respected; he would see things through. Lying in a nursing home in Bangkok, Thailand, on his thirty-sixth birthday, "watching dextrose solution dripping into my veins," he composed a long, reflective letter to his Harvard '52 classmates for inclusion in the fifteenth class reunion report. Wedged between the comments of a philosophy scholar and a space engineer, Ellsberg's message seemed peculiarly that of a man of action; it also seemed to indicate that he had reached a turning point in his views on Vietnam. "I have virtually decided to go home and make my contribution to the Vietnam problem we all share from there," he wrote. He reviewed his career, citing for all to see the now impressive pay scale he had reached in government work, equivalent to that of a lieutenant general. "My real status," Ellsberg pointed out, "has been properly menial for most of my time [in Vietnam]: distinctly down in the engine room rather than the bridge, and, it soon turned out, in a small, lonely ship in the convoy."

"I'm proud to have served with Lansdale," he continued, "and I've learned fully as much as I hoped: and learned to care deeply for this tortured country, Vietnam (whose countryside, I think, is the most beautiful in the world: a fact that rarely seems to be mentioned), its children, its people, and their future. But much of the knowledge is painful; I don't seem to have the temperament of a pathologist. It has been, most of it, an intensely frustrating and sad year and a half, though with a good deal of excitement and moments of hope.

[52]

. . . I'm more convinced than I could have been before that Lansdale's basic thoughts on political development, on nationalistic and democratic rivalry with Communists for leadership of revolutionary forces, and on counterguerrilla tactics are sound, relevant to Vietnam, and desperately needed here; but *none* of them are being applied, in any degree. . . ."

Ellsberg returned to the Rand Corporation and another life, settling in a beach cottage in Malibu. He would become close to Russo, also back from Vietnam, who had become too politically radical for the Rand management and was now being edged out. Russo was becoming concerned with the problems of Los Angeles ghettos; his transformation on the war was a total and rapid one, and he would thus be a convenient vehicle for Ellsberg's more gradual, self-conscious shift in attitudes. Ellsberg had a lively Southern California social life, staying less within the confines of the Rand elite than he had before.

Although he is unable to pinpoint specific stimuli, Ellsberg concedes that he changed a great deal during this period. Externally, it was noticeable: his hair grew longer; he looked less the part of the ex-marine. (The change was obviously not without hesitation and was occasionally clumsy; in his report to the Harvard class of '52, Ellsberg pointed out that "if I keep the beard I've started growing in the hospital, I'll look more contemporary than any of you.") He was eager to maintain his credibility and acceptance on all sides, remaining very close to Henry Rowen, the former Assistant Secretary of Defense who was president of Rand. Ellsberg's relationship with Rowen permitted him perhaps more running room than others had; lower-level supervisors were more inclined to tolerate his eccentricities because they knew he was listened to at the top.

Ellsberg became friendly at Rand with Vu Van Thai, a wealthy and urbane Vietnamese who had served for years in the Diem government and, more recently, as then-Premier Nguyen Cao Ky's Ambassador to the United States from late

1965 through early 1967. Thai never returned to Saigon after a falling out with Ky over domestic Vietnamese politics; instead he stayed on in the United States, serving as a consultant to the Brookings Institution in Washington and to the Rand Corporation. Ellsberg took many of his cues about Vietnamese affairs from Thai, according to friends, and frequently quoted him in conversation. Increasingly rejecting the hard anti-Communist line of the governments he had served, Thai, in his papers for Rand, was arguing for "a flexible position" which would divide Vietnamese Communists and for greater openness toward the National Liberation Front from the Saigon government. Ellsberg and Thai talked often about how the war might be ended.

Late in 1967, at just about the time he was called to Washington to contribute to the Pentagon Papers, Ellsberg flew to Bermuda to attend a conference on the Vietnam war sponsored by the Carnegie Endowment for International Peace. His views were rather more extreme than those of the other participants at the conference, but that was not obvious from the general, mildly dovish statement issued at its conclusion. Subsequently Ellsberg participated in the early 1968 Pentagon meetings that preceded President Johnson's cutback in the bombing of North Vietnam and his announcement that he would not run for reelection. Paul Warnke, then Assistant Secretary of Defense for International Security Affairs, recalls visits from Ellsberg at the Pentagon: "He came in to talk to me about Vietnam a couple of times, representing himself as John McNaughton's former special assistant. . . . I thought he was quite bright and very interesting on the subject of Vietnam, because he had spent so much time there. I was interested in particular in his analysis of Vietnamese reactions, which was something that I always thought it very hard to get any kind of a handle on. You could find an awful lot of Americans that had American reactions to Vietnam, but here was somebody who seemed to know a number of Vietnamese." They discussed the Vietnamese attitude toward the events of

the Tet offensive early in 1968 and the likely political consequences of it. "He was concerned," Warnke says, "about
whether or not what America had done in Vietnam was right
or wrong, but I had the feeling that he hadn't made up his
mind." Even then Ellsberg seemed "more concerned about the
tactics used to accomplish what he regarded as a legitimate objective rather than the legitimacy of the objective. I think his
feeling was that the effort to try and prevent South Vietnam
from being taken over by the Communists was desirable and
consistent with American interests; but I think he was terribly
troubled about the amount of devastation and just the general
disruption of Vietnamese life that had occurred as a result of
our intervention."

It was this theme that Ellsberg was to take up at another
conference he attended in the middle of 1968, at the University
of Chicago's Adlai Stevenson Institute of International Affairs.
But he stayed in the mainstream, hopeful that a new President
elected in 1968 might be willing to initiate drastic changes in
Southeast Asia.

Ellsberg could not resist trying to help formulate policy.
After Richard M. Nixon's election, his newly appointed national security adviser, Henry Kissinger, asked the Rand
Corporation for an analysis of the options open to the United
States in Vietnam. Rowen assigned the task to Ellsberg, who
knew Kissinger well. Ellsberg drafted a list of "A-to-Z options"
and then spent four days at Nixon's headquarters at the Hotel
Pierre in New York going over them with Kissinger. The list
included everything from dropping nuclear weapons on North
Vietnam to total unilateral American withdrawal from the
conflict. Ellsberg did not believe the United States should
open the full-scale peace negotiations then getting under way
in Paris with so bold an offer as total extrication, but he felt
strongly that the National Security Council should consider
it a legitimate choice for U.S. policy. When Kissinger submitted the list of options to the NSC, however, the prospect

of withdrawal was omitted—in an exact replay of the American approach to the problem for decades, no real alternative was permitted to reach the highest councils.

Ellsberg tried again. Kissinger had also asked him to prepare an exhaustive list of questions about Vietnam designed to elicit the views of all concerned agencies, including the State and Defense departments, the CIA, and the American Embassy in Saigon. When the answers came in after Nixon's inauguration—a total of about 1,000 pages—Kissinger called Ellsberg to Washington on a confidential mission to summarize them for the President. "I was the one who had written the questions; I knew the material better than anyone else," Ellsberg explained later. Kissinger assigned a team of people to help read the reports, under the direction of Morton Halperin (who had moved over from the Defense Department to the White House and stayed on for a time with the Republican administration), but Ellsberg claims that he was the only one to read the entire set. "I looked for particularly important conclusions that might be drawn from the answers and possible studies that might be done," Ellsberg says. His conclusions were approximately the same as before; but the project soon fell by the wayside, as Kissinger prepared for a trip to Europe.

Back at Rand early in 1969, Ellsberg embarked on a full-time study of the lessons that might be drawn from the American experience in Vietnam, in a sense an extension of his earlier work on crisis decision-making. One obviously useful tool in developing this study was the Pentagon Papers; Ellsberg obtained early drafts of some sections of the study well in advance of their official distribution. He contended later, in his interview with *Look* magazine, that this early access was "the price I asked for participating as a researcher. So I was given the commitment that I would be able to read this thing ultimately. No other researcher got that commitment on the study. . . . I was authorized by the Assistant Secretary of Defense to have personal access to the entire study."

[56]

Neither Leslie Gelb nor Paul Warnke remembers any such arrangement. "I did not in any way either say or imply that Dan would have access" when he came to work on the Papers, Gelb insists. But Ellsberg apparently arranged access on his own, taking the opportunity available to anyone at Rand who has top-secret clearance to request materials from the Defense Department that are relevant to his research work. According to Pentagon records, on March 3, 1969, Ellsberg was the designated courier to carry ten volumes of the Papers officially, including early drafts that differed from the final version, from Rand's Washington office to Santa Monica; the same arrangement was made for another eight volumes on August 29, 1969. Richard Best, a security officer at Rand, said later in a court affidavit in Los Angeles that Ellsberg was authorized to have possession of the volumes on those dates. But in another affidavit Jan Butler, "top-secret control officer" at Rand, said that the entire forty-seventy volumes of the Pentagon Papers came into her custody only on October 3, 1969. In yet a third affidavit on file with U.S. District Court in Los Angeles Daniel Ellsberg's former wife, Carol, noted that "in or about October 1969, I learned that my former husband . . . had been engaged in making xerox copies of a large number of documents some of which bore the classification Top Secret."

It was in September and October of 1969 that the polite, internal dissent about Vietnam boiled over at the Rand Corporation's normally quiet office building in Santa Monica. Five of the organization's top-flight researchers—including Ellsberg —were disturbed by the fact that their doubts about American participation in the war were not receiving the proper attention among their "clients" at the Defense Department and elsewhere in Washington. "We were talking about ways in which we could express our opposition to the war, ways in which we could in effect do something," Melvin Gurtov explains. They considered convening a conference modeled on the one that the Carnegie Endowment had sponsored in

Bermuda the year before, but they got nowhere with the idea. Rand associates ordinarily avoid publicity, but the period was one of intense public action; even Congressmen who were normally cautious had proclaimed open support of the Vietnam Moratorium on October 15, 1969, and of the massive Mobilization march against the war in Washington a month later. The Rand dissidents ultimately decided upon the most respectable form of establishment protest—a letter to the editor of *The New York Times*. "We went through a good many drafts, hammering things out," according to Gurtov. In the midst of drafting, a sixth person joined them. "Getting six people to sign anything is really something," as Gurtov puts it, especially when the six are academic experts with at least six different shades of opinion. Much to their surprise, Rand president Henry Rowen accepted the idea, so long as the six stressed that they were speaking only for themselves and not for their employer.

Rather than running the letter itself, the *Times* carried only a news dispatch on October 9, 1969, reporting that the letter had been written and that it "provided new impetus to the growing public demand for swift disengagement from Vietnam."

Three days later, however, the full text of the letter, signed by Ellsberg, Gurtov, Oleg Hoeffding, Arnold L. Horelick, Konrad Kellen, and Paul F. Langer, appeared in *The Washington Post*. "We believe that the United States should decide now to end its participation in the Vietnam war, completing the total withdrawal of our forces within one year at the most," the letter said. It then listed four basic objections to U.S. involvement:

> 1. Short of destroying the entire country and its people, we cannot eliminate the enemy forces in Vietnam by military means . . . What should now also be recognized is that the opposing leadership cannot be coerced by the present or any

other available U.S. strategy into making the kinds of concessions currently demanded.

2. Past U.S. promises to the Vietnamese people are not served by prolonging our inconclusive and highly destructive military activity in Vietnam. This activity must not be prolonged merely on demand of the Saigon government, whose capacity to survive on its own must finally be tested, regardless of the outcome.

3. The importance to the U.S. national interest of the future political complexion of South Vietnam has been greatly exaggerated, as has the negative international impact of a unilateral U.S. military withdrawal.

4. Above all, the human political and material costs of continuing our part in the war far outweigh any prospective benefits and are greater than the foreseeable costs and risks of disengagement.

The letter also warned that "the United States should not obstruct favorable political change in Saigon by unconditional support of the present regime. Yet, we believe, the United States should in no way compromise or postpone the goal of total withdrawal by active American involvement in Vietnamese politics. Such interventions in the past have only increased our sense of responsibility for an outcome we cannot control."

It was not just another letter to the editor. Here were men of unimpeachable credentials and experience, making judgments on the basis of government data within an organization that had been established under the auspices of the Air Force in 1946 and that still did 76 percent of its work for the Defense Department. There was a ripple of discontent from some high-ranking officers in the Pentagon, and somewhat less muted objections were voiced by members of the hawkish House Armed Services Committee. Within Rand the letter touched off what a temporary visitor there called "a great moral struggle"—memos, reply memos, and counterreply memos galore. The "physical sciences department" was outraged, citing

Rand's "special relationship" with the policy makers criticized in the letter and warning that their own "livelihoods"—Southern California was a luxurious setting for playing war games—were threatened.

Compared with going to jail for draft resistance or putting one's body on the line, as others were doing late in 1969 to dramatize their opposition, writing a letter to the editor was hardly a bold gesture. But from a Rand perspective it was a radical deed. Indications are that it stimulated more militant positions among the cool, calm inside dissidents. Gurtov, for example, a self-described hawk when he first came to Rand, began to examine Vietnam on previously taboo moral grounds. ("Of course, like many hawks who were in transition to becoming doves," he says, "my initial basis for a change of viewpoint was the strictly practical consideration that the war was not going well and perhaps we should be trying new things.")

Daniel Ellsberg has said that his intense exposure to the Pentagon Papers was the final step in his turning completely against the war; if so, it was the letter to the editor that marked his willingness to go public, very public, with his new position. The world outside the foreign affairs establishment began to hear Ellsberg's antiwar views expressed in laymen's terms, in terms that dealt with the human and social effects of the war, at home as in Vietnam. Ellsberg was introduced to Albert Appleby, chairman of the Southern California chapter and national vice president of Business Executives Move for Vietnam Peace (BEM), as a man who could help with the organization's programs. They met for lunch and talked nonstop for six hours. "I immediately realized," Appleby says, "that this guy was the most intelligent source on Vietnam that I had ever run across." What followed was a whirlwind tour of the West Coast business world to promote opposition to the war among those who had scarcely thought of questioning American policy. Appleby took Ellsberg to see the chairman of the board of the Bank of America (the nation's largest, where Appleby had once worked very successfully), the president of the San Francisco chamber of commerce, and the president of Hunt-Wesson Foods in archconservative Orange County. When Senator Mark Hatfield (R-Ore.) canceled his appearance at the organizational meeting of Home Decorators for Peace, Appleby had Ellsberg substituted. ("At first, they said: 'Dan who?' But he spoke for half an hour or so, and everybody was impressed.")

Ellsberg looked and acted the part of a man with a mission. Of medium height, slim and well-built, his curly hair graying at the appropriate points, he possessed a large measure of controlled intensity that drew his listeners to him. Whether in conversation or before a large audience, Ellsberg begins slowly and softly, gradually building in power and emotion and visiting a fixed stare on his listeners as he imparts the revealed word. His rhetoric has a personal rather than a carefully thought-through political tone.

On one occasion Appleby took Ellsberg to a meeting of the editorial board of the Los Angeles *Times*; it was a tense encounter. "They gave him shit for about an hour," Appleby recounts. "They said: 'We can't understand you, Ellsberg. We knew you when you were a real hawk, and now you come in here and tell us the war is no good.' . . . They worked him over and he got upset and mad; he really started talking about some way-out things. . . . He told them that it wouldn't surprise him if Nixon suspends the elections in 1972, things like that. They went crazy. . . ."

It was inevitable that the new Ellsberg and Rand would not last long together. By the spring of 1970 Ellsberg had had his fill, and so had the Rand hierarchy. "Frankly, Ellsberg was pressured to move on," says a high-ranking Rand official. "He had been very unproductive and had not delivered on some of his promises. . . . He was good at a first draft, but never followed through; his department head was increasingly unhappy with him from mid-1969 on."

There were several prospects. Ellsberg talked with the organizers of *Foreign Policy* magazine, an irreverent new quarterly that was challenging the role of *Foreign Affairs,* the bible of the establishment at New York's Council on Foreign Relations. But the most appealing opportunity was one that would return him to the free-wheeling academic world of Cambridge, Massachusetts, as a research fellow at MIT's Center for International Studies. "We had been too establishment," explains Everett E. Hagen, director of the center. "I said: 'Let's diversify, let's get somebody who may have a scholarly product from a different viewpoint; this clash of interpretation can't do anything but good.' So I took the initiative and I got the approval of my executive committee. . . . I had half a dozen names in mind, and Ellsberg looked like a good bet."

Ellsberg was signed on at the MIT research unit at the same time as William P. Bundy, the former Assistant Secretary of State who had a very different viewpoint, and their offices directly faced each other.

On August 8, 1970, Ellsberg married Patricia Marx, daughter of millionaire Republican toy manufacturer Louis Marx; during the previous year in California they had become emotionally and philosophically close to each other once again. About one hundred people attended their wedding—a standard Presbyterian ceremony performed by a college chaplain—at the idyllic estate north of New York City owned by Louis Marx, Jr., Patricia's brother. They went to Hawaii on a honeymoon (interrupted when Henry Kissinger asked Ellsberg to visit him in Washington, although the appointment was abruptly canceled) and then settled down in Cambridge. Ellsberg had a lot of work to do.

[CHAPTER IV]

Driving west out of downtown Los Angeles on Wilshire Boulevard, through Beverly Hills, through one after another barely
distinguishable well-manicured community, one comes eventually to the chalky white statue of Santa Monica, keeping watch
over the coastal city named for her. The city is quiet now,
calmer than in the boom days of the space and defense industries. But a few blocks to the south, occupying a full city
block at the intersection of Ocean Boulevard and Main Street,
there is one defense "industry" that has survived rather well,
merely adjusting its focus to the "late 1970s and early 1980s."

The orange and buff many-winged building that houses the
Rand Corporation, across from the Santa Monica city hall and
the Santa Monica County headquarters, could almost be a
Holiday Inn or a new office building for advertising agents and
insurance salesmen. The casual visitor is confronted by stiff,

vigilant security guards at any of the several entrances; they watch through sunglasses while the visitor fills out an identification card that includes questions on "affiliation" and "citizenship." The visitor would ordinarily prefer to abandon a tape recorder at the door rather than go through a clearance that seems to include everything but a phone call to the Pentagon (the person being visited, whatever his rank, has no authority to permit such equipment to be carried beyond the extrathick inner glass doors). An escort is required at all times, even to walk down a corridor past the occasional alcoves with photocopy machines, which have locks and signs warning that it is forbidden to copy classified material. Until the summer of 1971, however, employees could come and go without their briefcases being searched.

Associates of the Rand Corporation work in stark, silent private offices at any hour of the day, any day of the week; they communicate with one another primarily in carefully drafted memoranda. The rules dictate that unless they are away on official business, they must spend at least an hour in the office on any workday to avoid having it counted as leave (thus permitting individuals who are working on outside projects or who want to beat the system to come in from 11 P.M. to 1 A.M. and get credit for two days' work). Most of the research conducted at Rand is defined by specific requests from its government "clients," but there is invariably extra time between assignments, enviable flexibility, and a good deal of personal prerogative.

It was in this context, during the first eight or nine months of 1969, that Daniel Ellsberg had an opportunity to concentrate almost exclusively on reading and analyzing the Pentagon Papers. He had apparently completed at least one full reading before most of the Papers were even entered into the Rand security system, but after that and until he left the job Ellsberg was authorized to store the Papers in the "top-secret safe" in his own office. Rand security records indicate that for an extended period of time Ellsberg had access to all forty-seven volumes and exclusive custody of twenty-seven. Once the documents were integrated into the Rand files, Ellsberg signed receipts certifying that he would neither reproduce nor alter them.

What Ellsberg read convinced him beyond any doubt that the information in the Pentagon Papers, if widely available, would be explosive. The last part of the study to reach him was that covering the earliest period of American involvement in Vietnam—from U.S. support of the French after World War II to the early 1950s and the building up of the Ngo Dinh Diem regime—and he found it the most revealing of all. "It's that early material that changes the entire view as to the legitimacy of the war, of our intentions and our involvement," Ellsberg says. "One thing that is very clear is that there was no real junction in '54; the policy was a seamless one from a fundamental point of view. . . . It changed locale to some extent. Various things changed in '54, but nothing very fundamental about our aims or our commitment to the struggle. To find us joining what we clearly perceived to be a counter-independence and anti-independence movement, an attempt by the French to reestablish the colonial rule that had in fact been overthrown in 1945, is to see our policy stripped of all the pretensions of legitimacy that it acquired after 1954."

Ellsberg found the notion of North Vietnamese aggression against the South "thoroughly overthrown by the Pentagon Papers." He also came to reject the notion, popular in the peace movement, that the United States had merely intervened on its favored side in a civil war: "Probably a majority of people, if some sort of free peaceful choice were possible, would prefer some other leadership to that of the Viet Cong; but that does not mean that they'd be fighting a civil war to prevent Viet Cong leadership, any more than the Tories in this country [during the American Revolution], who may have been as much as a third or half the population in areas like New York, had it in mind to take up arms and fight the rebels. That was not a prospect at all, and exactly the same is true in Vietnam. . . . There would not be a civil war in Vietnam if we withdrew our money and arms. Differences would be resolved, and not primarily by force."

With the added perspective of what he saw as the total continuity of U.S. policy over more than two decades, he became convinced that the Vietnam story was "a case of aggression indeed. Our aggression entirely, our intervention. Ours is the foreign intervention in that situation. The other intervention, even by the Chinese and the Russians, is just negligible by comparison."

The more appalled he became by the war in Vietnam, the more Ellsberg worried about his own contributions to the decisions, to the devastation and destruction, to the deaths of Americans sent off to fight in a hopeless war and of Vietnamese in both North and South who had no choice. He became preoccupied with a sense of "personal responsibility" for the war and felt that he himself might come to be considered a "war criminal"; Ellsberg sought out a means to atone for this. He wanted to have a personal hand in helping to end the war, and—unrealistic as the notion may have been—he thought that disclosure of the Pentagon Papers could have that effect.

Anthony Russo had left the Rand Corporation in January 1969, having been fired six months earlier and given the customary grace period to complete any pending work and find a new job. He was convinced that his dismissal was "political," because he had consistently written reports criticizing the South Vietnamese government and recommending the cancellation of American-supported programs. Russo was somewhat bitter toward Rand and was also becoming increasingly radicalized through his work in the black ghettos of Los Angeles; he became part of Ellsberg's new circle of friends. Russo had a girl friend named Lynda Sinay, who ran a failing Los Angeles advertising agency. At Russo's urging, she rented out the agency's xerox machine to Ellsberg late in September 1969. Working entirely at night, when no one else was in the office, Ellsberg—with the assistance of his two children, Robert and Mary, and Russo—copied thousands of pages from the Papers. Utilizing an old trick devised by government bureaucrats for keeping copies of documents they work with or for leaking them selectively to the press, they covered over the "Top Secret," "Secret," or "Confidential" marking on each page before putting it through the machine, or sometimes cut off the classification afterward. Additional copies were subsequently made elsewhere, and the original pages, some from early drafts and some from the final version of the Papers, were systematically returned to the Rand files.

Carol Ellsberg learned of her former husband's activities through the children. As she explained it in a court affidavit later: "I spoke to my former husband about this and told him that I was extremely concerned since in my opinion this was a criminal act and he could go to jail for it. Daniel Ellsberg told me that he had done nothing illegal because there was no official secrets act in this country. I asked him what he thought would happen if he were to go to prison and he replied that he did not think there was much stigma to that anymore. He further said that people did this sort of thing all the time in their memoirs and that they mentioned things in print that had been top secret. My former husband at that time told me that he was very concerned about the war in Vietnam and that he was going to be actively working against it and that there were things that had not been disclosed which should be known. He then said that he would only give it to authorized people like Senators Fulbright and Goodell."

On November 6, 1969, during a visit to Washington, Ellsberg met with Senator J. W. Fulbright, chairman of the Senate Foreign Relations Committee, and several committee staff members. Fulbright, by that time committed to American withdrawal from Vietnam, was notoriously angry over **what** had been established as the purposeful deception of Congress during 1964 to obtain passage of the Gulf of Tonkin resolution, which became the "functional equivalent" of a declaration of war against North Vietnam. Ellsberg played on that anger, not only telling Fulbright about the existence of the Pentagon Papers but also turning over to him a brief portion that dealt with the Tonkin Gulf incident; he also gave the Senator notes on a separate command and control study of Tonkin, also secret and in the Rand files, which had been prepared by the Institute for Defense Analysis. Ellsberg urged that the Pentagon Papers be made public, perhaps through full congressional release of their contents, but Fulbright, who had never met Ellsberg before, expressed caution. "I didn't know what to do with [the Papers]," Fulbright recalled later. "I didn't want to get Ellsberg in trouble. I considered what to do with the portions he gave me—having executive hearings or something of that nature. But I decided that the best way would be to get them officially. Anyway, it wasn't clear then of what use they actually were in stopping the war."

The excerpts from the Papers were tucked away in the safe in the Foreign Relations Committee's offices on the fourth floor of the New Senate Office Building, but Fulbright lost no time acting on his promise to Ellsberg that he would try to do something about the study. Two days later he wrote to Defense Secretary Melvin Laird: "It is my understanding that the Department of Defense prepared a . . . history of the decision-making process on Vietnam policy covering the period from 1940 to April 1968. The project, I was informed, began under Secretary McNamara and was completed under Secretary Clifford and was confined to a study of written data. It appears that this study would be of significant value to the Committee in its review of Vietnam policy issues, and I would appreciate your making it, as well as any later studies of a similar nature, available to the Committee."

Laird promptly acknowledged Fulbright's letter, but then

took more than a month to write back refusing the request for access to the Pentagon Papers; the Secretary's letter of December 20, 1969, included the first formal confirmation by the Defense Department that the study even existed.

"In 1967, Secretary McNamara initiated a detailed history of the evolution of the present-day situation in Vietnam," Laird wrote. "It was conceived as a compilation of raw materials to be used at some unspecified, but distant, future date. On the basis of the understanding that access and use would be restricted, the documents were designed to contain an accumulation of data of the most delicate sensitivity, including NSC papers and other Presidential communications which have always been considered privileged. In addition, the papers included a variety of internal advice and comments central to the decision-making process. Many of the contributions to this total document were provided on the basis of an expressed guarantee of confidentiality."

"As intended from the start," Laird's letter continued, "access to and use of this document has been extremely limited. It would clearly be contrary to the national interest to disseminate it more widely. However, the Department of Defense is naturally prepared to provide the Committee information with respect to Executive Branch activities in Vietnam for any portion of the period covered by this compendium. I hope you will appreciate the reasons why we are unable to comply literally with your request."

Fulbright did not exactly appreciate Laird's reasons. The Senator wrote again on January 19, 1970, noting that he had hoped that previous satisfactory experience with Laird in connection with requests for other documents had "marked the beginning of a more cooperative attitude within the Executive Branch on problems of this nature."

"The issue involved here," Fulbright stressed, "is not merely that of allowing Committee members access to the documents but is far more fundamental, going to the heart of the continuing problem of striking the proper Constitutional balance between the Legislative and Executive branches, particularly on foreign policy matters. If the Senate is to carry out effectively its Constitutional responsibilities in the making of foreign policy, the Committee on Foreign Relations must be allowed greater access to background information which is available only within the Executive Branch than has been the case over the last few years. The history of the decision-making on Vietnam policy would be of great value to the Committee in appraising the policy-making machinery of our government and in studying ways to insure that the mistakes of the past are not repeated. Since this study was not initiated by President Nixon but by former Secretary McNamara and the doctrine of Executive Privilege has not been invoked, I again urge that you provide the Committee with these materials."

That argument might have been expected to appeal to Laird, himself a former Congressman from Wisconsin; but he apparently paid absolutely no attention. Except for a pro forma letter of confirmation sent to Fulbright on February 18, 1970, which promised to "be back in touch with you on this matter as soon as practicable," Laird remained silent on the subject for months.

Ellsberg, meanwhile, was searching for other people holding high office who might be willing to take dramatic action to help end the war. Late in 1969, after the massive Moratorium and Mobilization demonstrations in Washington, Congress was becoming increasingly disenchanted over the fact that, despite substantial troop cuts, President Nixon was continuing U.S. participation in the war and even stepping up bombing activity in Laos and South Vietnam. It was in this period that a number of outspoken legislators began to assert congressional prerogative in foreign policy for the first time in years; there was a rash of legislative proposals in the Senate, such as the effort by Senators John Sherman Cooper (R-Ky.) and Frank Church (D-Ida.) to cut off funding for American operations in Laos and by Senators George S. McGovern (D-S. Dak.) and Mark O. Hatfield (R-Ore.) to set a date for a pullout. One of the earliest and most brash of these bills was offered by Charles E. Goodell—the moderate Republican Congressman from upstate New York who had undergone his own conversion on the war after being appointed to fill the Senate seat of Robert F. Kennedy. He introduced legislation that would have required complete withdrawal by December 1970. Goodell was unable to find a single co-sponsor for his bill, but it became a *cause célèbre* in the peace movement. Ellsberg was impressed, and he enlisted to help Goodell drum up support.

Working with a group of other consultants to Goodell, but using his detailed acquaintance with the Pentagon Papers, Ellsberg helped draft the statement which the New York Senator used as lead-off witness before the Senate Foreign Relations Committee on February 3, 1970, when Senator Fulbright opened a new series of hearings on the war. In a few places, it was obvious that Goodell fudged while bending over backward to avoid using classified material in the speech; but the testimony was laced with references and conclusions which drew heavily on Ellsberg's point of view: "As a foreign intruder," Goodell said, "we have polarized the political situation in the South and driven many nationalist elements toward the NLF. Our withdrawal could help foster a depolarization that would create a more favorable environment for negotiations and a genuine political settlement." Goodell's predictions of U.S. force levels in Southeast Asia, which often proved to be accurate later, cited "informed sources" and were actually based on Ellsberg's own calculations.

At no point during his brief contact with the senator did Ellsberg tell Goodell that he had a copy of the Pentagon Papers; in fact, he never became aware of their existence until June 13, 1971. Goodell, who lost his Senate seat in the 1970 election to Conservative James L. Buckley after a three-man race including Democrat Richard Ottinger, later said he was sorry that Ellsberg did not tell him about the Papers, "because I think it would have made quite a difference if Congress had that information." Goodell acknowledged, though, that "I don't know what I would have done with them." In any event, Ellsberg felt that he must continue to work behind the scenes through the Foreign Relations Committee.

As the months passed, Ellsberg sought to prod Fulbright into action on the Papers. Late in February 1970 he submitted a large chunk of the contents—at least 3,000 pages photocopied from about twenty-five volumes of the study—to Norvill Jones, one of Fulbright's aides on the Foreign Relations Committee staff. Some of it he simply mailed from a post office in the Brentwood section of Los Angeles.

Fulbright reconsidered what he might properly do. But outright disclosure still seemed an unacceptable course of action to him: "I thought there would be a big to-do by the administration on the question of classification, which might divert from the contents of the Papers. I thought that if we used them without [official] release, the big attack would be on the procedure. . . . If I had done it, this would have brought a good deal of criticism on the Committee; certain Republican members would have raised hell. . . . I still thought they should be the subject of legitimate hearings." As chairman of one of the most prestigious committees in the Congress, Fulbright had a special problem and saw direct release as possibly counterproductive. Despite his frustrations, on many occasions he does receive classified material from the executive branch in closed sessions; any breach of security on his part could be used as a basis for denying him such material in the future. Then he in turn might be answerable to his colleagues in the Senate for their inability to learn that little bit of the inside story to which they were accustomed. And besides, whatever his policy views, Fulbright is a well-accepted member of the Senate "club"; he is not one to breach the standards and the etiquette under which it operates. He was in the bizarre position of having seen the Pentagon Papers but of feeling constrained not to quote publicly from them; instead he simply continued asking that they be made officially available. Fulbright wrote to Laird again on April 20, 1971. He got no reply.

By then, however, Ellsberg was exploring other means of getting the contents of the Papers into the public domain. He attended a conference on "war crimes" sponsored by retired Army general Telford Taylor and stressed to the international lawyers there that if any trial, or even mock trial, on the issue should be initiated, he knew of the existence of papers that corresponded—in his mind, at least—to the Nuremburg documents used after World War II. Ellsberg went as far as describing the Pentagon Papers to some of the lawyers and suggested that he could be named personally as a defendant or a witness in an attempt to get the Papers subpoenaed. He urged other constitutional lawyers to initiate civil suits and attempts to obtain court injunctions against the conduct of the war, offering the Papers as a dramatic piece of evidence. But no one was interested enough to pursue it.

In May 1970 American forces crossed into Cambodia with South Vietnamese troops on a mission that the Nixon administration promised would wipe out "enemy" sanctuaries within thirty days. The upheaval of protest throughout the nation was enormous. Four students at Kent State University in Ohio were shot and killed by National Guardsmen during a demonstration at the campus ROTC building; the Kent State deaths added more fuel to a mass march on Washington and an antiwar rally on the Ellipse behind the White House. Many universities, including some that had experienced relatively little antiwar protest previously, were forced by student strikes to close down a month ahead of schedule. Much more discreetly, Anthony Lake, a member of Henry Kissinger's national security staff at the White House, resigned in protest over the Cambodian invasion. The American troops would indeed withdraw into South Vietnam after thirty days, but vast numbers of people refused to believe the administration's proud declarations that the incursion had been a total "success." The Nixon credibility gap on the war yawned as newspaper correspondents reported that the American patrols had found scarcely any Viet Cong in Cambodia and not nearly the amount of war materiel that had been predicted. From then on opinion polls would reflect the clear sentiment of a large majority of the people that the war in Vietnam was no longer in the national interest.

The Cambodian adventure came in the midst of Senate Foreign Relations Committee hearings on the impact of the war in Southeast Asia on the American society and economy. The Senator from Arkansas was characteristically frustrated and angry that, constitutional niceties aside, the legislative branch had not been consulted on what seemed to be a widening of the war. Two days before the Cambodian incursion, in fact, there had been an executive hearing of the committee to discuss "a request by the Cambodian government for assistance," but no mention was made of the invasion plans by the administration witnesses. "They don't even deign to deceive us now," Fulbright said with a laugh.

Daniel Ellsberg testified before the Foreign Relations Committee at Fulbright's invitation on May 13, 1970, and his message was a gloomy one. He said he was proud of the protest over Cambodia, "but I am afraid that we cannot go on like this, as seems likely unless Congress soon commits us to total withdrawal, and survive as Americans. There would still be a country here and it might have the same name, but it would not be the same country. I think that what might be at stake if this involvement goes on is a change in our society as radical and ominous as could be brought about by our occupation by a foreign power."

Ellsberg pointed to the continuity of U.S. policy in Vietnam over the years and, in an exchange with Fulbright, said that "having studied the documents of a number of administrations and found the internal rationales in terms of strategic interests palpably inadequate, I have more and more come to look at the domestic political contexts in which those decisions were made year after year." Pointing out one of the weaknesses of the still secret Pentagon Papers, he added: "This is something which rarely gets into the internal documentation and if it is even talked about in the executive branch, that is done very privately, one or two people at a time." Extending his theory to the actions of the Nixon administration, Ellsberg observed that "this administration is no less ready than earlier ones to incur escalating risks and domestic dissent to avoid or postpone . . . 'humiliation.' The rhetoric has changed, and I refer here to the fact that we talk more about self-determination than we did in some recent years, but the policy has not. It is one that condemns Vietnam to endless war and Americans to endless participation in it in support of a corrupt and unpopular military dictatorship."

The interchange between Fulbright and Ellsberg inevitably turned to the Gulf of Tonkin incidents, and they jointly chastised the Defense Department for refusing to make studies of past events public. The Senator complained of the mystery surrounding the command and control study of Tonkin compiled by the Institute for Defense Analysis: "Here is a study made at government expense, paid for by the taxpayers, and withheld from the Committee. I don't see any justification for such classification." Ellsberg accommodatingly replied: "It is important that such few attempts at learning from our experiences should be exploited, be understood by those people who are involved in decision-making. I would wish, first of all, that President Nixon could have access to the information in that study and in other studies that were done directly for Mr. McNamara of our involvement. I would doubt very much whether anyone on the National Security Council staff has taken advantage of those." Fulbright concurred knowingly: "I can't subscribe to this extension of the concept of classifica-

[75]

tion to prevent our knowing about the past. . . . It doesn't give democracy an opportunity to function at all."

Ellsberg also congratulated Fulbright for publicly expressing "shame" over his part in ramming the Gulf of Tonkin resolution through Congress. "The voters of the country and the youth of this country, everyone, must hear statements from their leadership that imply that those leaders have a sense of personal values and of personal responsibility and are capable of acknowledging it," Ellsberg said. He urged that no one "refrain . . . from the indignities of 'mea culpas.'"

While he waited for the hearings that he felt certain Fulbright would call for the specific purpose of examining and exposing the lessons of the Pentagon Papers, Ellsberg also made them available, through intermediaries, to scholars from the Institute for Policy Studies, a radical-left think tank in Washington. They had been working since February 1970 on a two-volume study of the planning of the Vietnam war. A team of interviewers helping Ralph Stavins prepare the section entitled "Washington Determines the Fate of Vietnam: 1954–1965" received some documents from Kennedy and Johnson advisers with whom they spoke, but the availability of the Papers meant that assertions could be reliably checked against an existing historical study. For about a year the institute would make free use of the Pentagon Papers without any controversy. They were not hidden away in any peculiarly secretive maner; visitors remember having no trouble seeing them. But preparation of the book would take a long time—one volume was scheduled for release in the summer of 1971 and a second in the spring of 1972—and in any event this was not the kind of dramatic war-stopping disclosure that Ellsberg had in mind.

Fulbright, a man of delicate and gentlemanly persistence, was still trying. He wrote to Defense Secretary Laird again on July 10, 1970, asking that the Papers be made available to the committee. "It seems to me that the [Defense] Department has had ample time to consider this matter," he said. On July 21, a full six months after Fulbright had asked reconsideration of the decision not to make the study available, Laird wrote back to say no. He gave no additional reasons, nor did he answer Fulbright's point about sharing power over foreign affairs in the legislative and executive branches. "My letter of December 20, 1969," Laird said, "indicated that access to and use of this document, as intended from the start, has been and remains extremely limited. For the reasons expressed in that letter, I have again concluded that it would be clearly contrary to the national interest to disseminate the compendium more widely." That, under the rules permitting Cabinet officers an extraordinary degree of latitude in classification matters, was that.

Still stirring no public attention and being careful not to breach security himself, Fulbright took the Senate floor on August 7, 1970, and denounced Laird's decision on the Papers. "The Executive Branch—in what has become a reflex action—has again slammed the door on Congress," Fulbright said. He warned, though, that "as the old saw goes: 'Nothing is secret for long in Washington.' I hope that the first enterprising reporter who obtains a copy of this history will share it with the Committee."

Ellsberg had already been talking with one reporter, David Halberstam, formerly of *The New York Times* and then a contributing editor of *Harper's* magazine, who was compiling a book about the evolution of American policy on Vietnam. Although Ellsberg never showed Halberstam the Papers, he alluded to many of the documents in them.

Shortly after taking up his position at MIT in the fall of 1970, Ellsberg attended a seminar on "making news" given by Edwin Diamond, a former *Newsweek* writer lecturing on political science at the university; afterward he pumped Diamond with questions about *The New York Times*: "Where is power at the *Times*? Who runs what?" Diamond responded by mentioning the often publicized rivalries between the daily news operation of the *Times,* the editorial page, and the Sunday edition. Others recall similar conversations with Ellsberg at the time, conversations in which he expressed more than his usual amount of curiosity about the internal structure and operation of newspapers, especially the *Times.* On occasion Ellsberg even called Ben Bagdikian, assistant managing editor of *The Washington Post* and a friend, to ask him how to get information concerning Vietnam to the appropriate reporters at the *Times.*

When Ellsberg had something to say about the war and wanted to make sure it was read by the people he was criticizing, he would, like other East Coast intellectuals, write a letter to the *Times.* On November 26, 1970, for example, he wrote a bristling attack on the Nixon administration's Indochina policy. "Nixon's clearly announced and demonstrated strategy entails not only prolonging but vastly expanding this immoral, illegal, and unconstitutional war," he said in a letter endorsed by other MIT faculty members. "American casualties may decline, unless we invade the North. Yet the price of thus protecting Nixon from his fear of charges, borrowed from his own past, of 'losing Indochina to communism,' will be millions more refugees and hundreds of thousands more dead in Indochina, many more thousands of Americans dead, and the moral degradation of our country. To refuse any longer, wishfully, to believe that Nixon really means what he says and does, or to fail to resist his policy, is to become an accomplice."

In the meantime, Ellsberg had continued to work with the Pentagon Papers and hardly made a secret of that fact. In September, 1970, at the sixty-sixth anual meeting of the American Political Science Association in Los Angeles, he delivered a seventy-page paper called "Escalating in a Quagmire." In a long footnote to the paper Ellsberg said that his "assertions and speculations on U.S. decision-making" reflected his long experience in Defense and State department jobs as well as "research since that time, in part as a consultant with official access." He apologized for making "generalizations . . . without specific citation," but said that approach was less unsatisfactory than "to rely entirely on the public record or to pretend to do so, to forego generalizations or to subscribe to wrong ones." The paper, which would later be awarded a $250 prize as the best one delivered at the meeting, attracted widespread attention and later appeared in revised and abridged form in *Public Policy*. It was perhaps the most cogent statement of Ellsberg's conclusions about the decades of American involvement in Southeast Asia.

In his paper Ellsberg refuted the widely accepted notion—advanced, among others, by Arthur Schlesinger, Jr., the historian who had served as a White House aide to John F. Kennedy—that the United States had stumbled unknowingly into a "quagmire" in Vietnam and simply never knew how to get out. On the contrary, Ellsberg said, the "internal record" indicates that each successive American President was "striding with his eyes open into what he *sees* as quicksand, renewing efforts and carrying his followers deeper in, knowingly." He went back to a speech on the House floor on January 25, 1949, when then Congressman John F. Kennedy urged his colleagues to "assume the responsibility of preventing the onrushing tide of communism from engulfing all of Asia." As an alternate model of the "quagmire" theory, Ellsberg suggested that what had been operating was the "stalemate machine," a policy that involved doing "what was necessary at any given time to avoid losing, and not, at that time, much more." He inferred that a crucial "rule of the game" had been operating for all Presidents: "Do not lose the rest of Vietnam to Communist control before the next election." That interpretation certainly rang true to those who had noticed President Nixon telling the public repeatedly that he would not be the first American President to preside over a defeat of the nation at the hands of a foreign power.

Before he ultimately took things into his own hands, Ellsberg made a last flirtation with the actual decision-making process in government. Early in August 1970 he had lunch in Washington with Henry Kissinger and Lloyd Shearer, the roving editor of *Parade* magazine, a Sunday newspaper supplement with one of the largest readerships in the country. Kissinger indicated his interest in talking with Ellsberg alone about the war. Several subsequent appointments were made (including the one that interrupted the Ellsbergs' honeymoon in Hawaii), but according to Ellsberg they were canceled each time by Kissinger at the last moment. They did meet for half an hour at the Western White House in San Clemente in September, and as Ellsberg recounts it their conversation focused on the Pentagon Papers. Ellsberg learned that Kissinger had been one of the original advisers on the structure of the war history and that a copy of the final version was available to him. But Kissinger said he had not read the Papers, because they had little relevance to formulation of current policy. Ellsberg, citing his own reading of the Papers, disagreed. He pressed Kissinger, urging him to assign at least one person the task of reading and analyzing the entire study. Kissinger promptly offered that job to his visitor. Ellsberg refused: "My feeling was that I'd been through all that before and I wasn't going to get in the position of being a staff worker for him."

Later, when the Pentagon Papers were disclosed, Kissinger was quoted as denying any knowledge of them.

The last confrontation between Ellsberg and Kissinger came in late January 1971 at a weekend conference in suburban Boston sponsored by MIT and several businessmen to discuss "the foreign policy crisis." Kissinger, one of the main speakers, told the group that "there are no good choices left in Vietnam" and that "this administration has been the best protection of those who most loudly deplore our policy." After several other people asked Kissinger questions, Ellsberg stood and pressed him to say whether the administration had estimated the number of Asian dead and wounded that might result from "Viet-namization," just as it had estimates of expected American casualties. When Kissinger began to speak of "options," Ells-berg said, "I know the option game, Dr. Kissinger . . . can't you just give us an answer or tell us you don't have such estimates?" Kissinger did not reply. The meeting was broken up, and the next day South Vietnamese troops entered Laos on operations heavily supported by American troops from the air—a showpiece of Vietnamization.

The Laos operations became the subject of one of Ellsberg's angriest public attacks on American policy, an article in the *New York Review of Books* in March 1971. He wrote of "a coherent inner logic" to American policy: the old rule of "a decent interval" between American troop withdrawal and the fall of the Saigon government. "How many will die in Laos?" Ellsberg asked. "What is Richard Nixon's best estimate of the number of Laotian people—'enemy' and 'non-enemy'—that U.S. firepower will kill in the next twelve months? *He does not have an estimate.* He has not asked Henry Kissinger for one, and Kissinger has not asked the Pentagon; and none of these officials has ever seen an answer, to this or any com-parable question on the expected impact of war policy on human life. And none of them differs in this from his predeces-sors."

Whenever Ellsberg consulted lawyers, they advised him that he would be in a much safer position legally if he persuaded a member of Congress—protected by legislative immunity—to disclose the Pentagon Papers rather than doing it himself. As he became discouraged over the prospects with Fulbright—some of whose staff members began advising against holding hearings based on the Pentagon Papers—Ellsberg next chose Senator George McGovern, sponsor of a major end-the-war amendment and the first declared candidate for the 1972 Dem-ocratic presidential nomination. Ellsberg called on the Senator in January 1971, saying he had classified material that would expose American policy in Vietnam so thoroughly as to end the war. According to Ellsberg's version of the story, McGovern agreed that he would probably want to accept the Papers but later backed down after consulting with Senator Gaylord Nelson (D-Wis.), a good friend of McGovern and a lawyer. Later Ellsberg would attack McGovern for not having the courage to help flush out the truth on the war.

But McGovern's recollection of their relationship is substantially different. "I concluded after talking with him for a while that he was a hawk with a bad conscience," McGovern says. "I've had a dozen professors and preachers and foreign service officers give me memoranda in the past that they said would end the war if disclosed. . . . I had no idea what he had, and I didn't know if his judgment was good or bad. I didn't even know whether he was rational." McGovern says he also pointed out to Ellsberg that it would be better to approach someone other than a candidate for President, in order to avoid the impression that the release was for purely partisan political purposes. McGovern, who was proud of a long record of voting against the war in the Senate, resented Ellsberg's argument that everyone should be willing to go to jail in order to end the war: "I figured that if anybody was to go to jail, it would be better for him to go than me, since I was a United States Senator, doing what I think is important work." John Holum, McGovern's legislative assistant, did not like Ellsberg. "There are a lot of people you encounter who are recent converts on the war," Holum observes with the passion of a long-time believer. "They usually don't have much to offer." He and other staff members were offended by Ellsberg's manner and the knowledge that he had already "told off" Senator Nelson. McGovern denies that he ever encouraged Ellsberg or even looked at the papers before making his decision. According to McGovern, he urged Ellsberg to go instead to a large newspaper, such as *The New York Times* or *The Washington Post*. In retrospect, however, he concedes that if a member of

Congress had been willing to act, the press and the people might have been able to obtain and digest the information in the Pentagon Papers much more easily.

Ellsberg felt at that time that he had exhausted the major prospects in Congress. The press seemed to be the only solution, and the *Times* was his natural choice. It was simply a matter of choosing the right person to receive the material. That became easier when Ellsberg learned that Neil Sheehan—a former UPI correspondent whom Ellsberg had met in Vietnam and who was now working in the Washington bureau of the *Times*—was preparing an essay on thirty-three antiwar books for the *Times*'s book review section. Sheehan's piece, entitled "Should We Have War Crime Trials?", appeared in the newspaper on March 28, 1971. The men directing the war in Washington and Saigon, Sheehan observed, had "never read the laws governing the conduct of war . . . or if they did, they interpreted them rather loosely." Looking at the thirty-three books, he said, "if you credit as factual only a fraction of the information assembled here about what happened in Vietnam, and if you apply the laws of war to American conduct there, then the leaders of the United States for the past six years at least, including the incumbent President, Richard Milhous Nixon, may well be guilty of war crimes."

That was enough for Daniel Ellsberg. Neil Sheehan and his wife, Susan, a writer for *The New Yorker*, visited Cambridge late in March 1971; after a brief stay at the Treadway Motel there, they returned to Washington with an enormous bundle of disorganized photocopies of government documents, the Pentagon Papers.

Ellsberg did not make available to the *Times* the last four volumes of the Papers, which chronicled American diplomatic contacts through other nations aimed toward a negotiated settlement of the Vietnam conflict and release of prisoners of war, considered the most sensitive part of the study. He held back the "diplomatic volumes," Ellsberg explained later, because "I didn't

[83]

want to get in the way of the diplomacy. . . . I wanted to get in the way of the bombing and killing."

On March 7, 1971, the Sunday edition of the Boston *Globe* carried a front-page story by Thomas Oliphant describing the nature of the study McNamara had commissioned. The headline read: "Only 3 Have Read Secret Indochina Report; All Urge Pullout." The three people to whom Oliphant referred were Morton Halperin, Leslie Gelb, and Daniel Ellsberg. The last, described by Oliphant as "by far the most vocal in his opposition to the war," told the reporter in an interview that during his six years in government and consulting jobs "I was participating in a criminal conspiracy to wage aggressive war." Oliphant's story included quotes from Ellsberg's scathing article in the *New York Review of Books,* but not from the Pentagon Papers themselves. Nonetheless it was quite a scoop; except for a brief mention in the October 25, 1970 issue of *Parade* magazine, Oliphant was the first to write publicly about the Papers. But no one else picked it up.

There would still be a long wait. Daniel Ellsberg, who had paid attention to little else for a year and a half, was near despair.

[CHAPTER V]

When Neil Sheehan walked into the Washington bureau of
The New York Times late in March 1971 with the results of
his "investigative reporting"—the euphemism that was later
devised by the *Times* to give him primary credit for obtaining
the Pentagon Papers—the reaction was hardly one of overwhelming excitement. After Sheehan had been offered access
to the Vietnam war history by Daniel Ellsberg, but before he
actually traveled to Cambridge to pick it up, he had described
what he knew about it to his bureau chief, Max Frankel. The
sheer notion of obtaining thousands of pages of government
documents that were classified top secret was an intriguing
one, enough to quicken the heart of any devoted reporter or
editor on an independent newspaper. But there were basic
journalistic questions to be answered first. As one high-ranking
Times executive put it: "We had to wonder, 'What are we

going to learn from yet another Pentagon history? What confidence can we have of its authenticity and comprehensiveness?'" Interest was clearly waning among the American public in articles about Vietnam; even the American-supported South Vietnamese invasion of Laos had faded rather rapidly from the front pages; there was no longer the keen competition among reporters for the country's major newspapers to be assigned to cover the war. New antiwar protests were in the works, to be sure, but President Nixon, by withdrawing substantial numbers of troops from Vietnam, had succeeded to a remarkable extent in convincing the American people that the war would soon be over.

There was also some concern at the *Times* over the reliability and the motives of Sheehan's sources. Contrary to the later assertions of the Justice Department and Nixon administration officials, there is a tradition among newsmen of integrity to protect the confidentiality of their sources; reporters, even if they are the best of friends, frequently refuse to tell one another and their editors where they have obtained particular bits of information. Earl Caldwell, a *Times* reporter, had risked an indefinite term in prison by refusing to testify before a federal grand jury in San Francisco about his sources of information for a series of articles on the Black Panther Party. Thus, initially at least, the editors of the *Times* did not press Sheehan to reveal Ellsberg's identity. (Some would insist even nine months later, long after Ellsberg's public declaration of responsibility for the news leak, that they were not sure who provided the material to Sheehan.) They did seek to establish, however, that Sheehan was absolutely confident that he was not being used irresponsibly, a question that took on greater significance with the knowledge that the Papers had been virtually dropped in his lap, rather than ferreted out on his own initiative.

Sheehan had established a reputation as a hard-hitting journalist in the early 1960s as a UPI correspondent in Vietnam;

there, along with David Halberstam of the *Times* and Malcolm Browne of the Associated Press, he was one of the "fearless
threesome," the reporters who infuriated the Kennedy White
House with their full and frank disclosures about Ngo Dinh
Diem's regime in Saigon. Sheehan was hired by the *Times*
after many representations on his behalf by Halberstam and
others. His career at the newspaper was not without its difficulties; Sheehan seemed to suffer more than most from the
internal politics at the *Times*. At one point, after joining the
Washington bureau, he was denied permission to return to
Vietnam for several months to work on a magazine article.
When Sheehan was sent back to Vietnam by the *Times*, he
was subsequently passed over for the position of bureau chief.

In the spring of 1971, however, Sheehan's problems were of
a different order: some editors openly expressed displeasure
over his "war crimes" essay in the Sunday book review, feeling
that he may have gone overboard and damaged his reputation.
The editors of the daily newspaper persistently rejected the
requests of the Sunday book review editors that the unusual
essay be publicized in advance in order to draw maximum
attention to it. They were also annoyed that it often took
Sheehan longer than most reporters to turn out a major story.

Although it was not immediately noticeable, there may also
have been an element of defensiveness in the reluctance of
some editors at the *Times* to hop onto the internal Pentagon
Papers bandwagon. Critics of the American war effort had
long complained that, despite its reputation for thoroughness
and straightforwardness, the *Times*, like many other major
American newspapers, was slow to question the Kennedy and
Johnson administrations' lines about the war. In 1964, after the
Gulf of Tonkin incidents, the *Times* editorialized about "the
beginning of a mad adventure by the North Vietnamese Communists." It gave scant coverage to Senator Fulbright's Foreign
Relations Committee probe into Tonkin, having already ignored several reports, by the Associated Press and others, that

provided evidence to contradict the official government version of the facts. Members of the growing journalistic subculture of "media critics" frequently charged that the front page of the *Times* often resembled the Soviet Union's *Pravda*, uncritically reporting every word and deed official Washington offered about Vietnam without checking thoroughly or allowing reasonable space for the views of those who disagreed. Halberstam, who left the *Times* in 1967 to write magazine articles and books, contends that the Pentagon Papers showed, as much as anything else, how the newspaper had failed to turn up the full inside story of Vietnam. "A good newspaper is supposed to initiate coverage," Halberstam observes. "The editors of the *Times* were very good at initiating coverage of scandals in the poverty program in Harlem. It would seem to me that the origins of the decisions to escalate a war in Vietnam were just as serious a question for the nation."

But if Sheehan had personal and institutional obstacles to overcome, he did so before long. His supervisors and editors were impressed. "As the onion peeled, as Neil got a look at some of the stuff," says Max Frankel, "I pressed him for some samples of the rhetoric, of what it looked like and what it sounded like, what periods it covered, what the documents were like. . . . Then I finally got a look at some of the material from 1964 and 1965, only a couple of documents, but mainly the chapters of analysis. Because I had been intimately involved in covering the same stuff myself, I was able very quickly to reach the judgment that this was high quality and that it was fair, it was not grinding too many axes, it was not a bunch of Vietnam doves sounding off or anything like that. . . . I remember saying to Neil very early on that 'if this is the quality of most of the thing, it's a gold mine.' He thought it was."

Frankel moved quickly to brief *Times* managing editor A. M. Rosenthal and others in New York, advising that it would be "a mammoth reading job" and would require a lot of help. The Washington bureau chief, who had risen from rewrite man to one of the most prestigious jobs on the newspaper, commanded a great deal of influence in the main office, and he was in a hurry to move with Sheehan's story. Ellsberg had made it clear to Sheehan that Senator Fulbright had the Papers—on March 31 Ellsberg visited Fulbright and Foreign Relations staffer Norvill Jones, pressing them to take some bold action at last because the Papers were bound to surface elsewhere soon—and that the Institute for Policy Studies was also working with them; what Ellsberg did not confide, however, was that Fulbright was reluctant to take any action without official release of the history and that IPS was working on a long-range project that would not be completed before the summer. Frankel feared that the *Times* would be scooped by a U.S. Senator or that the radical scholars at the institute would leak parts of the Papers to politicians they favored. He also found it inconceivable that the Papers would not soon fall into the hands of another newspaper, most likely either *The Washington Post* or the Los Angeles *Times*.

The basic instincts of the editorial hierarchy at the *Times* left little room for doubts over the propriety of publishing classified government documents. It was standard practice for high-ranking Washington officials, even the President himself, to leak secret material purposefully to achieve domestic or international political goals; malcontents in the federal bureaucracy often passed classified memoranda on to opposition Congressmen, who in turn made political hay through floor speeches or selective leaks to the press. Senator Henry M. Jackson (D-Wash.), for example, regularly provided inside information to reporters that indicated, in his view, that the Soviet Union was rapidly passing the United States in one area or another of defense capacity. What is more, many of the most famous *Times* newsmen had built their careers on story after story based upon classified data, some of it American and some of it foreign in origin. James Reston, who epitomized the reputation of the *Times* and was now a vice president of the newspaper, had won wide acclaim in 1954 for his revelations of the Yalta Papers, leaked by the State Department in the Eisenhower administration, which allegedly documented secret deals between President Roosevelt and Soviet Premier Joseph Stalin during World War II. Sydney Gruson, now special assistant to *Times* publisher Arthur Ochs Sulzberger, had in the course of his long career as a newspaperman broken a number of secrets in major stories, including details of the draft charter of the North Atlantic Treaty Organization (NATO) and the new German-American policy in 1963. ("My life was spent trying to get secrets," Gruson acknowledges. "I never felt badly about getting them. I never felt that I had ever endangered anything by publishing.")

Still there seemed to be something a little different about the Pentagon Papers. They were history, yes, but they also risked aggravating the deep wounds in American politics over the war in Vietnam. And the sheer volume, the enormity of the apparent breach in government security, posed a unique and unprecedented problem; the decision on how to use the Pentagon Papers would not be as easy as it first appeared.

Times foreign editor James L. Greenfield, a man with State Department experience during the Kennedy administration and one of managing editor Rosenthal's closest allies, was given overall charge of the assignment, enticingly labeled "Project X" from the start. He dispatched one of his assistants, Gerald Gold, to Washington to work with Sheehan on planning and developing the stories. On April 5, 1971, Gold checked into a two-room suite at the Jefferson Hotel on Sixteenth Street in Washington, five blocks from the White House; Sheehan dropped out of sight from the bureau, an occurrence that in itself was not extraordinary. Sheehan and Gold worked together at the hotel for two weeks, attempting to determine what was new in the Papers and what was not and drafting an ambitious plan for a long series of articles that would require as much as ten to twelve pages a day in the *Times,* including the publication of selected documents from the Papers. When they took their plan to New York, the top editors decided that Sheehan and Gold had better stay there to work on the articles, with additional help to be provided.

After being disappointed elsewhere, Ellsberg was not about to hedge his bets on the *Times.* Even while Sheehan had the Papers and was working with them for the *Times,* Ellsberg continued to seek another avenue of release, one that might place him in less jeopardy and provide at least a tentative umbrella of congressional immunity. He went back to Fulbright and Norvill Jones, urging them again to act and hinting that he had already entered into negotiations with a newspaper in order to be sure that the Papers got out one way or another.

On April 19, 1971, Ellsberg appeared at a conference at Princeton University on the same program with Senator Vance Hartke (D-Ind.) and Congressman Paul N. ("Pete") Mc-Closkey (R-Cal.). McCloskey, who had launched a "Dump Nixon" movement within the Republican party and had recently returned from Laos, told the conference how shocked he had been to find that the executive branch had deceived Congress about American military operations there. The Congressman had to leave before Ellsberg spoke, but he remembered the *New York Review of Books* article about Laos. Ellsberg visited McCloskey at his Capitol Hill office about a week later, bringing along a sheaf of xeroxed documents from the 1962–1964 period of the Pentagon Papers. There was no visible sign that they had been classified. Testifying before the Senate Foreign Relations Committee late in April, McCloskey—unaware that Fulbright already had requested several times that Laird release the study—suggested that the committee chairman do exactly that. McCloskey read about half of the material Ellsberg had given him and then returned it. But then, early in May, by prior arrangement Ellsberg and Mc-Closkey sat next to each other on a plane trip to and from California. Ellsberg gave the Congressman additional excerpts from the Pentagon Papers, and they had long discussions about the war and about the best means for making the Pentagon study public. Like Senator George McGovern, McCloskey rejected the notion that he should take it upon himself to release the Papers. "I told him that it would have interfered with what I was trying to do" in opposing President Nixon, McCloskey recalls.

Months later, discussing his encounters with Ellsberg, Mc-Closkey said that he had the impression during the plane trip that Ellsberg had provided the Papers to *The New York Times* but felt he had maintained the personal option of telling the newspaper when it was "authorized" to go ahead with publication (a feeling, needless to say, that was not shared by the editors and reporters at the *Times*). At one point, McCloskey said, he considered offering his excerpts from the Papers on the floor of the House for inclusion in the Congressional Record, as a means of testing the congressional system and finding out how his colleagues would react. Instead, however, he decided to follow the Fulbright route and request them through the House Foreign Operations and Government Information Subcommittee, of which he is a member. In the meantime, McCloskey stored the Papers Ellsberg had given him in his safe in the Longworth House Office Building and had a young staff member sleep in front of the safe every night as a watchman. The subcommittee hearings at which McCloskey planned to unveil portions of the Papers were repeatedly postponed until after the *Times* had published. Once Daniel Ellsberg had been indicted on criminal charges, McCloskey sent his copies back to the source; if he had kept a set of the Papers, they could have been subpoenaed as evidence against Ellsberg.

It was late in April that publisher Sulzberger was first approached through the *Times*'s complex chain of command and informed of the news department's ambitious plans for publishing the Pentagon Papers. James Reston first told him by telephone. But through his executive aides—Harding Bancroft, a former diplomat without a trace of newspaper experience; *Times* vice president Ivan Veit, who had worked for the paper since 1928; and Gruson—"Punch" Sulzberger was advised of the complex legal dilemma that the stories might present, of the possibility that the government could take legal action against the newspaper on such a sensitive project. As one *Times* executive characterized the mood: "You had to. wonder at a time like that as to the outcome and what damage might be done to the newspaper as the kind of newspaper people consider it. . . . I couldn't help wondering whether we were going down a path that could lead to God only knows what consequences for the paper. We knew we were probably going to be in for a very bitter fight in the courts, and one didn't know at this time which way public opinion would sway. We hoped that the necessity for publishing, as we saw it, would be understood by the public."

Sulzberger clearly had misgivings from the start, given the scope of the project and the stakes involved, and he made it clear that the final decision would be in his hands. Without indicating how his feelings were running, the publisher told the news department in effect: "Go away, do the work you feel you have to do, come back to me when you have something to show me that you want published." In the meantime, he launched none-too-subtle consultations with the *Times*'s legal staff and with Lord, Day, and Lord, the Wall Street law firm that handled most of its legal business.

Rosenthal and Greenfield, sensing that there might be trouble looming, assumed personal direction of the preparations, occasionally calling Frankel up from Washington to help them deal with Sheehan, whom they found to be eccentric and

[93]

brooding. Greenfield was in an unusual position for a newspaper editor. He had served in the government for five years, much of that time as Assistant Secretary of State for Public Information, and had attended some of the very meetings that were described in the Pentagon Papers. "What I tried to do from the very beginning, and what Abe [Rosenthal] wanted me to do," Greenfield recalls, "was really to revert back as if I was in the government, what I would think [of the material] and the consequences of publication." During a period of ten days he and Rosenthal scoured forty-two books written by former government officials—among them Arthur Schlesinger, Jr., Theodore Sorensen, Roger Hilsman, and Chester Cooper—to discover whether they had written about and revealed comparable, or even the same, classified information. According to Greenfield: "We discovered that if there had been any confidentiality among them and the way they dealt with each other, it had been very well moved over and walked over and revealed." After also looking at books written by people outside government, the editors determined that the "principle" of protecting classified information, specifically with regard to the Vietnam war, "had become almost academic."

At the same time, the *Times* launched an extravagant library project of reviewing ten years' worth of the newspaper, to measure what the public was being told at each step along the way against what was described as happening in the Pentagon Papers. Events were listed on a huge chart, and an enormous card file was developed as a cross-reference for newspaper stories and decisions. The documents in the Pentagon Papers were "rated" and "gradiated." In Greenfield's words: "We decided that many were nothing but kibitzing along the line, while others quite clearly led to decisions." In the narrowing-down process the editors subjectively eliminated from consideration some of the more sensational items, such as a statement by Admiral Harry D. Felt, commander in chief of Pacific forces, suggesting that the United States should be prepared to use atomic weapons in Vietnam (a statement that subsequently appeared in a Boston *Globe* story on the Pentagon Papers). Felt's comment was omitted on the grounds that it had never been given serious consideration and might distort the perspective of the articles. The *Times* reporters and editors, relying on their experience in journalism and government, searched for material they thought might be considered dangerous to national security—battle plans, secret weapons, ongoing negotiations. But they found almost nothing in that category. They were sure that none of the documents would permit a foreign power to break an American code but nonetheless took the precaution of removing the time groups from the top of each document that might be used.

Originally "Project X" was to be worked on in an obscure corner of the *Times* building on West Forty-third Street near Times Square. But within a few days the lack of quiet, of space, and of appropriate provisions for secrecy led to a decision to move it elsewhere. Peter Millones, Rosenthal's assistant, was dispatched to find a hotel sufficiently large to camouflage the project and to keep the reporters and editors anonymous among tourists and conventioneers; he selected a three-room suite at the New York Hilton, outfitting it with desks, chairs, typewriters, file cabinets, and even safes. *Times* security guards were sent to the hotel to keep watch whenever one of the rooms was empty.

Hedrick Smith, scheduled to take up assignment in Moscow for the *Times*, delayed his departure to join Sheehan in New York; Ned Kenworthy also took a mysterious leave from the Washington bureau. Fox Butterfield, who had reported from both North and South Vietnam, was called in from Newark. (As Sydney Gruson puts it: "At the *Times* we never use few reporters when many will do.") They were all directed not to appear at the *Times* office but to work only in the Hilton, where the "Project X" headquarters eventually expanded to five rooms, all in assistant foreign editor Gold's name. One

Times editor recalls that each of the reporters characteristically brought in dozens of old notebooks to cull for additional detail; however, they were warned not to get off onto a "*New York Times* history of the war," but rather to stick closely to the content of the Pentagon Papers without embellishment. In another precise instruction, the reporters were warned not to phone any of the authors of the Papers or participants in the decision-making process on Vietnam to check details, lest the secret of the *Times* scoop get out. That was a kind of reporting and writing alien to them, and they became in effect prisoners of their own source material. Perhaps the most onerous requirement was that they maintain copious cross-referenced notes so that, if challenged, they could point to the basis of every assertion in their articles. Rather than follow the chronological order of the Papers and the years they covered, the reporters were to assign their priorities on the basis of newsworthiness. The Johnson administration's decisions involving covert warfare and bombing of North Vietnam were singled out as the subject of Sheehan's first installment. Showing the strain of their confinement, the foursome—and the several copy editors who joined them at the Hilton—quarreled frequently. They were under constant pressure from Greenfield and Rosenthal to produce copy, but despite twelve-to-fifteen-hour workdays the process moved even more slowly than expected. "We were just tormented by the notion that somebody else would dribble this stuff," Frankel says.

While the reporters worked with the Papers, an assistant picture editor for the *Times* built up a comprehensive archive of photographs detailing the decades of American involvement in Vietnam. His work would be in vain, however, because the stories about the Papers would ultimately squeeze out the pictures.

The official *Times* position would later become that there was never any doubt about whether the newspaper would publish, and thereby disclose, the top-secret Papers. In retrospect, it might be more accurate to say that until two days before publication there was never any certainty that it would. For as the team of reporters and editors labored away in the Hilton, and for the most part unknown to it, there ensued a very lively debate indeed in the *Times* building a few blocks away. One executive refers to it as "one of the healthiest arguments within this newspaper that I have ever known"; but a high-ranking newsman at the *Times* describes it less euphemistically as "a wild and almost ignorant argument."

Harding Bancroft for one had strong doubts, and early in the debate opposed publishing the Papers altogether. Bancroft's opinion automatically carried a good deal of prestige; like Greenfield, he was listened to on the basis of his long experience in government—as a naval officer in World War II, a State Department official, a deputy representative to a United Nations committee under President Truman, and a legal adviser to the International Labor Organization in Geneva. But perhaps more important, ever since "Punch" Sulzberger's accession to the publisher's job in 1963 on the death of Orvil Dryfoos, Bancroft's name had appeared second on the *Times* masthead; appropriately so, since he was one of Sulzberger's key advisers and had operational control of the newspaper in the publisher's absence (an arrangement that would be triggered at the height of the eventual crisis over the Papers). Bancroft, a dignified and soft-spoken man, was concerned over the possibility of revealing codes and of diplomatic embarrassment to the country. His reservations were magnified in the advice offered Sulzberger by the newspaper's law firm, Lord, Day, and Lord, whose senior partners were Herbert Brownell, U.S. Attorney General during the Eisenhower administration, and Louis Loeb, by this time almost seventy-three years old, a former general counsel of *The New York Times*. In no uncertain terms they told the *Times* not to

[97]

publish the material at all, warning that to do so would trigger vigorous, almost surely successful, legal action by the government.

But the *Times* executives also had to reckon with the advice of their own full-time legal department, now headed by thirty-eight-year-old James C. Goodale, a tireless, informal man who had made it a point to meet many reporters on the newspaper and who considered himself as much a newsman as a lawyer. Goodale had originally come to the *Times* through the good offices of Lord, Day, and Lord, where he was a junior associate, but he had long since developed a view of "publishing law" far different from that of Brownell and Loeb. His view as vice president and general counsel of *The New York Times*, unlike that of the lawyers for many other newspapers, is: "There's always a way to get [a story] into print, everything that comes to you." In the case of the Pentagon Papers, he too had special qualifications for making a judgment, having served in a strategic intelligence research group while in the Army reserve. "I've done histories like the Pentagon history," Goodale says. "I haven't done one on Vietnam, and I'm not going to say which ones I have done, but I've written many just like it and taken *New York Times* articles and used them as footnotes, just as these guys did, and stamped the result classified. Having gone through that process and in effect classified *The New York Times*, I was just sure as hell there was something from the *Times* in there which had been classified Top Secret. My analysis really began with this concept: If in fact there was *New York Times* material in there, how could the government prohibit you from publishing what you had already published?"

Goodale prepared a thorough legal memorandum for the executives and editors of the *Times* setting out the justification for publishing the Pentagon Papers. He felt confident that as long as the stories were handled carefully, no injunction against the *Times* or criminal conviction of the newspaper or its reporters could ultimately be sustained by higher courts. But Goodale had a sense that among the newspaper executives "no one agreed with me. I wasn't making any headway whatsoever with the non-news people who make the decisions, because I guess I was battling against Louis Loeb. I was at wit's end . . . I was about to throw in the whole towel." Goodale's wife had a baby in May, and he took off a full week, convinced when he left that the *Times* would not be running anything substantial based on the Pentagon Papers.

In the meantime, another powerful voice at the *Times* and perhaps one of the most influential voices in American journalism, James Reston, was also arguing strongly in favor of publication. Reston had mixed feelings, retrospectively, about having intervened in 1961 with then publisher Orvil Dryfoos to tone down a story about the impending American-financed Bay of Pigs invasion in Cuba. Over the angry objections of the editors at that time, Reston and Dryfoos had the Bay of Pigs story buried deep inside the paper with a drab headline and purged it of all references to the imminence of the invasion and CIA involvement. But after the Bay of Pigs adventure failed, even President Kennedy acknowledged that perhaps the *Times* had been too protective of American national security; had the full truth been told in print, the President admitted, the invasion might have been canceled, a fiasco avoided, and many lives saved. During his career Reston had squelched other stories, such as the knowledge that the United States was flying U-2 planes over the Soviet Union during the Eisenhower administration; he knew, but did not write, that story for a year, until a U-2 piloted by Francis Gary Powers was shot down by the Russians. Even if he had not had second thoughts about his earlier judgments, Reston saw a clear distinction between those situations and the Pentagon Papers. All evidence seemed to point to the fact that the Papers were almost pure history and could have little effect on current national security. Reston served as a conduit to Sulzberger for the opinions of the rank-and-file reporters on the *Times*.

Despite the internal security, rumors began to spread that the *Times* was corporately considering a weak position; the reporters' attitude was hardening—not only did they feel it was utterly essential to publish; they also urged adoption of the position in advance that the *Times* was willing to defy a court injunction and continue publishing in the name of freedom of the press. Reston, when he recognized the editors' hesitation, escalated his own position; he said that if the *Times* did not use the Pentagon Papers he would publish them in the *Vineyard Gazette*, the newspaper he recently purchased on Martha's Vineyard, off the coast of Massachusetts. (During the vacation season, when many of the most influential members of the Washington–New York establishment are on the island, the Papers might have had almost as much impact there as in the *Times*.)

Contrary to Daniel Ellsberg's later private claims, the *Times* officials had no notion that they were under obligation, as a condition of obtaining the Pentagon Papers, to use them in a particular way. To permit a source to control absolutely how the stories must be handled, they observed later, would have been a breach of normal journalistic standards; and if the *Times* was to bear the brunt of any legal repercussions, the central decisions would have to be its own to take. Thus the newspaper considered several possible ways to handle the stories, should Sulzberger eventually decide to grant permission to proceed with publication of the Pentagon Papers.

One option favored by more conservative elements within the *Times* management was to run a series of articles that described the Pentagon history but merely paraphrased the documents that accompanied it rather than quoting directly from them—or, as an alternative, quoting brief excerpts from the documents in the articles but still not printing the confidential documents themselves. This technique, it was argued, would have the advantage of appeasing the government by making the security breach appear less blatant than it had been, and the Justice Department might then be less eager to take legal action in the courts. Among the proponents of this approach were John Oakes, a direct descendant of Adolph Ochs—the man who bought the *Times* in 1896—with great power on the newspaper by virtue of his position as editor of the editorial page. Oakes ordinarily observes the strict separation between the news and editorial operations, but he was inevitably drawn into the discussions about the Pentagon Papers. Another vigorous advocate of leaving out the documents was Lester Markel, the man who had built the Sunday edition of *The New York Times* into a separate "institution within the institution" and then ruled it with an iron hand until he was replaced by Sulzberger in 1964. Markel, now chairman of the *Times's* Committee of the Future, declared that any use of the actual documents in the newspaper would be "irresponsible."

But the editors and reporters argued that any decision to use the Pentagon Papers without their internal documents would be catastrophic. Even to quote briefly from them, they complained, might risk taking certain statements out of context; not to quote from them at all would deny *Times* readers the flavor and tone of official communications on the Vietnam war. They were discouraged by the attitudes of the conservative lawyers for the *Times,* whose advice they felt was intimidating the executives into taking a less than forthright position for the sake of avoiding trouble with the government. General counsel Goodale originally agreed that printing the documents might "aggravate the risks" taken by the *Times,* but "after reading the documents," he later acknowledged, "I was so stunned that I changed my mind." His judgment on this point, as a newspaperman's lawyer rather than a lawyer's lawyer, was apparently influential in the *Times's* decision to use the documents after all.

On another level the discussion revolved around the number

of stories to be written and the way they were to be presented. Sheehan and Frankel had always envisioned a series of ten consecutive daily articles, and Greenfield and Rosenthal accepted that as the best way to handle the Papers. Goodale, on the other hand, despite his confidence in his legal analysis, argued forcefully in favor of a single, massive one-day package, perhaps a supplement to the newspaper or an entire edition of the *Times* Sunday magazine. Although to do so would not avert the danger of after-the-fact criminal prosecution, it would render impossible any government attempt at advance restraint on publication—and also remove the competitive problem of other newspapers falling into possession of the Pentagon Papers and scooping the *Times* on one or more installments of a series. "Journalistically speaking," Goodale realized, a series was the most sophisticated way to handle the story; but he objected to the argument of some editors that the sheer volume of a one-day presentation would be too much for the readers. "We certainly don't publish the Sunday paper to convenience the reader," he observed. "If we did, we wouldn't publish so goddamn many pages. Is the argument that intellectually the reader isn't up to reading a mammoth story? Is it too much for him to struggle through? . . . That argument, carried to its logical extreme, means a complete mediocrity in the content of the paper."

To the editors and writers, Goodale recalls, his proposal for a one-day presentation "was the end of the world." Frankel's objections, though, were philosophical as well as journalistic: "I think we found offensive the idea that we ought to be running with one eye on the sheriff. We felt that what we were doing was eminently right . . . and that we ought not to distort our presentation to beat a rap or prevent an injunction. . . . If we were doing the right thing and if we decided that the reader can only take so much and let's give it to him in the kind of hunks that even the *Times,* in its voluminous habits, regards as maximum digestable amounts, then let's not distort and contort ourselves because we have to be sneaky about it and worry." There was another, less commonly verbalized objection to a single story—that the editors would have to surrender their exclusive jurisdiction over what they regarded as the biggest story in years to the much detested "Sunday department," now run by Daniel Schwarz. There was a danger, they feared, that in the tradition of Lester Markel, the Sunday editors would tamper with the articles or insist that their own set of guidelines be followed. After all that work, it was too difficult to hand over the prize to your internal rivals.

Sulzberger tentatively accepted the notion of a series of of articles, backed up each day by selected documents; but about a week before he was scheduled to leave for London he called a meeting in his office to review some other details —among them, how much space the *Times* should devote to the Pentagon Papers story. The publisher wanted to see the lead-off article by Sheehan, a request that worried the editors since the story was still not in very polished form. They made a few frantic revisions and submitted it to Sulzberger. "We ourselves were not ready to print it in that form," one of the editors confided, "and we were sorry about that because not only the publisher but presumably some of the people he showed it to did not catch the full excitement that we had." There were new discussions among the executives at this point, with some of them, clearly disappointed in Sheehan's draft, asking: "Is this really worth it?" A few days later, apparently as the combined results of pressures and new doubts, Sulzberger declared that the upper limit on space was to be six pages a day. It was a compromise figure, based in part on the cost of the project and in part on the publisher's concern that the *Times* should not appear to be going overboard.

The reporters were furious. They had always been aiming toward Sheehan and Gold's original estimate of ten to twelve pages daily. Sheehan's draft itself was long enough to fill four pages in the *Times,* and the drafts of some later installments would have filled at least three pages each, not including the documents, which had also been selected to fill much more space than was now available. The practical effect of Sulzberger's edict was that almost everything had to be cut in half. That was a reasonable task for the documents, since many superfluous ones could be eliminated and others cut down, but for the articles themselves it meant substantial and time-consuming revision. Moreover, further pressure was added to a situation already at the breaking point at the Hilton when the editors stressed that Sulzberger had been let down by Sheehan's draft and that "the goddamn stuff has to be in much better shape in the next four or five days, so that before the publisher gets on the plane, he can sign off the whole project and be done with it."

Sulzberger did not sign off until the last moment, however, and called another meeting with key editors on Friday morning June 11. He still seemed to be vacillating and in the previous twenty-four hours had sought reassurance from Reston, Rosenthal, and Frankel, among others. Frankel and Rosenthal were very nervous that morning, and in the elevator on their way to the publisher's suite on the fourteenth floor of the *Times* building they rehearsed what they would say and do. "He hasn't heard as much from you," the managing editor said to his Washington bureau chief, "so if we get into a brawl, you speak up—hearing it in new words from a new guy might help the cause." What if the publisher declared at the last moment that the documents could not be printed but had to be incorporated into the articles? They determined that they would ask for an hour to think about their answer if it came down to a choice between "that or nothing." They ruminated, asking themselves as they had previously: "Are we just on an ego trip or is this worth the trouble?"

The final meeting was brief. Sulzberger began by saying, jokingly: "Gentlemen, I've decided to run only the documents and not the stories." After a short discussion of the issues with

Rosenthal, Greenfield, and Frankel, the publisher turned to the managing editor and said blankly: "I've decided to go ahead the way you planned it"—a ten-part series, still with the six-page daily limit. The editors reiterated their intention to play the articles as low-key as possible and to supervise the headlines carefully to avoid any sensationalism (the word "secret," for example, never appeared in a headline over the *Times* stories). There was one final condition: Bancroft, the former diplomat and the man who would be in charge while Sulzberger was in London, was to be given a last look at all the stories and would have the right to suggest changes.

Late in May the technical department of the *Times* had been alerted that it might have to handle a top-secret rush job. On Tuesday June 8 John Werner, the production manager, Richard Rogers, the manager of general services, and John Schwarz, the space coordinator for the *Times* building, found an empty office on the ninth floor, recently vacated by Allan Ullman, the director of the book and educational division of the *Times*. The next day, on managing editor Rosenthal's go-ahead, the room was stripped of its furniture, drapes, rugs, and built-in bookcases. The walls were covered with masonite and the soft indirect lights were replaced with bright fluorescent units. Straining the limit of the floor, built to withstand 250 pounds per square inch, they moved in a huge page-proof press, six automatic typesetting perforators, a galley-proof press, a printer's saw, a storage cabinet, make-up tables, a proofreading desk, and a paper shredder to destroy any extra proofs. A watchman was posted at the door to the microcosmic composing room and was instructed to admit only those people on a special secret list. The typesetting began Thursday night June 10, even before Sulzberger had given his final approval for the project; between then and Saturday the specially designated printers worked around the clock, having been warned not to talk about what they were doing.

When the "dummy" of *The New York Times* for Sunday

June 13, 1971, was prepared in the news room on Saturday afternoon, a gaping blank four columns wide and five inches deep was left on the front page, marked only with the word "Neil." The six inside pages containing the Pentagon Papers stories and documents were wheeled into the main composing room on Saturday afternoon for final corrections, and the front-page portion of Sheehan's story was dropped into the printing form at the last possible moment.

On Sunday morning the Papers were public, and Sulzberger left for London on schedule. But Rosenthal was still uncertain and uneasy about his publisher's true reaction and wondered what would happen if the government were to ask the *Times* to cease publication of the classified material. The managing editor thought it might be a good idea to bolster Sulzberger's morale while he was overseas, to make him feel that the *Times* had done the right and good thing. On Monday two *Times* editors called friends at another major newspaper to ask if they would send Sulzberger a congratulatory cable in London. The cable was sent, the *Times's* journalistic coup was firmly established in the eyes of the public and the administration, and Rosenthal had a happy publisher.

[CHAPTER VI]

To obtain a copy of the Sunday edition of *The New York Times* in Southern California on the same day that it is published, one must get up shortly after dawn and pounce on one of the few locations in the Los Angeles area where several copies of the paper are available. Anthony Russo did not do this on Sunday June 13, 1971, and thus he was unaware all day that the project on which he had labored with Daniel Ellsberg— duplicating the Pentagon Papers in order to make them public —had finally come to fruition.

Another person who was not aware of the big news on the East Coast was Robert C. Mardian, Assistant Attorney General in charge of the Internal Security Division of the Justice Department. Mardian, a conservative Republican from Southern California who had come to Washington with the Nixon administration, had delivered a speech in Los Angeles on Thursday June 10 sharply criticizing the American news media for allegedly contributing "to the growing tolerance of lawlessness and the indifference to the obligations of citizenship that exists in America today." Now he was resting in Pasadena for the weekend before returning to Washington for what he expected to be an ordinary week. Among other things, there was a conspiracy case to be developed against the antiwar demonstrators who disrupted the nation's capital during the Mayday protest week and the ongoing investigation of Catholic militants charged with conspiring to kidnap President Nixon's national security adviser, Henry Kissinger.

Neither Russo nor Mardian was given any assistance by the press in finding out how totally their lives would be changed over the days and weeks to come. Newspapers, wire services, radio, and television brought Californians hardly any word about the disclosure of the Vietnam war history; nor would there be any information in the weekly newsmagazines that are sometimes available in California on Monday morning. Russo finally heard a brief mention on the radio late Sunday night, but his efforts to reach Ellsberg for fuller details failed. Mardian had an uninterrupted flight back to Washington that night, and only on his arrival in his office at 8 A.M. Monday did he discover something unusual in *The New York Times*— installment number two in the Pentagon Papers series, an article by Neil Sheehan headlined "Vietnam Archive: A Consensus to Bomb Developed Before '64 Election, Study Says." Mardian was stunned and sent for a copy of the Sunday edition of the *Times;* he immediately phoned Attorney General John Mitchell, who had known about the *Times* series for twenty-four hours but had not taken any action until the normal business week began, despite an alarmed phone call on Sunday from Secretary of Defense Melvin Laird before his appearance on a television interview program. Both Mitchell and Mardian would subsequently consult several times with William H. Rehnquist, an Arizona conservative who was then Assistant

Attorney General in charge of the Justice Department's Office of Legal Counsel and would later be named to the Supreme Court by President Nixon.

Whatever the Justice Department did, it was bound to be acting in the dark. As one high department official put it later: "There wasn't a soul at Justice who had ever heard of the Pentagon Papers, much less seen them." In planning government legal action, he observed, "It doesn't do much good to know there's a colonel over in the Pentagon who's been working with them for two years."

Indeed, there appeared to be more than just a lonely colonel contributing to the immediate concern at the Pentagon. Laird phoned the Attorney General a second time on Monday; the Secretary of Defense was due to appear before the Senate Foreign Relations Committee, and reporters were certain to quiz him about the Papers even if the committee members did not. Once again Mitchell advised Laird merely to say that the matter was under consideration at the Justice Department; after the meeting Laird said just that—and it was the first formal tip-off that the administration might take legal action. Although Laird had never read the Pentagon Papers, he knew very well that they had been prepared at McNamara's request and sensed that the top-secret study could rekindle the furor over the war. At Mitchell's request, Laird ordered a memorandum—itself promptly classified top secret—explaining what the Papers were, who had contributed to their preparation, and who had received the fifteen copies, and describing the circumstances of some previous leaks of classified material to newspapers. But since Laird had trouble locating an expert on the Papers within the Pentagon, the memorandum included only a general assertion of the harm that publication might conceivably do to the national security. The Justice Department received the hastily drawn Defense Department memo late in the afternoon of Monday June 14, and Mardian subsequently conferred about it with J. Fred Buzhardt, a former aide to

Senator Strom Thurmond (R-S.C.) who was serving in the Pentagon as general counsel to Laird.

As the military and the civilians in the Pentagon pushed for a strong reaction, and as the State Department began its own deliberations about the consequences of disclosure of the Papers, influential Republican politicians in the capital weighed the Papers from their own vantage point. The chairman of the Republican National Committee, Senator Robert Dole of Kansas, argued against going into court; he foresaw an enormous bonanza for the Republicans if they could exploit the Papers for what they revealed about their Democratic predecessors in the White House. After all, the more sensational aspects of the study—and they were the only ones that had thus far been presented in the *Times*—included revelations that were intensely embarrassing to former President Johnson and his top advisers. And the scope of the Papers ended early in 1968, which automatically excluded the Nixon administration from scrutiny. President Nixon was inclined to that view himself and expressed it openly at the regular Tuesday morning White House meeting of the Republican congressional leadership. But a contrary attitude was developing among key White House advisers, especially in the office of Henry Kissinger.

The middle of June 1971 was perhaps the most sensitive period in American diplomacy in years. Unknown to the public, the Congress, and even some high officials, the White House, with the help of the Pakistani government, was negotiating with the People's Republic of China for a confidential visit to Peking by Kissinger—with the eventual goal of arranging an invitation for President Nixon to visit China. Although the country would not learn about it until January 1972, Kissinger was also involved at that time, as he had been for two years, in top-secret Vietnam war negotiations with North Vietnamese officials in Paris; on his way back from his secret visit to Peking, in fact, he stopped off in Paris for one of those secret sessions.

The President was urged to consider the prospect that the

Chinese would back out of the arrangements because of an impression that the United States could not be counted upon to negotiate secretly and keep confidences with other nations. Nixon, proud of his various initiatives with the Communist powers and Eastern European satellites, had often expressed the concern that success in such endeavors as the strategic arms limitation talks with the Soviet Union depended on strict confidentiality. Others in the White House also pointed out that unless the administration took a firm stand, even at the risk of further alienating the press, it was liable to establish a dangerous precedent; reporters might feel encouraged to probe ever more deeply for secret documents on American foreign policy. To blink at such a massive breach of security, it was argued, might weaken the administration's strong law-and-order record. Presidential press secretary Ronald L. Ziegler, confronted with complaints from reporters about overclassification of material within the Defense Department, made the point this way: "Disagreement with a particular classification, in this case . . . is beside the point. There has been improper handling of classified material, apparently, and unauthorized disclosures specifically prohibited by the law. We have an obligation to move as we are moving."

The American republic had long been buffeted by controversy over the proper balance between the rights of the press and its obligations to the government, especially in time of crisis. During the Civil War, when the press was far more mischievous than in current times, there were repeated conflicts; at one point General William Sherman, commander of the Union forces, arrested a battlefield correspondent for the New York *Herald* and ordered that he be shot as a spy. Only President Abraham Lincoln's intervention saved the reporter's life. Perhaps the most celebrated government legal attack on a newspaper in recent years arose over a story in the fiercely antiwar Chicago *Tribune*, run by Colonel Robert R. McCormack. The story, published on June 7, 1942, described in

intimate detail the American victory over the Japanese at the
Battle of Midway, making it clear to anyone acquainted with
such matters that the United States had recently broken the
Japanese code. Once the Japanese learned this, it was argued,
they could change their code completely and deny the Americans an opportunity to reap further military advantage from
the break. President Franklin D. Roosevelt's Attorney General,
Francis Biddle, launched a federal grand jury i. vestigation in
Chicago at the urging of the Department of the Navy. In order
to remove any political considerations from the affair, Biddle
even appointed William D. Mitchell, Attorney General during
the administration of Herbert Hoover, as a special prosecutor
in the *Tribune* case. The investigation fizzled out, however,
and it was acknowledged years later that the Japanese had
apparently never noticed the story.

But after-the-fact prosecution was a different matter from
the issue that would be involved in any immediate Justice
Department action against *The New York Times* in June 1971.
The government would have to seek an injunction against
the newspaper's continuation of its series of articles—a "prior
restraint" on publication. Since 1931, when the Supreme Court
decided the landmark case of Near v. Minnesota, the strictest
conditions had defined the government's power to prospec-
tively prevent a newspaper from printing anything. The Near
case involved the successful state prosecution of the publisher
of the *Saturday Press* of Minneapolis, a blatantly and viciously
anti-Semitic newspaper, on the grounds that the paper was
"largely devoted to malicious, scandalous, and defamatory articles." The articles at issue contended that "a Jewish gangster"
controlled gambling, bootlegging, and racketeering in Minneapolis and St. Paul and that most of the local elected and appointed officials were in cahoots with the alleged gangster.
Publisher Near, in a chain of legal actions financed largely by
Colonel McCormack of the Chicago *Tribune*, invoked the protection of the due-process clause of the Fourteenth Amend-

ment to the Constitution. Chief Justice Charles Evans Hughes, writing the opinion of a divided 5–4 Supreme Court, declared that the Minnesota statute allowing suppression of a newspaper "is unusual, if not unique, and raises questions of grave importance transcending the local interests involved in the litigation." Hughes affirmed that "liberty of speech, and of the press, is . . . not an absolute right, and the State may punish its abuses"; but he denounced the "effective censorship" implied in the Minnesota state court decisions against the *Saturday Press*. Even "miscreant purveyors of scandal" are guaranteed freedom of the press, the Chief Justice added. But in words that would become the only available standard for measuring prior restraint, he said that "no one would question but that a government might prevent actual obstruction to its recruiting service or the publication of the sailing dates of transports or the number or location of troops." The four justices dissenting from the Near decision in 1931 warned at the time that such a stringent standard for prior restraint would expose "the peace and good order of every community and the business and private affairs of every individual to the constant and protracted false and malicious assaults of any insolvent publisher who may have purpose and sufficient capacity to contrive and put into effect a scheme or program for oppression, blackmail, or extortion." Nonetheless, the Near standard held for forty years, and as late as May 17, 1971—only a month before the *Times* published the Pentagon Papers—Chief Justice Warren E. Burger reaffirmed it in a decision upholding the right of an interracial group in Chicago to distribute leaflets charging a real estate broker with "blockbusting" sales tactics. Burger reiterated the "heavy presumption" against "the constitutional validity" of any prior restraint of expression.

If one of the several preceding administrations had taken legal action against a newspaper, there can be little doubt that

it might have been greeted with a somewhat less emotional reaction and response. It could have been seen—by lawyers,
scholars, and even some elements of the press—as a confrontation between well-intentioned forces, as a rational test of constitutional principles in a political cauldron. But the strong
presumption of legal observers was that no other administration of the post–World War II period, including the one that
Richard M. Nixon served as Vice President, would have been
quite as eager as this one was to take the press to court. And it
was impossible to view the crisis over the Pentagon Papers in
perspective without considering the overt hostility of the Nixon
administration toward the press and the inhibiting effect that
hostility had produced.

The administration's sustained two-year assault on the press
was ably led by Vice President Spiro T. Agnew, the little-
known Governor of Maryland who was President Nixon's
surprise choice as a running mate at the 1968 Republican National Convention in Miami. Agnew was furious over his treatment by *The New York Times, The Washington Post,* and
other liberal-leaning newspapers during the 1968 campaign
and promptly proceeded to accumulate evidence against them
as well as against the national television networks. (During the
campaign Agnew had sworn to file a libel suit against the *Times*
in retribution for its remarks against him; he renewed the
threat several times but never actually filed the suit.) In November 1969, after only ten months in office, he aimed his fire
at the newsmen he so thoroughly detested in speeches to audi-
ences carefully selected for their receptivity to assaults on
the "Eastern establishment press." In Des Moines, Iowa,
Agnew chose the Midwest Regional Republican Committee as
his forum for an attack on "a small and unelected elite" of
television newsmen for allegedly abusing their influence over
public opinion. In a reference that would become notorious,
the Vice President complained that among television news

commentators "a raised eyebrow, an inflection of the voice, a caustic remark dropped in the middle of a broadcast can raise doubts in a million minds about the veracity of a public official or the wisdom of a government policy." Agnew's stimulus had apparently been a set of "instant analyses" by the networks after a presidential speech on Vietnam policy on November 3. Disclaiming any interest in censorship, he proclaimed that "a form of censorship" already existed on the part of "a handful of men" working for the networks; the disclaimer of censorship was immediately suspect, however, when Agnew implied that the networks should no longer be allowed to "wield a free hand in selecting, presenting, and interpreting the great issues of the nation." If its hand was no longer "free," the press wondered, what were the alternatives?

The newspapers had only to wait a week for Agnew to erupt. For his homily against the *Times* and the *Post* he picked the chamber of commerce in Montgomery, Alabama, in the heart of the Deep South, which had never forgiven the newspapers for bringing the civil rights crises of the 1960s to the public on their front pages. Agnew hit a sensitive nerve when he pointed out that The Washington Post Company owns the largest newspaper, one of four major commercial television stations, and an all-news radio station in Washington, as well as *Newsweek* magazine—"all grinding out the same editorial line . . . four powerful voices harken[ing] to the same master," Katherine Graham. (His assertions about the uniformity of opinion were demonstrably untrue, as anyone who worked for the "master" was able to document. A potentially valid point about concentration of power in the media was blunted by the Vice President's standard exaggeration and overkill.) He then took out after the news judgment and editorial policies of the *Times*, suggesting that his generation had been unjustly denigrated in favor of a younger, protesting one and contending that news favorable to the President was purposely suppressed.

On comfortable ground, Agnew also renewed his mocking, bitter criticism of those who protest against American involvement in Vietnam.

Taken as a whole, Angew's wanderings and musings came to resemble a veritable crusade—an attack on the "zoo of dissidents," in St. Louis; an accusation that the media win prizes with innuendos while overlooking the "evils of communism," in the Virgin Islands; a singling out of his most hated list of "illiberal, self-appointed guardians of our destiny," in Houston; instructions on the rules of rhetoric, in Detroit; a charge that all his critics resort to "mud-slinging and hate-peddling," in Chicago; a renewed assault on the networks and the CBS documentary "The Selling of the Pentagon," in Boston; a complaint that the media give "preponderantly negative" coverage to the Vietnam war, in Los Angeles; and, once again quite safely in the arms of a receptive audience, a diatribe against the "editorial doublethink" of the "Seaboard Media" before the Mississippi House of Representatives, and a discussion of the merits of *The Washington Post* before the national convention of the Society of Former FBI Agents in Atlanta. There was a strong body of opinion within the American press that repeatedly argued that Agnew should be ignored, perhaps treated like a naughty exhibitionist child. Counterbalancing this, however, was the worry that a substantial majority of the American people—who, if tested, might even disapprove of the First Amendment—would actually believe everything Agnew said, would accept the notion that the media were creating rather than reflecting many of society's problems. Agnew was generally answered by the press, often emotionally but with the conviction that responses are required if an era of repression against the news media is to be avoided.

Some members of the fourth estate would argue that the repression had already arrived by the summer of 1971. Former *Times* newsman Fred Powledge, in a report prepared for the American Civil Liberties Union, observed that "in a relatively short period of time, the press in the United States has moved, and has been moved, from what many considered a position of extreme security to one of extreme vulnerability. There are some who say freedom of the press is now in the greatest degree of danger of being lost in America; there are others who say it is all but lost already." While the apocalypse may actually be distant, the incursions and intimidation since Agnew's original speeches have been substantial and varied: the files and unused photographs of several newsmagazines were subpoenaed during the investigation of the Weathermen faction of Students for a Democratic Society; virtually every area of the media was hit by subpoenas for information concerning the Black Panther Party, some of them complying; the House Committee on Interstate and. Foreign Commerce sought to investigate the making of the CBS documentary "The Selling of the Pentagon" (the House eventually refused to vote a contempt citation against CBS and its president, Frank Stanton); undercover policemen and FBI agents began posing as newsmen at press conferences and demonstrations; an FBI investigation was ordered at the State Department to determine the sources of "stories harmful to the national interest." CBS news president Richard Salant told Powledge that at one point there were so many attacks, complaints from the Federal Communications Commission, and other problems to handle, that he had to employ more lawyers than newsmen. Although there was no overt censorship, the administration substantially succeeded in making the press more timid. There was a clearly observable "chilling effect" as the news media began to neglect stories (the networks, for example, hardly covered the November 1969 Mobilization against the war, which occurred a few days after Agnew's Des Moines speech), cut back on coverage of controversial subjects, and scrape for the "good news" favored by the administration. Despite the issuance of "guidelines" by Attorney General Mitchell, subpoenas continued to be served against the media. Between January 1969 and July

1971 CBS and NBC received a total of 122 subpoenas for film or reporters' testimony in grand jury or court proceedings.

But almost as important as the mood of government-press relations at the start of the Pentagon Papers confrontation were the general policies of Attorney General Mitchell's Justice Department. Despite frequent assertions, public and private, that high Justice Department officials are blind to bias and make their choices and decisions utterly objectively, the department's record was, by the summer of 1971, undistinguished with regard to civil liberties and open to frequent charges by critics of a cynical use of the federal courts and the nation's judicial machinery for clearly partisan political purposes.

One astonishing sequence of events revolved around a Washington demonstration planned by the Vietnam Veterans Against the War (VVAW) in late April 1971, just before the Mayday antiwar protests. Well aware that jurisdiction over a pending lawsuit on the validity of Interior Department regulations governing protest permits lay at the time with U.S. District Judge George L. Hart, Jr., an outspoken conservative with impeccable Republican credentials and a well-established dislike for protesters, the Justice Department filed for an injunction against the VVAW's mock Vietnam encampment on the Mall in front of the U.S. Capitol. The injunction was granted but then reversed by a three-judge panel on the U.S. Court of Appeals for the District of Columbia Circuit. Despite the reluctance of Solicitor General Erwin N. Griswold to do so, the Justice Department made an emergency appeal to Chief Justice Warren Burger in his capacity as circuit justice for the District of Columbia. (One motive, it was speculated at the time, might have been Mitchell's eagerness for a legal victory over his predecessor, Attorney General Ramsey Clark, who represented the antiwar veterans.) Burger, acting before Clark's opposition papers even had time to reach him, reinstated the injunction; but then, as President Nixon began to have qualms over the image of policemen driving the veterans—some of them amputees—off the Mall, the Justice Department failed to enforce the injunction. An angry Judge Hart finally called the government lawyers into court, upbraided them for abusing the courts, and withdrew the injunction on his own accord.

Critics of the Mitchell regime at the Justice Department inevitably drew a contrast between the Attorney General's willingness to prosecute demonstrators and his refusal to institute legal action against, or even convene a grand jury investigation of, the National Guardsmen who shot and killed four students at Kent State University in Ohio during a demonstration against American entry into Cambodia. Mitchell endorsed the view of the President's Commission on Campus Unrest (whose report was totally scorned by the administration) that the rifle fire that killed the students was "unnecessary, unwarranted, and inexcusable," but he rejected out of hand compelling evidence, developed by the FBI among others, that there had been an advance agreement among the Guardsmen to fire into the crowd of student protesters at Kent.

That the initial decisions and responsibility for reacting to the newspapers lay within the jurisdiction of the Internal Security Division was, in and of itself, a revealing aspect of the Justice Department's priorities under Mitchell and Deputy Attorney General Richard G. Kleindienst. Under previous Attorneys General, the case would almost surely have been assigned to the Civil Division of the Department, which had a number of experienced trial attorneys. But Mardian, who initially served the Nixon administration as general counsel to the Department of Health, Education and Welfare, had been transferred to Justice with a mandate to beef up the Internal Security operation. He brought in new young lawyers, gave public speeches on the need for "domestic intelligence" and accrued substantial influence in the policy-making process in the Department. After nearly a full day of intradepartmental consultations on Monday June 14 that for some reason did not include Solicitor General Erwin N. Griswold—even though it was clear that any legal action against the newspapers was bound to go to the Supreme Court, where it would become his responsibility—John Mitchell and Robert Mardian met at the Attorney General's home in the Watergate apartment complex in Washington to hammer out the text of a telegram to the publisher of *The New York Times* asking that the newspaper cease publication of the series of articles and threatening legal action as the alternative. The telegram from Mitchell read:

> I have been advised by the Secretary of Defense that the material published in *The New York Times* on June 13, 14, 1971, captioned "Key Texts from Pentagon's Vietnam Study" contains information relating to the national defense of the United States and bears a top-secret classification. As such, publication of this information is directly prohibited by the provisions of the Espionage Law, Title 18, United States Code, Section 793. Moreover, further publication of information of this character will cause irreparable injury to the defense interests of the United States. Accordingly, I respectfully request that you publish no further information of this character and advise me that you have made arrangements for the return of these documents to the Department of Defense.

Just in case, Mardian decided to phone the text of the telegram to Sulzberger; when he called the *Times* at 7:30 P.M., however, he was told that the publisher was out of the country and was referred to Harding Bancroft. It was two hours before press time for the first edition; they spoke briefly, and the executive vice president promised to get back to Mardian within an hour.

The Justice Department later complained that it took Bancroft two hours to return Mardian's call; that would be no surprise, given the new argument that ensued at the newspaper.

James Goodale, "thinking we were clear for another day," left the *Times* shortly after 7 P.M. on Monday June 14. He arrived at his apartment on the East Side of Manhattan to hear the phone ringing, but he was too late. He guessed what the problem might be and immediately called Bancroft, who told the general counsel of the Attorney General's ultimatum. Goodale reacted instinctively: "That's easy. We won't stop publication. We don't do that." But Bancroft, the former diplomat, said: "I'm not too sure." They agreed to meet back at the *Times*.

By the time Goodale arrived at the newspaper office Sydney Gruson and Abe Rosenthal, according to one participant in the session, were "screaming and yelling at each other. It was like a movie." Gruson, the publisher's assistant, was feeling "very judicious" and had been arguing that the *Times* would gain nothing by continuing with the series and possibly further aggravating the administration; he urged suspension of the articles pending resolution of the issue by a court. But Rosenthal was in a frenzy over the suggestion, warning that it would create the impression that the *Times* was knuckling under to government pressure. Bancroft called Louis Loeb, senior partner in Lord, Day, and Lord, to ask his advice. Loeb, who had been against publication of the Papers in the first place, said the *Times* should accede to the Attorney General's request. Bancroft, buttressed by Gruson, was inclined to accept that advice, but Rosenthal insisted that "Punch" Sulzberger have the definitive word.

Sulzberger was roused from his bed at the Savoy Hotel in London. Rosenthal, worried that Gruson and Bancroft would carry the day, pleaded with Goodale to intervene; the general counsel took the phone and told the publisher that "we cannot afford for the future of this newspaper to stop publication now. It would be terrible." Sulzberger went along and gave the order for the third installment to appear in the *Times*; he also decided to cut his European trip short. The *Times* editors hastily drew up a statement to transmit back to the Justice Department and to release publicly:

We have received the telegram from the Attorney General asking the *Times* to cease further publication of the Pentagon's Vietnam study. The *Times* must respectfully decline the request of the Attorney General, believing that it is in the interest of the people of this country to be informed of the material contained in this series of articles. We have also been informed of the Attorney General's intention to seek an injunction against further publication. We believe that it is properly a matter for the courts to decide. The *Times* will oppose any request for an injunction for the same reason that led us to publish the articles in the first place. We will of course abide by the final decision of the court.

On Tuesday June 15, 1971, *The New York Times* appeared with a third Neil Sheehan story on page one: "Vietnam Archive: Study Tells How Johnson Secretly Opened Way to Ground Combat." The lead article, however, was a story datelined Washington by Max Frankel; the five-column headline, which gave the news department an opportunity to stress its in-house victory of the night before, read: "Mitchell Seeks to Halt Series on Vietnam But *Times* Refuses." "Think what it would have meant in our history and in the history of the newspaper business," Abe Rosenthal said months later, "if the headline had been 'Justice Department Asks End to Vietnam Series and Times Concedes.' I think it would have changed the history of the newspaper business." The decision to play the story about the confrontation over the Pentagon Papers so prominently may also have shifted the focus of future attention to and interest in the Vietnam history. Never mind what the Papers said; were the papers entitled to publish articles based on them?

The *Times* had no way of knowing exactly what nature the government legal action might take, but mention of the Espionage Act in the Attorney General's telegram was a clue. Goodale had prepared a basic legal memorandum, but he would need help in defending the newspaper in court. The general counsel called Louis Loeb, who promptly passed him along to Herbert Brownell. As President Eisenhower's Attorney General, Brownell had had a hand in drafting Executive Order 10501, the basis for the ongoing classification of confidential documents. For that reason, Brownell said, and because the *Times* had disobeyed the consistent advice of the firm on how to handle the Pentagon Papers, Lord, Day, and Lord would not be representing the *Times* in court the next morning. Goodale was stunned to have the lawyers drop out of the case at 11 P.M. on the night before they would be urgently needed. ("It was like eating a piece of Mexican food," he said later. "It woke you up a little bit.") Goodale had an idea: only the day before, he had lunch with Yale law professor Alexander M. Bickel, a constitutional scholar and a political moderate who was preparing the *amicus curiae* brief of the *Times*, NBC, CBS, and other news organizations for the argument at the Supreme Court in the case of *Times* reporter Earl Caldwell. Bickel had made flattering remarks about the *Times* series on the Pentagon Papers during lunch and expressed the view that the newspaper was fully entitled to publish the articles. "He was an obvious guy to get," Goodale said, and Bancroft agreed. But there was a problem: Bickel could not be found at the Yale Club of New York as expected. Giving up the search after an hour, Goodale finally returned home, assuming that he would have to reach Bickel the next morning before going to court. First, however, Goodale called Floyd Abrams, a former student of Bickel's who was working at the New York law firm of Cahill, Gordon, Sonnett, Reindel, and Ohl and was also a lawyer in the Caldwell case. Abrams said that he would work on the *Times* case—and he thought his whole firm would—if Bickel went along. Once given the task, the night rewrite desk in the *Times* news room took only twelve minutes—and a battery of phone calls to New Haven, Connecticut, and Palo Alto, California—to find Bickel at his mother's apartment on Riverside Drive in Manhattan. Bickel accepted the case, despite a commitment to testify the next morning, Tuesday June 15, before a congressional committee in Washington.

Bickel and Abrams met at the Cahill, Gordon office at 2 A.M. and worked through the night. As they arrived in Goodale's office at the *Times* at 9:30 A.M. with a ten-page brief, Whitney North Seymour, Jr., U.S. Attorney for the Southern District of New York, called to say that the newspaper's representatives should be at the federal courthouse in Foley Square within half an hour.

The complaint for injunction under the Espionage Act, rushed up to New York from Washington (having been thrown together under such emergency conditions that Mardian had to drive to the Alexandria, Va., police station in the middle of the night to have his affidavit notarized) and served on *The New York Times*, was a general one, alleging that the installments about the Papers already published had "prejudiced the defense interests of the United States," and that additional articles would further prejudice those interests and "result in irreparable injury to the United States." There were no specifics, and neither Seymour nor Michael D. Hess, chief of the civil division in the U.S. Attorney's office, could provide them; all they knew about the Pentagon Papers they had read in *The New York Times*. Initially, the government lawyers attempted to file their legal papers directly with U.S. District Judge Murray I. Gurfein, who had been sworn in only a few days earlier and was serving his first day on the bench; but Gurfein insisted that they follow the standard procedure of going through the court clerk's office. An additional delay developed when it was discovered that the government had cited the wrong subsection of the Espionage Act in the complaint, and Gurfein postponed until after lunch the hearing on the government's request for a temporary order restraining further publication.

The court argument was brief and spirited. Hess told the judge that "serious injuries are being inflicted on our foreign relations, to the benefit of other nations opposed to our form of government"; he argued that the *Times* should at least be required to suffer "slight delay" in its publication schedule until the case could be heard on its merits later in the week. Bickel responded with a protest against what he considered a "classic case of censorship," complaining that the Espionage Act had never been intended by Congress for use against newspapers. He refused Gurfein's suggestion that the *Times* submit voluntarily to a temporary restraining order until the case was heard. "A newspaper exists to publish, not to submit its publishing schedule to the United States government," Bickel said.

Gurfein conferred briefly with the lawyers in his chambers and ruled a short time later. Reserving any judgment on the merits of the case, the judge nonetheless granted the restraining order because "any temporary harm that may result from not publishing during the pendancy of the application for a preliminary injunction is far outweighed by the irreparable harm that could be done to the interests of the United States government if it should ultimately prevail." Gurfein refused, however, to require seizure of the *Times's* copy of the Papers, as urged by the government (but vigorously objected to by the newspaper, lest its source be revealed through fingerprints or other markings), saying that he did "not believe the *The New York Times* will willfully disregard the spirit of our restraining order." The judge ordered both sides back for a full hearing on the basis of substantial legal briefs on Friday morning June 18.

It was the first time in the nation's history that a newspaper was restrained in advance by a court from publishing a specific article. The issue was joined.

[CHAPTER VII]

On Wednesday June 16, 1971, for the first time in four days, *The New York Times* was missing its four-column front-page box and six inside pages on the Pentagon Papers. Ironically underscoring one lesson of the Papers, their place on page one was taken in part by a report that the Nixon administration was launching "a broad policy review aimed at determining courses of action that might improve South Vietnam's ability to withstand military assaults next year, after most American forces have been withdrawn." The old rule number one was as apparent as ever: Do not lose Vietnam to communism before the next election. "The Administration is also concerned," wrote *Times* reporter William Beecher, "about the effects a major South Vietnamese military defeat in the spring of 1972 might have on Republican fortunes in the Presidential election in November." One general told Beecher that "next summer is the make-or-break period. If we can get the Saigon government successfully through the dry season, they'll have almost another year to further bolster their position. And, not incidentally, it should also carry us safely past our own November elections."

The Papers were still in the news, to be sure. Spread across five columns in the *Times*, in fact, was a three-deck headline for the lead story of the paper: "Judge, at Request of U.S., Halts *Times* Vietnam Series Four Days Pending Hearing on Injunction." The newspaper's ace Supreme Court reporter, Fred P. Graham, had been summoned to New York on Tuesday to cover the proceedings against the *Times* before Judge Gurfein, and instead of the Vietnam war study the "documents" inside the *Times* on Wednesday were the texts of the Justice Department's complaint and legal memorandum and of Gurfein's ruling granting a temporary restraining order. Gurfein's courtroom in the federal courthouse on Foley Square in Manhattan had been packed with reporters on Tuesday afternoon, and even newspapers that had totally ignored the Papers initially were now taking notice of the legal confrontation surrounding them. The government versus the press; relatively simple, very dramatic.

Daniel Ellsberg was angry. He had struggled for more than a year and a half to get the Pentagon Papers before the public, and now that he had succeeded, the story was cut off after only three days. Ellsberg's anger was directed not so much at the Justice Department—he did not expect anything different from the Nixon administration—as at the *Times*. He felt strongly that for the Papers to have maximum impact a newspaper had to be willing to defy an injunction against publication, at least for a day or two, even at the risk of being found in contempt of court; Ellsberg had told U.S. Senators that they ought to be willing to go to jail to end the war, and he had no difficulty extending that principle to cover the publisher of a newspaper. As an alternative to outright defiance he thought it might be effective if the *Times*, following a practice he had seen in Saigon newspapers, left white space wherever an article was censored; that would have been devastating in an American newspaper, he felt.

Ellsberg found the restraining order issued by Judge Gurfein especially untimely, since the Senate was about to vote on the McGovern-Hatfield end-the-war amendment and a battle was under way in Congress over whether to renew the military draft. He had enormous faith in the influence the Papers might have on policy, if only they were available to and read by all members of Congress. (McGovern-Hatfield, in fact, was beaten in the Senate by a vote of 55 to 42 on Wednesday June 16, the day after Gurfein's restraining order; a milder substitute offered by Senator Lawton Chiles (D-Fla.) was also turned back by a vote of 52 to 44. The Pentagon Papers were scarcely mentioned during the floor debate over those measures.)

"When the *Times* obeyed the restraining order, I could foresee that the thing could be stopped for weeks while it went to the Supreme Court," Ellsberg says. "That would lose the momentum of it, and the Supreme Court might rule against it, in which case it would be totally blocked, and I was particularly anxious that it not be blocked, having revealed only the Johnson era, because it seemed to me that the most important message to be conveyed was that this was not a matter of just one party or one administration, but that it had covered a number. It was essential that at least one other administration be brought out, preferably of a different party." With that in mind, Ellsberg began to look elsewhere.

One prospect was television. The networks would presumably treat the Pentagon Papers more thoroughly if they were given their own copies rather than having to rely on what was reported in *The New York Times*, and it was difficult to imagine how the Justice Department could follow the same procedures in trying to enjoin "publication" on the airwaves. Ellsberg was impressed to find that the NBC nightly news had featured a photograph of Julian Goodman, president of the network, and quoted him as supporting what the *Times* had done in publishing the classified study. "So I decided to give him a chance to try this material out himself," Ellsberg relates, "and that was done through a third party. . . . Goodman turned it down within half an hour." The same thing happened at ABC, where James Hagerty, who had been President Eisenhower's press secretary, is a vice president. CBS, according to Ellsberg, took longer to refuse: "They went through quite a long process of soul-searching and spent a full day of meetings, deciding what to do." That network's decision, ultimately, was based on the fact that the House of Representatives was about to vote on the recommendation of a committee that CBS be charged with contempt of Congress for refusing to turn over to an investigation the unused film ("outtakes") from its controversial documentary on military public relations, "The Selling of the Pentagon." Ellsberg was sympathetic to that problem and appreciated the fact that CBS at least thought things over before refusing to accept the Pentagon Papers; it was on that basis that, after receiving invitations to appear on all three networks, he later accepted the opportunity to be interviewed by Walter Cronkite on the CBS evening news.

The networks' reluctance to touch the Papers was perhaps the clearest evidence of the extent to which they felt intimidated by the Nixon administration's attitude toward the press; judging from past statements by Dean Burch, chairman of the Federal Communications Commission and a former campaign aide to Senator Barry Goldwater (R-Ariz.), they knew how easy it was to spark a costly and threatening investigation by the FCC, which controls their broadcast licenses. Sander Vanocur, the nationally known television newsman who left NBC in the summer of 1971 to join public television, later related in *Center* magazine an inside story of how timid the networks are with such touchy matters and how their coverage is invariably oriented to the "official" view of events. After Ellsberg appeared on CBS with Cronkite, Vanocur said, he complained to his superiors that NBC should have made an effort to beat out or match CBS. The idea was rebuffed; so was Vanocur's suggestion that the CBS "exclusive" resulted from "the view of the peace movement that CBS had been fairer in its reporting of the Vietnam war and the opposition to it than we had been." An executive insisted that Ellsberg's preference of CBS over NBC was based instead on the fact that Cronkite's news program had higher "ratings" than its counterpart on NBC. Subsequently, NBC was offered an opportunity to interview Ellsberg for half an hour during prime time, but according to Vanocur "Reuven Frank, president of NBC news, . . . found every reason under the sun why NBC should not give Ellsberg the time." Ellsberg did eventually appear on the morning "Today" show for about twelve minutes; former Secretary of State Dean Rusk was given an hour of prime time on NBC to refute the image of the development of U.S. war policy that was presented in the Pentagon Papers.

The Washington Post, still feeling egg on its well-respected, well-connected face after the *Times*'s weekend scoop, had been trying for several days to catch up on the Pentagon Papers story in some other way than merely rewriting its competitor's articles. The editors at the *Post*, after redoing the *Times* story of June 13, had considered and rejected the idea of sending one or two qualified reporters to New York to get an early edition of each day's *Times* and rewrite each installment before the 12:30 A.M. deadline for the *Post*'s largest edition. But that hardly seemed worth the effort. Instead, the content of each day's *Times* story was evaluated and rewritten on the basis of any other information available to *Post* reporters and published a day later, with credit necessarily given to the *Times*. For the most part, as Chalmers Roberts puts it, "we were crying on each other's shoulder" about having to handle the story that way.

There were at least two false starts for the *Post*. On Sunday afternoon June 13, 1971, the day the *Times* first published the Papers, executive editor Benjamin C. Bradlee got a phone call at his country home in West Virginia from Marcus G. Raskin, one of the three authors of the Institute for Policy Studies book based on the Pentagon Papers, *Washington Plans an Aggressive War*, which was then in production. Raskin was obviously shaken—he hadn't counted on Ellsberg's finding another outlet for the secret Pentagon study before the IPS book appeared, and he was anxious to save it from obscurity. Raskin was "hush-hush and secret," Bradlee recalls, but he wanted to have breakfast with the *Post* editor on Monday. Bradlee agreed: "The score was thirty-six to nothing, and we were trying to get even." At breakfast Raskin and co-authors Richard J. Barnet and Ralph Stavins made it clear that their book had been based on access to the Pentagon Papers and offered their manuscript to the *Post* for serialization. Bradlee, a clever negotiator, expressed enough interest to get the manuscript delivered to the *Post* building on L Street in Washington by noon, so that the newspaper's own experts could evaluate it. The IPS authors said they no longer had their "source material" but might be able to get it back, depending on how the *Post* handled their book.

Bradlee looked over the manuscript and was not very impressed—"they were in the war criminal racket." Chal Roberts, who had been covering diplomatic stories for decades, was even less taken by it. He advised Bradlee that it was "just atrocious. . . . It was infuriating because they kept paraphrasing things, or they'd take one sentence out of quotes, and you never knew what the rest of [a document] said. It smelled like they'd grabbed out what they wanted to prove their own case. . . . I told Ben I wouldn't touch it with a ten-foot pole;

[131]

I'd rather be murdered on the story." So much for that and, consequently, for the IPS "source material."

That same Monday Philip L. Geyelin, editor of the *Post*'s editorial page, received a call from a friend in Boston, who commiserated with the situation the *Post* found itself in. He said he thought he might be able to help out: he had some excerpts from the Pentagon Papers that had not yet appeared in the *Times*, including a long memorandum from McGeorge Bundy urging escalation of the American effort in Vietnam. Geyelin reacted enthusiastically, and within hours an anonymous woman walked into his office at the *Post*, deposited a plain brown envelope containing about two hundred pages on his desk, and promptly turned around and left. This time another *Post* diplomatic correspondent, Murrey Marder, was given the task of looking the material over. Marder spent much of Monday night reading and analyzing it—there seemed little question that it came straight from the Pentagon Papers— and felt that it would merit working up a story the next day. On Tuesday morning, to the amazement of Marder, Geyelin, and his source, the same material appeared in the third installment of the *Times* series. The *Post* was back where it started, except that it now had evidence that the Papers were in fairly wide private circulation.

Once the *Times* was enjoined from publication, the *Post* began trying even harder; if it could pick up where the *Times* left off, not only would it save substantial face for the *Post* but it would also score some points for freedom of the press. Like anyone else who had ever known or worked with Daniel Ellsberg, Ben H. Bagdikian, the *Post*'s assistant managing editor for national affairs, had thought immediately of the intense and troubled defense researcher after the Papers appeared in the *Times*. Bagdikian, a former staffer of the Providence *Journal* who had established an eminent reputation as a media critic (and who was hired by the *Post* after he had sharply criticized that paper), overlapped with Ellsberg during a two-year period he spent at the Rand Corporation writing a book about the media and the future of mass communications. The revelations in the Papers, Bagdikian observed, seemed to reinforce arguments that Ellsberg had long advanced about decision-making on the war in Vietnam. Bagdikian tried unsuccessfully several times to reach Ellsberg on Wednesday June 16, but kept leaving messages. That evening Bagdikian was phoned by a friend of Ellsberg, who would not speak in much detail until Bagdikian called him back from a pay telephone. (Many employees of *The Washington Post* have long suspected that their home telephones and perhaps even extensions at the newspaper are tapped, so the request was not a surprising one to Bagdikian.) The editor went across L Street to the Statler Hilton and phoned Boston from one in a long row of exposed coin telephones separated from one another by flimsy plastic partitions; once he made it clear that he was "interested," he was given another number—also to be called from the public telephone—where he could reach Daniel Ellsberg.

Bagdikian and Ellsberg spoke at length, and on the former's assurance that the *Post* would use the material once it was obtained, Ellsberg spelled out elaborate arrangements for how he could be reached and found if Bagdikian flew to Boston that night. Ellsberg said he should bring a large suitcase. Ironically, as Bagdikian hung up the telephone and turned to go back to the *Post*, he ran into a vice president of the Rand Corporation whom he had not seen since moving to Washington from Santa Monica late in 1969; the Rand executive asked whether the *Post* would be catching up with *The New York Times* on the Pentagon Papers story, and Bagdikian shrugged his shoulders. He was in a hurry.

Back at the *Post*, Bagdikian spoke first with Eugene C. Patterson, then managing editor of the newspaper; Bradlee was out of town for the day, so Patterson was in charge. They sat next to each other on a couch in Patterson's glass-enclosed office but did not close the door, lest they stir up too much curiosity in the cramped *Post* news room. "If I can get a solid chunk of the Pentagon Papers, will we publish them Friday morning?" Bagdikian asked. Patterson, a former editor of the Atlanta *Constitution* and a relatively conservative newspaperman, thought for a while and then said: "Yes. Go get them." They agreed, however, that Bagdikian would have to check with Bradlee that night for confirmation. Bagdikian left his deputy, Peter Silberman, in charge of the national news operation and rushed to National Airport across the Potomac River in Virginia. In keeping with the time-honored newsmen's code of respecting one another's sources, no one asked Bagdikian where he was going or who his source would be.

After missing the first plane to Boston, Bagdikian called Bradlee from the airport to ascertain that the venture had his endorsement. Bradlee, who has virtually absolute control of the news operation at the *Post*, replied that "if we don't publish, there's going to be a new executive editor of *The Washington Post*." It was an assertion that would come very close to being translated into a threat in the next twenty-four hours. "By the way," Bradlee added, "say hello to Southern California."

Bagdikian, unaccustomed to operating in the cloak-and-dagger fashion of those awaiting him in the Boston area, flew north with a ticket in his own name. There was a complicated chain of contacts to be made on arrival, and after being awake almost all night he ended up with a disorganized mass of photocopied sheets completely out of sequence and with very few page numbers. The suitcase he had brought along was inadequate, and the Papers were dumped instead into a huge bulky cardboard box. Bagdikian slept for about two hours and, getting up at daybreak, asked the hotel desk clerk for twine to secure the box; the only thing that could be found, however, was a length of rope that had been used to tie a dog to a fence a few days earlier.

Ellsberg specified terms for the *Post*'s use of the Pentagon Papers. "I hadn't expected to give them to any more than one paper," he explains. The first condition was that the *Post* not scoop the *Times* on the next scheduled installment in its series, announced as "The Kennedy Administration Increases the Stakes"; the *Post* was to begin its own series of articles, Ellsberg said, with a selection from the earlier period covered by the Papers, the part that he found most revealing and that had not yet appeared in the *Times*. His other condition, as he remembers it, was "that it not be a small news story, that they would give it a number of pages per day." Ellsberg also claims that, without asking, he was promised that the *Post* would print not only the narrative in the papers but also the documents and that the paper was prepared to defy any court injunction that might be imposed at the government's request. *Post* officials later emphatically denied, however, that any such agreement was made with regard to the documents or an injunction.

When Bagdikian arrived at Logan Airport in Boston to claim the two first-class seats to Washington that he had re-served—one for himself, under a fictitious name, and one for the unwieldy "package"—he inadvertently ran into Stanley Karnow, a China expert and former *Post* correspondent in Hong Kong who was coming to work for Bagdikian on the national staff of the newspaper after spending a year at Harvard writing a book. Karnow and his wife were flying to Washington to look at houses, and Bagdikian initially had a hard time avoiding detailed conversation with them. Karnow came up to talk with him in the first-class section of the plane but found Bagdikian reluctant to move the package and make room for his colleague. Finally, Karnow's jaw dropped and he said: "Oh, you've got it!" "Got what, Stanley?" Bagdikian asked with a long look. They agreed it would be "better to talk later."

That Wednesday night would become an important juncture in the new life of Daniel Ellsberg, quite apart from spreading the circulation of the Pentagon Papers. It was the start of his twelve days "underground," and it was the night when the already poorly kept secret that he was the source for the leak of the Papers would break wide open. Much to Ellsberg's amazement, reporters from both the *Times* and the *Post* called him on Wednesday to ask whether he had provided the Papers to the press. It was a curious, unprecedented situation: reporters being asked to compile news stories about their own newspapers, asked to look elsewhere for information that their own colleagues or editors could have provided but were honorbound not to reveal. The word was out, however, that *Newsweek* had found Ellsberg for an interview and that the St. Louis *Post-Dispatch* would report in its edition of Thursday June 17 that he was the source for the Papers. On Wednesday night, well before any official government announcement was made to the American public, the FBI also subtly contacted foreign journalists working in the United States to tell them that Ellsberg had leaked the Papers.

For some newspapers, like the *Post* and the *Times*, identifying Ellsberg posed a peculiar dilemma: if they really believed their credos about reporting the news fully and frankly, they were obligated to tell their readers this essential piece of information, which was becoming widely known. And yet to reveal their own source would breach a fundamental journalistic principle and perhaps institute a chain of legal difficulties for Ellsberg and others connected with the disclosure of the Papers. The dilemma was resolved for them when a maverick journalist named Sidney Zion, a former reporter for the *Times* and an editor of the defunct *Scanlan's* magazine, appeared on a radio talk show in New York and calmly revealed that his own reporting efforts had turned up the information that Daniel Ellsberg leaked the Pentagon Papers. Zion had set about finding the identity of the source after he visited the news room of the *Times* on Tuesday afternoon June 15 in the midst of the excitement over Judge Gurfein's restraining order. He attempted to write the story for the London *Daily Express,* but it was refused because of England's strict libel laws. Zion later acknowledged that he had gone after the story "to satisfy my ego" and had revealed it on the radio because he was not connected with an institution that would print the report.

Zion's action became one of many bizarre incidents in the course of the controversy over the Pentagon Papers. He was attacked from all sides for breaking the news, and for doing it in such an unusual manner. Columnist Pete Hamill of the New York *Post* called him "scummy" (but later retracted the remark). Arthur Gelb, metropolitan editor of the *Times,* warned Zion that he was "never to set foot into the *Times* again." Zion's former associate at *Scanlan's,* Warren Hinckle III, denounced him as a "publicity seeker." Alexander Bickel labeled Zion, his former law student at Yale, "an animal making his way in the jungle." Later, writing his own side of the story in *Women's Wear Daily,* Zion accused his critics of hypocrisy; he pointed out that if he had provided the name of a source for, say, scare stories about alleged Communists in the State Department, he might have been treated as a hero instead of a villain. "What bedeviled the reporters—and, as I later was to learn, many people outside the media—was the fact that I wasn't working for a paper or a TV station. I don't know how much of it was conscious," Zion wrote, "but the clear-cut feeling was that you don't go around breaking stories unless you've got a job. I always thought all you needed was a pencil, or only a voice."

The fact was that Zion had revealed something that was about to become widely known anyway. And Ellsberg later said that he bore no resentment against Zion, because he fully intended all along to claim "personal responsibility" for disclosing the Papers, just as he claimed responsibility for helping develop American policy in Vietnam. But Zion's announcement did help force Ellsberg underground; after giving the Papers to the *Post* Ellsberg spent almost two weeks successfully evading the FBI—which sought him for questioning—by staying in five different places, including a very public motel on the banks of the Charles River in Cambridge. Ellsberg thus gained the time he needed to continue orchestrating disclosure of the Papers to the public.

Ben Bagdikian had phoned Ben Bradlee from the airport in Boston early Thursday morning June 17 to say that he was on his way home with "the stuff." Bradlee was delighted and instructed Bagdikian to bring the huge carton directly to the Bradlee home in the Georgetown section of Washington. Avoiding the Karnows and anxious not to see anyone else he knew, Bagdikian raced into a taxi at National Airport. By the time he got to Bradlee's house the executive editor had also summoned three of the newspaper's most knowledgeable reporters on the subject of Vietnam, Chalmers Roberts, Murrey Marder, and Don Oberdorfer, as well as two secretaries who would help sort out and identify the material—which was, as Roberts put it, "a trash heap." At the same time other editors of the *Post*, including editorial page editor Philip Geyelin and his deputy, Meg Greenfield, converged at Bradlee's house to discuss the general question of how to handle the Pentagon Papers; they were joined by Roger Clark and Anthony Essaye, Washington representatives of the *Post's* New York law firm, Royall, Koegell, and Wells. (Until he was named Secretary of State by President Nixon in 1969, William S. Rogers had been a senior partner in the firm and served as chief counsel to *The Washington Post*.) Later in the day Frederick R. Beebe, chairman of the board of The Washington Post Company, who was coming to Washington from New York for a farewell party at Katharine Graham's home in honor of retiring *Post* business executive Harry Gladstein, would also join the deliberations.

In effect the *Post* editors had one day, or two days if they cared to be extravagant about it and take the risk that other newspapers might also obtain the Papers, to go through two simultaneous processes that had taken almost three months at *The New York Times:* sorting out, analyzing, and reviewing the material in the Papers (the *Post* had been given approximately 4,400 pages from the mammoth study) in order to decide how best to present it in readable fashion in a newspaper with somewhat more limited resources than the *Times;* and working out the legal issues in order to strike a balance between minimizing the risks to the *Post* and doing justice to the First Amendment guarantee of free speech. On the one hand, the legal problem was easier for the *Post* because the *Times* had already blazed the trail and shown the frailty of the argument that any classified material must automatically be kept away from the public; on the other hand, the *Post*'s problem was also more complicated—there was already an outstanding court order against one newspaper, and any bold action might be interpreted as defiance of the law and disrespect for the court.

It was also argued that the potential corporate problems of the *Post* were particularly grave, especially in June 1971. Although The New York Times Company is also a large and diversified institution. The Washington Post Company is the epitome of the "communications conglomerate" that had come under strong attack since the Nixon administration took office. In addition to the newspaper, the company was full owner of *Newsweek* magazine and *Art News* magazine, three television stations (in Washington, Miami, and Jacksonville), two AM radio stations (in Washington and Cincinnati), and one FM radio station (in Washington); half owner of the Los Angeles *Times–Washington Post* news service (with about 345 domestic and foreign client newspapers); one-third owner of the *International Herald Tribune* in Paris; owner of 49 percent interest in the Bowaters Mersey Paper Company Ltd. of Canada (which provides most of the newsprint on which the *Post* is printed); owner of an 85 percent interest in a terminal and warehousing business in Alexandria, Virginia (where the *Post*'s newsprint arrives and is stored); and half owner of *Book World,* a Sunday book review supplement to the *Post*, the *Chicago Tribune,* and other newspapers. Several of the company's broadcast licenses were up for review by the Federal Communications Commission in 1972, and executives could not help but note that anyone convicted of a felony is not permitted to hold a broadcast license. There was also a special problem, which was very much on Beebe's mind: on June 15, 1971, only two days earlier, The Washington Post Company had "gone public" for the first time, with an offering of 1,354,000 shares of Class B common stock. It had taken two months to construct the exact terms of the offering, including arrangements to list the stock on the American Stock Exchange, and the underwriting agreement with Lazard Freres would not take full effect until a week later. One clause in that agreement provided for possible cancellation of the stock issue should some "disaster" or "catastrophic event" befall the compay during that week. Since no precise definition of those terms was included, it was impossible to predict whether the underwriters would claim that an injunction against the newspaper or criminal prosecution by the government fell into the category. And yet there was a paragraph in the stock prospectus that seemed to deal with just that point:

> The Washington Post has the reputation of being an outspoken observer of local, national, and world events. The management of the Company and the editorial staff of the *Post* place great emphasis on the newspaper's public responsibilities, as expressed in the Company's Certificate of Incorporation, which states that it is the Company's purpose "to publish any newspaper owned by the Company as an independent newspaper dedicated to the welfare of the community and the nation in

keeping with the principles of a free press." Publishing the Post in keeping with those principles has involved and will continue to involve substantial expenses (not necessarily compensated for by increased revenues) incurred in endeavoring to achieve and maintain editorial excellence and independence and to provide outstanding news collection and reporting.

Beebe, a lawyer and a long-time associate of The Washington Post Company, had written the certificate of incorporation in 1948 along the lines directed by Eugene Meyer, Katharine Graham's father, and as he flew to Washington on Thursday June 17 he knew that business and editorial concerns could not necessarily be separated. Were not the Pentagon Papers to be included in the category of "outstanding news collection and reporting?" But what about a "disaster?"

The *Post*'s decision-making processes took place in the living room and an adjoining library in Bradlee's house. The original plan was that the *Post* would begin catching up by running two articles based on the Pentagon Papers the first day, Friday—one by Marder explaining, as the Papers showed, that President Johnson had instituted various halts in the bombing of North Vietnam not in an effort to bring about negotiations but as a means of mollifying domestic public opinion; and another by Roberts describing early U.S. efforts to block elections in North and South Vietnam out of concern that the Communists would win them. The latter was based on a combination of principle (dealing with the early period of the Papers was one of Ellsberg's conditions for giving the material to the *Post*) and practicality (Roberts was an expert on the Geneva conference of 1954, which he covered personally; he had been the first to report, on June 7, 1954, that the United States had twice proposed sending American planes to help the French in Indochina but that the British had blocked the plan). At the same time Oberdorfer, who had just completed a book about the 1968 Communist Tet offensive in Vietnam, pulled together material from the late

Johnson years and other parts of the Papers that would be the basis for later installments in the newspaper's series.

It soon became clear that two stories would be impossible to produce. Marder, a slow, deliberate writer who often stayed in the *Post* news room until after midnight to finish long pieces, had an enormous amount of reading to complete before he could begin putting words on paper. But Roberts felt at ease in such a crisis situation and even seemed to thrive on it. In his dry, grinding voice he told Bradlee: "Look, Ben, I can produce a story for you in time to make the second edition. It's not going to set the world on fire like the Johnson stuff, but it's a story if you want a story." Bradlee was desperate to begin repairing the public part of the *Post*'s ego; he wanted a story, any story. "Write it, write it, write it," he replied to Roberts. Like the other reporters in the library, Roberts ignored what was going on in the living room: "I had my nose buried in the typewriter. We were all going blind because there was no light in the place. It was terrible." The only comic relief of the day was provided by Bradlee's ten-year-old daughter, Marina, who did a booming business selling lemonade to the extraordinary horde of people visiting her father on a weekday.

The reporters and editors made several policy decisions from the start of their work: the *Post* stories would be based primarily on the actual documents in the Pentagon Papers rather than on the commentary of the Vietnam History Task Force ("I was distrustful of the narrative," Roberts said). The newspaper would not, however, publish the documents themselves as the *Times* had; there simply was not enough space immediately available in the newspaper to do so, but the decision was also based on the editors' feeling that a story without documents would be a more "digestible" one for readers. The lawyers too felt that the courts might make a distinction between the alleged sins of the two newspapers if one had printed the full texts of classified documents and the other had not.

Initially, Bagdikian spent most of his time in the library

supervising the reporters' work. His euphoria began to fade after he made several trips through the living room. "All the faces were gray," Bagdikian noticed, "and it just dawned on me that something serious was going on. . . . So I began to spend more time sitting in the living room, and as I tuned in I realized that this was a very fundamental conversation about whether or not the *Post* should publish the Papers." Much as their counterparts in New York had done with the *Times*, Roger Clark and the other *Post* lawyers were fervently counseling against any publication of the Papers at all. They argued that the *Post* should await the outcome of *The New York Times* case, since the issue of freedom of the press would be adequately handled there. Besides, said Clark— a dignified, well-put-together young lawyer who invariably looked out of place in the *Post* news room advising harried, disheveled reporters on the potentially libelous content of their stories—how could the *Post* possibly be sure it was avoiding danger to national security when it was trying to do in one day what had taken the *Times* nearly three months? The lawyers complained of the "unseemly haste" of the reporters in the library and scoffed at the notion that "competition" should be a significant factor in a story of such magnitude as the Pentagon Papers.

Bradlee and Bagdikian, supported by Geyelin, Meg Greenfield, and at times deputy managing editor Howard Simons (who would succeed to the managing editorship later in the summer when Eugene Patterson resigned from the *Post* to teach at Duke University), fought a running battle against the lawyers. Beneath the surface was the notion that the *Post* was getting ever closer to its goal of being a truly "national" newspaper, increasingly mentioned in the same breath as the *Times* by others besides Vice President Agnew. A failure on the biggest story of the year would obviously be a setback. But the argument followed other lines, as summarized later by Bagdikian: "All the newspapers in the country should not feel bound by a move the government made against the *Times*. . . . We had our own decision to make, we had information we believed to be of great importance to the public in our hands. . . . We had some of the best people in the country writing it; these people had been working in this area for ten to fifteen years. They were competent judges of what was dangerous to the country and what was not; they handled this kind of information every day. They were familiar with many of the documents to begin with, and they could understand the new ones in context. . . . If the issue of freedom of the press was involved, it was extremely important that the Papers be published, because if we did not publish it would appear as though we were not supporting *The New York Times*."

At one point Bagdikian uttered a phrase that would become something of a rallying cry against the persistent lawyers: "The only way to assert the right to publish is to publish."

The lawyers were unyielding, turning each new argument advanced by the editors into a reason not to go ahead with the Pentagon Papers. When Fritz Beebe arrived he tried to push the corporate concerns out of consideration, but he too felt that it would be imprudent for the *Post* to rush into print; reacting more as a lawyer than as a publishing executive for the moment, Beebe sided with the skeptics. By evening a "compromise" had been hammered out—the *Post* would not publish the Papers Friday but would notify the Attorney General of its intention to do so, either by telephone or by publishing a front-page box saying in essence: "We have the Pentagon Papers and are working on them and are going to begin publishing them on Sunday." It was just at that point that the reporters, hungry for dinner, emerged from the library and were apprised of the current state of affairs. There was, as one participant put it, "an explosive response." Oberdorfer unabashedly labeled the plan to notify the Attorney General "the shittiest idea I've ever heard." Marder looked as if he would become ill. Roberts, who by sheer seniority and a self-confident presence commanded enormous respect at the *Post*, may have saved the day. He accused the editors and lawyers of "crawling on your belly to the Attorney General." "If you don't want to risk running it," he said, "then to hell with it, don't run it." But if the *Post* didn't run the Papers, he warned, he would move his retirement ahead two weeks and turn it into a resignation, issuing a public statement disassociating himself from the decision of the newspaper where he had spent most of his professional life. Bagdikian leaned over to Bradlee, who was by now turning pale. "You're going to have a full-scale revolt from the staff of this paper," Bagdikian warned. "You know that you have a commitment to me to publish these Papers." As the assistant managing editor described his boss later: "I have never seen him so gray. His eye sockets seemed to get blacker and blacker."

A solution seemed far away, and it was determined to put the problem to Katharine Graham for a decision. From Bradlee's kitchen Beebe and the lawyers phoned her at her home a few blocks away. Paul Ignatius, president of the newspaper, came to the telephone first, because Mrs. Graham was in the midst of a farewell toast to retiring *Post* executive Harry Gladstein. A former Secretary of the Navy, Ignatius was quite new to the newspaper business and had rather little rapport with the journalists who worked at the *Post*; he pronounced himself against immediate publication. (Ignatius was relieved of his position later in the year as a result of internal executive disputes on other issues, including labor-management relations.) When Bradlee and Geyelin eventually spoke to Mrs. Graham on the phone, they warned that word would be out all over Washington that the *Post* had the Pentagon Papers but shrunk away from publishing them. Recalling the interminable and chaotic phone conversation later, Mrs. Graham said: "It certainly weighed very heavily in this rush decision that the editors were absolutely wild about this and the reporters felt incredibly strongly that we had to go ahead."

Beebe had begun to see that side clearly too. "I was convinced," the chairman of the board said later, "that it would have been a disaster from the point of view of the editorial staff. Their principle was that if you've got the news, you've got to print it."

With time pressing in, Beebe finally outlined the positions on both sides for Katharine Graham. She paused and said, with something of a gulp: "Okay, go ahead." "I felt a great sense of relief," Beebe said later. "I felt once the decision was taken that it was right."

But there would be another crisis later that night. Bagdikian, having raced downtown to the *Post* building with the last few pages of Chalmers Roberts' story, was in the composing room on the fourth floor, one below the news room, making sure that the story would get into the "late city" edition (the *Post*'s second and largest) when he got an urgent phone call. Roger Clark had found a new potential problem: Was there "collusion" with *The New York Times*? He demanded to know Bagdikian's source for the Papers; Bagdikian refused, asserting that it was utterly "confidential." Clark said Bagdikian would have to come back to Bradlee's house to discuss the matter further.

Bagdikian was unbelieving; he finally relented and, relying on the confidential lawyer-client privilege, told Clark, as his lawyer, that Daniel Ellsberg had provided the Papers to the *Post*, as he was presumed to have done to the *Times*. If the source was the same, Clark said, that amounted to collusion; he called New York and confirmed this view with William R. Glendon, a senior partner in the law firm. Any politeness that had remained through the long day was now gone, and Bagdikian and Clark shouted angrily at each other. The assistant managing editor accused the lawyer of "finding every excuse for not publishing." Clark phoned Katharine Graham's house, where Bradlee, Beebe, and other executives were now gathered. He refused to put Bagdikian on the phone but communicated to Bradlee the assistant managing editor's threat at 12:15 A.M. that he would quit unless the *Post* went ahead. At 12:25 A.M., five minutes before the press deadline for the "late city" edition, Mrs. Graham once again decided in favor of publishing the Papers.

Bagdikian was still unsettled. He called the national desk as soon as the first copies of the edition were scheduled to appear, to check whether the Roberts article based on the Pentagon Papers was there intact. Indeed it was; the headline across four columns read: "Documents Reveal U.S. Effort in '54 to Delay Viet Election." "First of a series" was the line above Roberts' byline.

[CHAPTER VIII]

The appearance of the Pentagon Papers in *The Washington Post* was received with mixed feelings at *The New York Times*. The editors of the *Times* were fiercely proud of their exclusive and resented losing their competitive position. "I was jumping up and down in here like a madman," said *Times* managing editor A. M. Rosenthal later, recalling his initial reaction on seeing the first installment in the *Post* series based on the Papers. (It is far more difficult to obtain the *Post* in New York than to get the *Times* in Washington, but each newspaper watches the other closely every morning to see if it has missed any important stories.) For Neil Sheehan and the other reporters who had worked on planning and producing the articles since early in April, there was a feeling of both annoyance and worry—it seemed possible that their work might have been in vain, that by the time the restraining order was lifted, if it was lifted, most of the revelations of the Pentagon Papers would have already appeared elsewhere, albeit not in "the *Times* way." The editors moved to reassure them that once the court case was settled, all installments in the ten-part series would be printed as originally contemplated, notwithstanding what other newspapers had printed in the meantime. But on Friday June 18 sentiment was perhaps stronger than ever at the *Times* that the management ought to have considered defying Judge Gurfein's injunction and printing the articles anyway.

At the same time anyone who moved beyond a simple feeling of competitiveness had to be pleased that the *Post* had followed in the tracks of the *Times*. Once he overcame his initial reaction, Rosenthal acknowledged: "I was glad they did it. I felt this would help us." Philosophically, there could be no better way of asserting the freedom of the press guaranteed by the First Amendment than for several different newspapers to assert it collectively; if different groups of reporters and editors made the same judgment simultaneously—that the Papers were not harmful to national security and, indeed, provided information wanted and needed by the public—the motives and the good sense of each separate group might be vindicated. And there could be little doubt that the expanding access to the Papers was an unambiguous assist to the *Times* in its legal battle; it demonstrated plainly to the Justice Department and the courts that news is news, that it might be utterly futile to attempt to cut off through prior restraint a story that had already caught on.

Inevitably, the charge was levied that the newspapers were proliferating the Pentagon Papers among themselves in order to frustrate the Nixon administration's legal maneuvers. High officials in the White House, including presidential aide John Ehrlichman, who were relatively unfamiliar with the internal operations of the American press were utterly convinced on that point and privately stressed that the first two newspapers to run the story, the *Times* and the *Post,* were both strongly anti-administration. The logical conclusion, for an administration whose attitude toward the press was best reflected in the tirades of Vice President Agnew, was that the two papers were in cahoots. Several influential members of Congress also believed this variation of the "collusion" theory.

Both Rosenthal and Benjamin Bradlee conceded that when they began to run into legal difficulty many of their colleagues at other newspapers called with offers to help out by carrying the torch and taking the Papers off their hands. But both editors emphatically deny that they ever took the offers seriously. The notion that they cooperated with each other strikes most people working for either newspaper as absurd; asserting the freedom to publish is one thing, they point out, but handing over the biggest story of the year to your chief competitor is quite another. What is more, under the terms of Judge Gurfein's initial temporary restraining order against the *Times,* it would have been of questionable legality to turn the classified material over to another newspaper. "I don't mind going to jail for freedom of the press," Rosenthal proclaims, "but not for being stupid. Besides, it's a monstrous idea as a newspaper editor. The idea of taking our story that the guys had worked on and saying: 'Ben, here, take it.' It's crazy."

However mixed the feelings may have been at the *Times* on June 18, there was jubilation at *The Washington Post.* Reporters and editors alike felt that they had caught up, and also that the *Post* had handled the Pentagon Papers capably in the short time available. By opening with Chalmers Roberts' story on the Eisenhower period, the *Post* also managed an exclusive of sorts. Preparations began immediately for the second installment in the *Post* series, Murrey Marder's article on the motivations for pauses in the bombing of North Vietnam during the Johnson administration, as well as for subsequent stories based on the Papers, with most of the work still centered at Bradlee's house. The first two articles were running about one full page each, compared with the six pages in the *Times,* and the *Post* editors felt convinced that they were presenting moderate-length pieces that were likely to appeal to a broad spectrum of readers. In its own assessment of how to avoid endangering national security, the *Post* made a policy decision not to quote any diplomatic or military cables fully and not to name any CIA agents.

Hand in hand with elation at the *Post* was a sense of anticipation for any government moves against the newspaper. Although legal action would be expensive and potentially threatening, half the excitement of the story had become the *Times's* confrontation with the government over freedom of the press; the case before Judge Gurfein was already a major front-page story in the *Post.* No one at the *Post* was saying it publicly, but the editors—and especially Bradlee, who delights in a good fight—would have been disappointed if the Justice Department had not dragged their newspaper into court too. Reporters covering the White House, the Justice Department, and the federal courts were alerted to watch for any signs that a request for an injunction against the *Post* was about to be filed. But Friday morning and early afternoon passed quietly, and it began to look as if the government had distinguished between the *Times* and the *Post* on the basis of whether the full text of classified documents had been printed.

The Justice Department had at least two options available in any legal action against the *Post.* Because the headquarters of *Newsweek* were on Madison Avenue in New York (and the *Post* also maintained a news bureau there), The Washington Post Company listed "principal executive offices" in both Washington and New York; that arrangement was confirmed in the stock prospectus issued on Tuesday June 15. Thus anyone suing the *Post,* including the government, could legally do so in either city; it would have been a simple matter for Justice Department lawyers to go before Judge Gurfein in New York and seek to add *The Washington Post* as a co-defendant in

The New York Times case. Even if an argument had ensued over the proper venue for sustaining legal action against the *Post*, Judge Gurfein would almost surely have enjoined publication of the Papers by the *Post* until that issue was resolved, if only to keep the two newspapers on an equal footing. Temporarily, at least, only *one* case would have been in litigation. But that course was apparently never even considered by the Justice Department, which was developing and implementing policy under crisis conditions.

Another possible course of action, Senate Minority Leader Hugh Scott (R-Pa.) later suggested, would have been for the Justice Department to file directly with the Supreme Court under the rarely used Declaratory Judgment Act for a ruling on whether publication of the Pentagon Papers could be considered "criminal" under the federal espionage law. That would have conserved resources on all sides, he pointed out, and permitted an early resolution of several major issues in the case, at the same time avoiding some of the controversy implicit in the government's civil suits against the newspapers. It would have had the disadvantage for the government, however, of risking full disclosure of the Papers while waiting for a decision to be rendered.

The suspense was cut off at *The Washington Post* at about 3 P.M. on Friday June 18, when Benjamin Bradlee received a phone call from William H. Rehnquist, Assistant Attorney General for the Justice Department's Office of Legal Counsel, the intellectually conservative "President's lawyer's lawyer." Bradlee recalls that Rehnquist was "friendly but formal" as he read the inevitable message from the Attorney General:

> I have been advised by the Secretary of Defense that the material published in *The Washington Post* on June 18, 1971, captioned "Documents Reveal U.S. Effort in '54 to Delay Viet Election" contains information relating to the national defense of the United States and bears a top-secret classification. As such, publication of this information is directly prohibited by

the provisions of the Espionage Law, Title 18, United States Code, Section 793. Moreover, further publication of information of this character will cause irreparable injury to the defense interests of the United States. Accordingly, I respectfully request that you publish no further information of this character and advise me that you have made arrangements for the return of these documents to the Department of Defense.

It was exactly the same wording that had been used in the ultimatum to *The New York Times* four days earlier, but for the *Post* there was no hesitation about the answer; the lawyers, despite their earlier misgivings, had made a clear commitment to defend the *Post* if the case went to court, and preparations were already under way. With publisher Katharine Graham and a crowd of other *Post* officials listening in his office, Bradlee told Rehnquist: "I'm sure you will understand that I must respectfully decline." He also refused to delay the rest of the series pending resolution of the *Times* case in New York. Rehnquist said that he understood and after hanging up contacted the *Post*'s lawyers and asked them to meet legal representatives of the Justice Department at U.S. District Court for the District of Columbia at 5 P.M.

At the federal courthouse on John Marshall Place NW in Washington it was not unusual in these days of government by injunction for a crisis to arise on a Friday afternoon, and routine steps had already been taken to keep the judicial apparatus functioning after hours. Joseph M. Hannon, chief of the civil division in the largest U.S. Attorney's office in the country, had been summoned six blocks down Pennsylvania Avenue to the Justice Department at 2:30 P.M. and returned to his office an hour later. A frequent seeker of injunctions and an expert in the procedures and politics of the federal courts, Hannon would be essential in greasing the wheels of the government's frontal attack on the *Post*. The Justice Department had also notified Chief Judge John J. Sirica, who was in the midst of a controversial trial of a burglary and fencing ring that had victimized the Georgetown homes of wealthy Washingtonians, and Sirica in turn informed James F. Davey, clerk of the court, that a late case filing could be expected. Davey alerted U.S. District Judge Barrington D. Parker, a Republican who had been named to the court a year earlier by President Nixon and had already carved out a reputation as a civil libertarian on the bench; as "motions judge" for June, Parker would have to take the case if the judge to whom it was normally assigned was unavailable for an immediate hearing. At the same time word was passed to the U.S. Court of Appeals for the District of Columbia Circuit, one of the most liberal federal appellate courts in the country, which has its headquarters on the fifth floor of the same building, that a major case was on its way and was almost certain to generate an appeal from one side or the other.

It made a big difference, in June 1971, which of Washington's fifteen federal district judges sat on a case. The court included several judges who simply had a blind spot when it came to any case involving antiwar protest. Some of the judges seemed to detest the press and went out of their way to avoid cooperating with reporters. A few members of the court were judicial activists who took a broad view of the Bill of Rights and had a national reputation for their willingness to challenge bureaucracies and institutions. For the sake of judicial efficiency and also to guarantee that cases would be distributed among judges of different ideological persuasions, the court had adopted an individual calendar system and random assignment process. The judge who would be assigned to a new civil or criminal case was determined by drawing a card from the top of a sealed deck in the clerk's office, and unless unusual circumstances arose he or she kept the case until a final verdict or ruling was made.

A phalanx of seven government lawyers walked into the clerk's office at the federal courthouse in Washington at about 5:15 P.M. that afternoon. The complaint they filed in what would become case number 1235-71 was similar in most details to the one that had been lodged against the *Times* in New York; it named as defendants everyone listed on the masthead of the *Post* and Chalmers Roberts, the author of the first article in the series. According to the lawsuit, which was drafted in legalese to match the espionage law, each of the defendants "knew, or had reason to believe, that such information [in the Pentagon Papers] could be used to the injury of the United States to the advantage of a foreign nation and notwithstanding such knowledge and belief did willfully communicate, deliver, and transmit said information by the publication thereof, to persons not entitled to receive such information." Attached were affidavits from two Defense Department officials, which stated without specifics that Roberts' article "has prejudiced the defense interests of the United States." In view of the damage already done, the government's legal memorandum stated, the *Post* and its editors would "suffer no injury if they cease to publish the contents of the study in their possession pending the determination of [the government's] motion for a preliminary injunction."

When the blue card was pulled from the deck to assign the case, it carried the name of Judge Gerhard A. Gesell. Hannon, who had lost many a government case before Gesell, winced noticeably. Roger Clark and two other lawyers representing the *Post* smiled discreetly at their good fortune. Gesell was one of the best-known and most widely respected members of the federal bench in Washington. He is the son of Dr. Arnold Gesell, the noted pediatrician. (The judge used his father's original examining table as working space in his chambers at the courthouse.) While an undergraduate at Yale, Gesell had been a stringer, or part-time correspondent, for *The New York Times,* and he had a close acquaintance with the newspaper business, having once served as a lawyer for the *Post* (before he was replaced by William S. Rogers. After a long legal practice in the nation's capital, beginning as a staff attorney for the Securities and Exchange Commission, Gesell was accustomed to evaluating the demands and assertions of the federal government. He also knew something of the nature of secret war documents, having served in 1945–1946 as chief assistant counsel to the Joint Congressional Committee on Investigation of the Pearl Harbor Attack. Gesell had dealt intensively with the military after being named by President Kennedy as chairman of the President's Commission on Equal Opportunity in the Armed Forces. His three and a half years as a judge had been marked by controversial decisions and attitudes: Gesell refused to sentence convicted killers to death, even in a case involving the murder of two FBI agents; he threw out the District of Columbia's archaic statute banning abortions (later to be partially reversed by the Supreme Court). More recently, in a case argued by some of the same lawyers from the Justice Department's Internal Security Division who would now face him over the Pentagon Papers, he had banned the Superintendent of Documents from distributing a list prepared by the House Internal Security Committee of so-called subversive speakers on college campuses because the list appeared to have no "valid legislative purpose"; he had pronounced an end to the long-standing practice of members of Congress holding reserve commissions in the armed forces. Only a few days before the Pentagon Papers case came to him, he ruled that the FBI must stop distributing personal arrest records—some of them uncorrected to show that people had never been convicted of the crimes with which they were charged—outside the federal government for purposes other than law enforcement. Gesell was delighted to have the Papers case.

At a conference in his chambers immediately after the lawsuit against the *Post* was filed, Gesell asked the newspaper to agree voluntarily to withhold publication while he weighed the case for two or three days; but Roger Clark refused, saying that the newspaper felt it was essential to "assert the principle" of freedom to publish rather than accommodate the schedules of others by cooperating in a delay. Gesell's courtroom was packed with *Post* executives, including Katharine Graham and Fritz Beebe, and interested outsiders for his seventy-five-minute hearing on whether to issue a temporary restraining order. The judge was stern with the lawyers for both sides as he rushed to deal with the case before the press deadline at the *Post* (Marder's story, the second in the series, was already being set in type when court convened just after 6 P.M.). Gesell chided Justice Department lawyer Kevin T. Maroney for suggesting that the *Post* was bound to have "reason to believe" the Papers would injure the nation "just because the U.S. government says so." Maroney insisted that government classifications must be respected and contended that "the situation here is not the normal situation of prior restraint of First Amendment rights. It's a question of whether or not . . . a newspaper should be permitted to publish classified information." He pleaded that at the very least Gesell enjoin the *Post* until Judge Gurfein ruled in the second hearing on the *Times* case in New York, which was going on simultaneously with the *Post* proceedings. Gesell acknowledged concern over "competitive fairness" between the two rival newspapers, but said that that could not guide his decision.

Clark pressed Gesell for a decision based purely on the First Amendment but stressed that the *Post* had reviewed the content of the Papers to be sure that national security would indeed be protected despite publication. "This case represents a critically important principle involving the relationship between the press and the government," the *Post*'s lawyer insisted. "For two hundred years we have operated under a system of a free press. We have two choices now: either we go on with it or we inject the courts into the relationship." In an argument that would become a telling one as time went on, Clark warned that "there's a leak in the dike" and that the Pentagon Papers could no longer be kept secret from the public. "There were at least fifteen copies [of the study] available before the *Times* and the *Post* got theirs. You just can't suppress information of this nature. It's going to get out one way or another."

The newspaper and government representatives paced the second-floor corridors of the courthouse while Gesell retired to his chambers with his law clerk for forty-five minutes to write an eloquent six-hundred-word opinion. When he returned to the drab courtroom at 8:05 P.M., he handed the *Post*—and the press —a stunning victory. Reaching back to Chief Justice Charles Evans Hughes's opinion in Near v. Minnesota, Gesell stressed "the historic reasons supporting the total freedom of the press to publish as guaranteed by the First Amendment of the Constitution." The government was misusing the Espionage Act, the judge said, since it was never intended to provide for "any preexisting restraint or censorship of the press; even if it had been so intended, "the Court has before it no precise information suggesting in what respects, if any, the publication of this information will injure the United States and must take cognizance of the fact that there are apparently private parties in possession of this data which they will continue to leak to other sources."

In an aside that caused the *Post* executives some chagrin, Gesell expressed his regret that they had been unwilling to give him more time, and he cautioned that "the *Post* stands in serious jeopardy of criminal prosecution"; but that, he said, not an injunction, "is the only remedy our Constitution or the Congress has provided." Gesell acknowledged that the "information [in the Papers] unquestionably will be embarrassing to the United States, but there is no possible way after the most full and careful hearing that a court would be able to determine the implications of publication on the conduct of government affairs or to weigh these implications against the effects of withholding information from the public."

Gesell refused even a momentary stay of his decision to

permit the government time for an emergency appeal to the higher court.

It would be an hour and forty-five minutes before the clerk of the U.S. Court of Appeals could round up a panel of three judges to hear the *Post* case, and during that time the first edition of the *Post* was going to press. Roger Clark warned Judges J. Skelly Wright, Spottswood W. Robinson III, and Roger Robb when the appellate hearing began at 9:45 P.M. that within forty minutes "the copies will be out of our control." The hearing lasted thirty-five minutes, and it was clear from the start that there was sharp disagreement between Wright and Robb about whether Gesell's decision should be reversed in order to give the government another opportunity to prove its case at a more extensive hearing in the lower court. Maroney, who stressed the *Post*'s "unlawful possession" of the Pentagon Papers and contended that Gesell's ruling amounted to "an abuse of discretion," pleaded for just that second opportunity. Clark, on the other hand, praised Gesell for a decision that "recognized the breadth of First Amendment rights." Wright, gritting his teeth, repeatedly scolded Maroney for "going a bit far" by, among other things, comparing disclosure of the Pentagon Papers to the Chicago *Tribune* story during World War II, which revealed that the United States had broken the Japanese code.

The judges retired to a conference room, and the *Post*'s press deadline came and went without any sign that a ruling was imminent. As it happened, the *Post* ran late that Friday night, and it was not until 10:43 P.M.—when Herman Cohen, the newsdealer who sells the first copies of the paper every night, hit the street with the first edition—that the newspaper was genuinely "beyond control." The Marder story on President Johnson's bombing pauses was out on the *Times-Post* news service wire as well, which meant that hundreds of other newspapers would have access to the story within minutes.

Meanwhile, in the conference room behind the courtroom of the U.S. Court of Appeals, a bitter fight for the vote of Spottswood Robinson was going on between Wright, a long-established civil libertarian who was often labeled a "radical judge," and Robb, a conservative who had represented the Atomic Energy Commission in the J. Robert Oppenheimer case. Robinson, an extremely thoughtful and cautious jurist, ordinarily voted with Wright and the liberal bloc of the appellate court, but he was deeply troubled by the procedural question of whether the government should not be given the same full opportunity to make its case in Washington as in New York. As their debate continued behind closed doors, the *Post* kept churning out copies of the Saturday paper—because of technical mishaps, more slowly than usual—but kept a telephone line open to a reporter in the courtroom, lest the press run have to be interrupted in the event of an adverse ruling.

A decision finally came at 1:20 A.M. Robinson had voted with Robb to reverse Gesell's ruling and literally to stop the presses. The *Post's* press room fell silent, and printers began lifting the Marder story out and remaking the front page. But Fritz Beebe, who had remained at court the entire time, and Roger Clark realized that the temporary restraining order was obviously ineffective since thousands of copies of the newspaper were already out. They rushed in with an emergency request that the appellate panel "clarify" its ruling; within moments the judges did so, saying that the order applied only to subsequent installments in the *Post* series after the second one. The Pentagon Papers story was put back on the presses—before any copies had actually been published without it—and they were started up again. The final edition of *The Washington Post* for Saturday June 19, 1971, a very late final edition at that, presented an ironic contrast on the front page: the lead story, at the right, said that the U.S. Court of Appeals had issued an order "preventing publication" of articles based on the Pentagon Papers; to the left, there appeared just such an article.

Later Saturday, after a few hours' sleep, Judges Robinson and Robb explained in a written opinion their decision to enjoin the *Post* and to require that Gesell hold an evidentiary hearing on the government lawsuit the following Monday to determine whether publication could "so prejudice" United States defense interests or result in "such irreparable injury" as to justify a prior restraint. "Freedom of the press, as important as it is, is not boundless," the judges said. "We do not understand," they added, "how it can be determined . . . without even a cursory examination of [the Pentagon Papers] that [they are] nothing but 'historical data' without present vitality." A prior restraint is not so serious if granted "for the shortest possible period," they concluded; the *Post*'s injury "from a brief pause in publication is clearly outweighed by the grave potentiality of injury to the national security."

Judge J. Skelly Wright, accusing his colleagues of precipitating "a sad day for America," dissented bitterly. The executive branch, he contended, "has enlisted the Judiciary in the suppression of our most precious freedom. As if the long and sordid war in Southeast Asia had not already done enough harm to our people, it now is used to cut out the heart of our free institutions and system of government." Wright complained of the vagueness of the government affidavits purporting to establish the damage to national security: "We are asked to turn our backs on the First Amendment simply because certain officials have labeled material as unfit for the American people and the people of the world. . . . To allow a government to suppress free speech simply through a system of bureaucratic classification would sell our heritage far, far too cheaply." Striking a note that was deeply felt by the newspapers themselves, he added that "at a time when the American people and their Congress are in the midst of a pitched debate over the war, the history of the war, however disillusioning, is crucial."

On Friday night June 18 the editors of the *Post* assigned reporters to cover every aspect of the developing confrontation over the Pentagon Papers—a story that had shown itself, in the *Post* as in the *Times* and other newspapers across the country, to be far more compelling than the articles based on the actual content of the Papers. Thus when it appeared possible that the U.S. Court of Appeals might affirm Gesell's ruling against the government, the man to watch became Chief Justice Warren E. Burger, who could have been called upon in his capacity as circuit justice for the District of Columbia to grant a stay to the Justice Department. Burger is very close to President Nixon—he prays regularly at the White House on Sundays—and sympathizes profoundly with the attitudes of the administration that named him to head the high court. He had already demonstrated, in the Vietnam Veterans Against the War case, his ability to act with lightning speed on the basis of very little documentary evidence to uphold the Justice Department's position. On another occasion, after writing the unanimous opinion of the Supreme Court affirming the constitutionality of busing to achieve racial integration in public schools—an opinion that displeased the White House and could have hurt President Nixon politically—Burger issued an unprecedented personal "clarification" in another busing case. The clarification, which could be interpreted as cutting back on the forcefulness of the busing opinion, was directed to the "personal attention" of every federal judge in the country.

Concerned that the Chief Justice might act on an emergency basis from his home on North Rochester Street in a wooded area of suburban Arlington, Virginia, the *Post* attempted to reach him by telephone but was unsuccessful. Shortly after 11 P.M. *Post* reporters Spencer Rich, who ordinarily covered the

U.S. Senate, and Martin Weil, an experienced member of the newspaper's metropolitan staff, were dispatched to Burger's house to keep watch for any action there. Going past the "No Trespassing" sign at the entrance to Burger's driveway, they knocked on the front door of the house. As Weil later put it in a staccato memo to his editor: "After about a minute or two, the Chief Justice opened the door. He was wearing a bathrobe. He was carrying a gun. The gun was in his right hand, muzzle pointed down. It was a long-barreled steel weapon. The Chief Justice did not seem glad to see us. Spencer explained why we were there. There was a considerable amount of misdirected conversation. It seemed for a bit that people were talking past each other. Spencer, who held up his credentials, was explaining why we were there, but the judge seemed to be saying we shouldn't have come. . . . Finally after a little more talk, everybody seemed to understand everybody. The Chief Justice said it would not be all right for us to wait for any possible Justice Department emissaries outside his door, but we could wait down at the street. He held his gun in his hand throughout a two- or three-minute talk. Sometimes it was not visible, held behind the doorpost. He never pointed it at us. He closed the door. We went down to the street and waited for about three hours. Then we went home."

The *Post* knew well that Chief Justice Burger was a law-and-order man in the image of the Nixon administration; but the notion that he would answer his door with a gun in hand was extraordinary. That was news. The *Post* was preparing a large package of stories on the Pentagon Papers controversy for the Sunday edition of June 20, and the daily news "budget" on Saturday afternoon originally included an article on the reporters' encounter with the gun-toting jurist; it was, after all, an unusual way to handle the press. But First Amendment or not, this seemed too hot a story to handle in the midst of a court case involving the *Post* that was sure to make its way to the Supreme Court. The story was killed by Bradlee before it

[163]

got far from the two reporters' hands; in fact, the story was destroyed lest it slip into the paper by mistake. It did not.

While the *Post* was rejoicing in its accomplishments on Friday June 18 and defending itself in the initial hearings before Judge Gesell and the three-judge panel of the appellate court, Judge Murray Gurfein was conducting his all-day trial on the merits of the government's case against *The New York Times*. Gurfein had already held an interim hearing the day before on the government's demand that the *Times* be required to turn over the Papers in its possession for inspection; the *Times*'s legal team vehemently objected, and the judge settled for the alternative of the newspaper providing a list of the material it had. *Times* lawyer Alexander Bickel opened the court proceedings in New York on Friday by pointing out that the story was now out in *The Washington Post* and in the client newspapers of its news service, notably the New York *Post*; that situation, he insisted, "radically changed" the case and seemed to render meaningless the government's request for a standing injunction. U.S. Attorney Whitney North Seymour and his assistant, Michel D. Hess, were clearly taken aback; their superiors in Washington had not even bothered to inform them before the 10 A.M. hearing began of the new disclosures in the *Post*.

Unlike Judge Gesell in Washington, Gurfein moved rather slowly and without an overabundance of self-confidence. It was, after all, his very first case as a judge—the extraordinary and somewhat humorous result of the case assignment procedure in U.S. District Court for the Southern District of New York and of new judicial appointments by President Nixon. The motions calendar of the Manhattan federal court, one of the busiest in the country, is rotated among judges every week rather than every month; for the week beginning Monday June 14, 1971, it listed Judge Walter R. Mansfield. But Mansfield had been elevated to the U.S. Court of Appeals for the Second Circuit only a few weeks earlier, when appellate Judge Leonard P. Moore retired to senior status. Unwritten custom dictates that when a vacancy occurs on the busy calendar on which all emergency matters are handled, the judge with the least seniority automatically fills in. Murray Gurfein had exactly two days' seniority when the *Times* first disclosed the Pentagon Papers on June 13. A close friend of Senator Jacob K. Javits (R-N.Y.), he had long been slated for a federal judgeship, but his nomination was substantially delayed by a dispute between Javits and newly elected Conservative party Senator James Buckley over other judicial appointments in New York State. Gurfein had finally been sworn in at the end of the previous week and had just installed himself in Spartan chambers on the twenty-ninth floor of the courthouse in Foley Square. Happily for the new judge, Monday June 14 was a quiet day; when the *Times* case reached him on Tuesday, his only prior judicial function had been to preside over the naturalization ceremony for a group of new American citizens.

Gurfein came to the confrontation over freedom of the press with an entirely different background from Gesell. He began his legal career as a prosecutor, working closely with Thomas E. Dewey, then the crusading District Attorney of New York. During World War II Gurfein served in the Office of Strategic Services, the forerunner of the Central Intelligence Agency; thus he had been fully exposed to military intelligence operations and secret documents. After the war, he was an assistant prosecutor to Justice Robert Jackson during the Nuremburg war crime trials of the Nazi German regime. Since that time, however, he had been out of the public glare, spending 70 percent of his time in "corporate counseling" and in charitable activities. His reputation among the New York legal community was that of a relatively conservative man who shunned controversy.

For Whitney North Seymour the issue before Gurfein was "a very simple one . . . whether, when an authorized person comes into possession of documents which have been classified under lawful procedures, that person may unilaterally declassify these documents in his sole discretion." The government subsequently presented several witnesses, including Dennis J. Doolin, Deputy Assistant Secretary of Defense for International Security Affairs, who was responsible for recommending to Defense Secretary Melvin Laird that Senator Fulbright's request for a copy of the Pentagon Papers be denied. Admiral Francis J. Blouin, deputy chief of naval operations for plans and policy, testified that the command and control study of the Gulf of Tonkin incidents—of which the *Times* acknowledged having a summary—was also classified top secret. William B. Macomber, Deputy Undersecretary of State for Administration, asserted that "a historic and present absolute essential to the conduct of diplomacy is the capacity for governments to be able to deal in confidence with each other and to have confidence that when they are dealing in confidence, that confidence will not be violated." George MacClain, director of the Security Classification Management Division in the Defense Department, was also in court to explain the labyrinthine intricacies of how government documents are classified. Despite the strenuous objections of the *Times*'s lawyers, Gurfein then heard several hours of testimony on classified matters in a secret session to which only two newspaper representatives were admitted.

Closing arguments began at 9:50 P.M. Bickel and Seymour were in substantial agreement by that time that some prior restraints on publication might be permissible, if the "facts" of a particular case were found to justify it. But Bickel stressed that "the burden of proof is on the government to show a crisis, an emergency," and he denied that any such situation had been demonstrated. The *Times*'s decision to publish the

Papers, he insisted, was one of "everyday garden-variety commonness."

The case would turn inevitably on fifteen affidavits submitted to the court by *The New York Times* attempting to demonstrate the frequency with which the American press handles classified material and publishes articles based on it. Perhaps the most forceful of these was that of Max Frankel, the *Times* Washington bureau chief who had worked for the newspaper for twenty years, ten of them in Washington. "I know how strange all this must sound," Frankel acknowledged in a disarmingly conversational style as he set out to explain the "cooperative, competitive, antagonistic, and arcane relationship" between "a small and specialized corps of reporters and a few hundred American officials."

"Without the use of 'secrets,'" Frankel contended, "there could be no adequate diplomatic, military, and political reporting of the kind our people take for granted . . . and there could be no mature system of communication between the government and the people. That is one reason why the sudden complaint by one party to these regular dealings strikes us as monstrous and hypocritical—unless it is essentially perfunctory, for the purpose of retaining some discipline over the federal bureaucracy." In the general scheme of things, he pointed out, "the Navy uses secret information to run down the weaponry of the Air Force. The Army passes on secret information to prove its superiority to the Marine Corps. High officials of the government reveal secrets in the search for support of their policies, or to help sabotage the plans and policies of rival departments. Middle-rank officials of government reveal secrets so as to attract the attention of their superiors or to lobby against the orders of those superiors."

Frankel cited several telling examples from his own experience as a reporter: President Kennedy revealing direct quotations from the classified record of his conversations with

Soviet Foreign Minister Andrei Gromyko in order to demonstrate the "toughness" of the American position on the Berlin Wall; President Johnson providing details of his secret conversations with Soviet Premier Aleksei Kosygin at Glassboro, New Jersey, in 1967; Secretary of State Dean Rusk telling Frankel in a private meeting in 1961 that "Laos is not worth the life of a single Kansas farm boy" and that "the SEATO treaty . . . was a useless instrument that should be retained only because it would cause too much diplomatic difficulty to abolish it." The rule of thumb that had developed over the years, Frankel observed, went this way: "The government hides what it can, pleading necessity as long as it can, and the press pries out what it can, pleading a need and a right to know. Each side in this 'game' regularly 'wins' and 'loses' a round or two. Each fights with the weapons at its command. When the government loses a secret or two, it simply adjusts to a new reality. When the press loses a quest or two, it simply reports (or misreports) as best it can." The Pentagon Papers controversy could be understood only in this context, Frankel insisted. It was merely a gross example of a standard operating procedure, a journalistic coup that hurt the sensibilities of the other side. To urge, as the Attorney General had, that the press publish "no further information of this character" was to tell reporters to stop doing their job.

Gurfein and his law clerk worked almost through the night to produce a seventeen-page opinion, released at 2:45 P.M. on Saturday June 19, that fully vindicated the actions of the *Times*. "The security of the nation is not at the ramparts alone," Gurfein lectured. "Security also lies in the value of our free institutions. A cantankerous press, an obstinate press, a ubiquitous press must be suffered by those in authority in order to preserve the even greater values of freedom of expression and the right of the people to know. . . . it is not merely the opinion of the editorial writer or of the columnist which is protected by the First Amendment. It is the free flow of information so that the public will be informed about the government and its actions. These are troubled times. There is no greater safety valve for discontent and cynicism about the affairs of government than freedom of expression in any form. This has been the genius of our institutions throughout our history. It is one of the marked traits of our national life that distinguish us from other nations under different forms of government."

The government's evidence during the secret hearing showed only that security agents and some foreign governments had "the jitters" rather than a sense of genuine danger, the judge said. "No cogent reasons were advanced as to why these documents—except in the general framework of embarrassment—vitally affect the security of the nation." Analyzing the Espionage Act and other related laws in minute detail, Gurfein said he doubted that they could be stretched to cover what the *Times* had done, even in a criminal prosecution. He specifically found that the Espionage Act ban on communication of normal defense information was never intended to preclude newspaper "publication," which was not mentioned in the act. "This has been an effort on the part of the *Times* to vindicate the right of the public to know. It is not a case involving an intent to communicate vital secrets for the benefit of a foreign government or to the detriment of the United States." Nonetheless, Gurfein's ruling was not an absolute one and conceded that under other, more pressing circumstances the government might be able to obtain a prior restraint of publication (a point that Bickel had already conceded); unlike Gesell, Gurfein extended his restraining order to give the government time for an emergency appeal.

The government managed with unusual speed to get what *Times* general counsel James Goodale later labeled the "elevator injunction," a further stay from the only member of the appellate court on duty in the courthouse that Saturday, Judge Irving R. Kaufman. Goodale and the other members of the

Times's legal team had not expected that and made what the general counsel called "our only mistake of the whole litigation" by phoning the editors after Gurfein ruled and telling them to prepare to resume the articles based on the Pentagon Papers. Kaufman was well known as a defender of the First Amendment, and in a brief hearing he made proud reference to his own lectures on the subject; he compromised that principle, however, because of the "institutional consideration" that the appellate court ordinarily sits in panels of three judges. Kaufman observed that his colleagues might have "a sound basis for saying I had usurped power" if he acted alone to refuse the government's petition. Stressing that he intended "to intimate no views as to the merits" he extended the restraining order until noon on Monday June 21.

Kaufman's interim decision kept the *Times* and the *Post* in the same situation—both restrained—and it was on that basis that the *Post*'s lawyers determined not to seek a reversal of the Court of Appeals restraining order from Chief Justice Burger but rather to go ahead with the Monday morning hearing before Judge Gesell.

Gesell was annoyed at being handed a task by the appellate court that he was quite sure would lead nowhere. Working with an imposed deadline of 5 P.M. Monday, he sought to hold court on Saturday and Sunday; but that was precluded by the fact that the air conditioning at Washington's federal courthouse had to be turned off for the weekend because of construction work. Instead, after weekend conferences with the lawyers on both sides, he arrived in his chambers at 5:45 A.M. on Monday June 21, and government affidavits based on the Pentagon Papers were delivered to him forty-five minutes later. The full-scale hearing began sharply at 8 A.M. and followed parallel lines to the one before Gurfein in New York. The government wheeled a full set of Papers into the courtroom, but never once consulted them. Gesell pressed the Justice Department to bring in the person who had originally classified the Papers "Top Secret–Sensitive" to explain his decision, but Maroney said that the government had no idea who it was. (The classifier, of course, had been Leslie Gelb, head of McNamara's Vietnam History Task Force, who was in town at the time and would have been available to testify had the government contacted him.) Once again MacClain and Doolin testified in the open court sessions; an attempt by *Post* lawyers to obtain a copy of Doolin's memorandum advising against release of the study to Fulbright was rebuffed because it too carried a top-secret classification. Gesell also reluctantly granted the government's request for a secret hearing lasting several hours, with black plastic placed over the windows in the courtroom doors to preserve security; unlike Gurfein, however, he permitted all defendants in the case and additional *Post* reporters with expertise in the area of national security to remain in the courtroom.

During the closed session Macomber again testified, along with Lieutenant General Melvin Zais of the Army, director of operations for the Joint Chiefs of Staff. Gesell continually stressed that for the purposes of the hearing he would assume that the *Post* had possession of the full contents of the Pentagon Papers, and he asked the government to demonstrate which information in them would most jeopardize national security. At one point government lawyers cited the account in the Papers of "Operation Marigold," the unsuccessful 1966 American peace initiative to Hanoi through a Polish diplomat, a subject that had already been widely written about publicly. (Former President Johnson later dealt his own blow to that example when he recounted details of "Operation Marigold" in his memoirs, *The Vantage Point*.) Representing the *Post* at this hearing was William R. Glendon, a senior partner from the New York office of Royall, Koegel, and Wells; each time the government cited a touchy item in the Papers, *Post* Pentagon correspondent George Wilson and other reporters in the courtroom passed on to Glendon an exact book-and-page reference to where that material had already been available to the public. Reporters and editors later remarked that their own lawyers had required a full-scale education on the extent to which classified information was stock in trade in daily reporting in Washington; they needed prompting throughout the hearing to challenge the government's seemingly plausible claims.

Like the *Times*, the *Post* also made that same point forcefully in affidavits from its staff. Executive editor Benjamin Bradlee recalled in his sworn statement that when he was a reporter for *Newsweek* magazine, President Kennedy revealed to him portions of a highly classified memorandum describing details of the 1961 conversations in Vienna between Kennedy and Soviet Premier Nikita Khrushchev. Murrey Marder noted that he had once suggested to presidential adviser McGeorge Bundy that only 5 percent of the material marked classified on Bundy's desk would actually prove to contain "secrets." Less than two years later, according to Marder's affidavit, Bundy observed that the estimate of 5 percent had been "high. . . . The importance of actual secrets in terms of their impact on national security was limited to a relatively brief time span—usually measured in hours or a very few days, before they either became known or their secrecy significance virtually disappeared." Chalmers Roberts, in his own affidavit, reiterated the view expressed by Max Frankel in the *Times* case: "There is, always has been, and must always be a built-in conflict between press and government. This is simply one of the checks and balances of our system." Some of the *Post* affidavits, however, were watered down by the lawyers to seem less extreme.

Glendon, pointing out that "nothing has happened" to the United States since the Pentagon Papers were first disclosed, cited Gurfein's denial of an injunction in New York as an appropriate resolution of the issues. Gesell also permitted Congressman Bob Eckhart (D-Tex.) to argue on behalf of himself and twenty-six other members of Congress as *amici curiae* with a "right to know" the contents of the Papers. Maroney, however, pleaded to the last that, at the very least, Gesell give the government "a few more days" to prove its case.

Gesell had no time to draft another opinion before his deadline; instead, after a recess, he returned to the bench at about 4:30 P.M. to deliver a twelve-minute oral opinion from written notes. Complaining that "the role of quasi-censor" had been imposed on him and that there were "no standards" enunciated for that role, Gesell said that in any event "there is no proof that there will be a definite break in diplomatic relations, that there will be an armed attack on the United States, that there will be an armed attack on an ally, that there will be a war, that there will be a compromise of military or defense plans, a compromise of intelligence operations, or a compromise of scientific and technological materials." The judge suggested that the Justice Department may have forgotten that "the interests of the government are inseparable from the public interest . . . the public interest makes an insistent plea for publication."

"In interpreting the First Amendment," Gesell said sternly, "there is no basis upon which the court may adjust it to accommodate the desires of foreign governments dealing with our diplomats, nor does the First Amendment guarantee our diplomats that they can be protected against either responsible or irresponsible reporting. . . . The First Amendment remains supreme."

Having asserted that "no one can measure the effects of even a momentary delay" in publication, Gesell noted that he would not "under any circumstances" nullify the meaning of his own decision by granting a long enough stay to guarantee appellate review. "You have twenty minutes," he told Maroney at 4:40 P.M. "I am sure they are waiting for you upstairs."

Two hours later the appellate court issued a brief order signed only "by the court" setting the case for argument before all nine of its judges at 2 P.M. the next afternoon. In the meantime, it granted an extension of its own temporary restraining order preventing publication of further articles in the *Post* pending resolution of the appeal; no dissent from that extension was noted, not even from Judge Wright, who had proclaimed "a sad day for America" the previous Saturday, when the restraint was initially entered.

Meanwhile, in New York a three-judge panel of the U.S. Court of Appeals for the Second Circuit had convened and decided to postpone consideration of the government's appeal in the *Times* case until all its eight judges could assemble in New York City (there was a vacancy on the court at that time). Appellate argument on the *Times* case was also scheduled for 2 P.M. on Tuesday June 22, and Kaufman's stay remained in effect. The newspapers had won stunning victories, but they were still under a prior restraint; seventeen appellate judges in two cities gave the government exactly what it wanted: a little more time to pull together some convincing evidence or arguments that might keep the Pentagon Papers out of the press.

[CHAPTER IX]

Tom Winship was hurting. There was something rather embarrassing about being editor of the Boston *Globe* and not having the biggest story in the country, a story that had in effect broken in his own backyard—among the intellectual community across the Charles River in Cambridge. The *Globe* had been the first major newspaper in the country to talk about the Pentagon Papers in any detail; on March 7, 1971, staff writer Thomas Oliphant wrote a front-page story about the fact that all three people who had read the complete "secret Indochina report"—Morton Halperin, Leslie Gelb, and Daniel Ellsberg—now urged a swift American withdrawal from Vietnam. Ellsberg had spoken rather freely about the Papers over two lunches with Oliphant, a savvy young reporter about to move to the *Globe*'s Washington bureau; but Oliphant, never imagining that Ellsberg might actually be willing to make the study available to a newspaper, did not press him for details of a distribution list or for advice on how a reporter might get to see some of the documents.

When Ellsberg moved a few weeks later to make the Papers public through the press, he apparently never gave serious consideration to the *Globe* as an option. That would not be the way of Cambridge readers, who follow *The New York Times* first. They can substitute for or supplement The *Times* with *The Washington Post*, whose final edition is readily available by 10:30 A.M. in Harvard Square and in Central Square near MIT. And for local news there is always the Harvard *Crimson*, a sophisticated daily most of the year.

But Winship, an impulsive, affable man who often orders up a story with much the same tone that others use to order their favorite drink, had worked hard since taking over the top position at the *Globe* to make the newspaper less parochial and more relevant to its potentially varied readership. He was proud of the fact that the *Globe* was one of the first major newspapers in the country to take a strong editorial stand against American involvement in Southeast Asia, and he had been relentless in recruiting young reporters who could help open lines of communication with leading antiwar news sources like Ellsberg and MIT linguistics professor Noam Chomsky.

When the *Times* published its initial installment of the Pentagon Papers story, the *Globe* had no illusions of being able to compete, and rather than embarking on a frantic search for a copy of the Papers, Winship sent a reporter to New York to write about the *Times's* phenomenal scoop. But as the week of June 13 wore on, and especially when the *Post* turned up with the Papers, Winship became eager to catch up and to join in the developing fight on behalf of freedom of the press. The main burden of the *Globe's* efforts fell to Oliphant, who had received an anonymous phone call during the night of Wednesday June 16 notifying him that Sidney Zion was about to identify Ellsberg as the *Times's* source on a New York radio talk show. On Thursday Oliphant wrote a story about Ellsberg, drawing in part on his notes from the springtime lunches, and he began his persistent but futile efforts to reach Ellsberg by telephone. Messages left for Ellsberg at his office and his home, with his answering service, and with friends had failed to produce any response by Saturday June 19, so Oliphant left on a previously scheduled trip to visit his parents in La Jolla, California. By that time the *Post* had been enjoined by the U.S. Court of Appeals in Washington, and Ellsberg and his friends were ready to move again; no sooner had Oliphant arrived at his parents' home than he received another anonymous call there, asking him to check on the status of the government's efforts to find Ellsberg and offering to discuss providing the Papers to the *Globe*.

That was the first of a long series of phone calls to Oliphant in California over the weekend, all but one of them collect; by Sunday he was able to phone editor Winship at his country home in Vermont to advise him that arrangements were under way. There was one condition from the start: Ellsberg was apparently concerned that his children would worry about his safety and wondered if he could use the *Globe* as a vehicle to pass on a message to them. ("It was a small price to pay," Winship said later, "and besides, it made a good story.") During a Monday morning call to Oliphant, two other conditions were established: that the *Globe* would strictly respect the anonymity of any and all intermediaries between Ellsberg and the newspaper and that, like the *Times* and the *Post*, the Boston newspaper would refuse to surrender its copies of the Papers in any court action. Oliphant agreed. This time the caller identified himself as "Bosbin" and promised to phone Winship in Boston at 10:30 A.M. in order to arrange details. At 10:30 precisely Winship's phone rang, and Bosbin had yet another set of conditions to impose: that the *Globe* promise to defy any court injunction and that it provide the services of its Xerox machine to help make extra copies of the Papers. Winship refused the first condition, causing a three-hour delay, but he readily accepted the second ("another cheap price to pay"). The editor imposed his own condition: the *Globe* wanted fresh material, particularly on the Kennedy administration (always good for Boston area readers), not just the documents that had already appeared elsewhere. That was agreeable to Ellsberg's representative.

When Bosbin called Winship back at 1:30 P.M. to say that the deal was on, he set up a system for passing on the documents that seemed to belong in a mystery novel. Although of all the newspapers that would get the Pentagon Papers the *Globe* was closest to the source, it had to go through the most complex intrigue to obtain them: Winship was to send one *Globe* staffer to a phone booth in Harvard Square and another to a phone booth in Newton, a suburb west of Boston; by 3 P.M. they were to call Winship and report their phone numbers. Five minutes later Bosbin would phone Winship to get the two phone booth numbers and then before 3:10 contact one of them (he didn't say in advance which one) to say that the Papers were on the way to his phone booth. The scheme worked exactly according to plan: the man in the Cambridge phone booth heard nothing, and at about 5 P.M. the man posted to Newton returned to the Globe offices with a large brown package enclosed in a zippered plastic bag; inside were 1,700 xeroxed pages from the Pentagon Papers.

The *Globe* had already decided to publish its first edition without the Papers but wanted to get them into the second one, which hits the streets in Boston at 1 A.M. That meant a copy deadline of 11 P.M.—or six hours to prepare, compared with the *Times's* three months and the *Post's* full day. A special task force of staff members, including *Globe* correspondent Matthew V. Storin, who had recently returned from Vietnam, and executive editor Robert Healy, was assembled to prepare four separate stories; in order to maintain security, none of the articles was sent to the composing room until the last possible moment. The later editions of the *Globe* for Tuesday June 22, 1971, carried a large photograph of President Kennedy on the front page; the headline next to it trumpeted: "Secret Pentagon Documents Bare JFK Role in Vietnam War." Individual stories discussed Kennedy's direct approval of covert military operations against North Vietnam, President Johnson's turn toward "Vietnamization" of the war after the 1968 Viet Cong Tet offensive, and CIA involvement in the war. In its own self-censorship, the *Globe* rejected publishing a particular ship location and material on a prisoner-of-war negotiation on the grounds that these details might indeed endanger national security. There was absolutely no argument at the *Globe* over whether the Pentagon Papers should be published, but Winship had the newspaper's lawyers on hand in the news room to handle any problems or questions that might arise.

Also appearing on the front page of the *Globe* on June 22 was Tom Oliphant's story, datelined San Diego, which said that Ellsberg "expects to comment publicly in a week or two on his role in the unearthing of the secret Pentagon study of the Indochina war." Citing "intermediaries known to be close friends of his," Oliphant said Ellsberg "did not want to divert public attention" from court battles over the Papers by speaking out too soon. As promised, Oliphant wrote: "Ellsberg said he wanted his two children who live in this state with his first wife to know that he is well and thinking of them. He also said he wanted his father, Harry Ellsberg, who lives in a Detroit suburb, to know that he is deeply grateful for the expressions of support he made to the press last week." Oliphant's story apparently turned the search for Ellsberg by the FBI and by several newspapers to the West Coast for a day—a total mistake, of course, since Ellsberg was still in the Boston area and Oliphant's story had been datelined San Diego only because that was where he was, visiting his parents.

After the *Globe* published, Winship panicked upon reading a UPI story saying that the FBI was investigating locations in Cambridge where the Papers might have been photocopied. "In a little fit of hysteria," he later revealed, "we gathered all of our Papers together and hustled them out to an unlit parking lot and locked them up in the back of a car. We just had visions of a bunch of marshals walking in and saying: 'Let's have it. Let's stop the presses.'"

The *Globe* did not have to wait long for a gentler version of Winship's fantasy to come true. The Justice Department was moving faster now, and Joseph Dineen, managing editor of the Boston *Evening Globe*, took a call at 5 A.M. from Assistant Attorney General Robert Mardian. Mardian, who had been up all night, asked if there would be more stories in the *Globe*; he was told that there would be. Later the same morning Winship received a call from the Attorney General himself. "Well, Tom" said John Mitchell, whom Winship had never met, "I see you're in the act too." "Well, General," Winship replied, "if you want to call it that, we did print this morning." Mitchell asked if the *Globe* would suspend publication of the Pentagon Papers "on a voluntary basis." Winship answered: "No, I don't think we can." Mitchell told Winship that the *Globe* would be hearing soon from the U.S. Attorney in Boston. As the editor recalls it, Mitchell said: "I just have to do this to you because if I didn't, the other papers would be upset; it wouldn't be fair to the *Times* and the *Post*." There was a tense moment for Winship while he was on the phone with the nation's chief law enforcement officer. His other telephone line lit up, and his secretary, Kathy Kennedy, came into his office and whispered: "Your man Bosbin is on the line and wants to talk to you." Winship paused from his conversation with Mitchell and thought for a moment: He wanted to get more of the Pentagon Papers, but should he risk being rude to the Attorney General? He asked the secretary to have Bosbin hold on. The mysterious source hung up after thirty seconds, however, and Winship never heard from him again. He had no number to call back. The *Globe* had to make do with the 1,700 pages of Papers it had stored in the parking lot.

While the *Times* and the *Post* were making their cases before the respective appellate courts in New York and Washington on Tuesday June 22, the *Globe* was appearing before U.S. District Judge Anthony Julian in Boston. The *Globe's* lawyers, from the Boston firm of Bingham, Dana, and Gould, put up a much less strenuous fight than had those for the other newspapers, and before long Judge Julian ruled that unless the *Globe* were restrained "immediate and irreparable injury" might result to the government and to national security; he set a full hearing for the following Friday, June 25. When Julian asked *Globe* lawyer Robert Haydock what harm might come to the *Globe* "if material not published for years were delayed a few more days," Haydock conceded: "No harm . . . but it is a matter of principle." Worse, however, the lawyers did not initially fight Julian's order that the *Globe's* copy of the Pentagon Papers be impounded by the court.

When Winship learned of the impounding order—a requirement that had not been placed on any other newspaper—he was very alarmed. Not only did that risk revealing the *Globe's* confidential source; it also violated the conditions that had been firmly agreed upon by Bosbin and Oliphant. The *Globe* refused to turn the documents over and instead hid them in a locker at Logan Airport. The newspaper went back into federal court on Wednesday June 23, seeking revision of the impounding order. Judge Julian relented, but only to the point of requiring that the Papers be locked into a vault at the First National Bank of Boston, with the *Globe's* lawyer and Winship's assistant, John Driscoll, having the only access. Even that provision worried some editors and reporters at the *Globe*, given the usual enthusiasm of banks to cooperate with FBI investigations and grand jury subpoenas. Nonetheless, the restraint imposed on the *Globe* remained the strictest of the three that had been granted; for a time the newspaper was not only forbidden to run its own stories based on the Pentagon

Papers but Julian's ruling also seemed to preclude publication even of wire service dispatches based on the disclosures in other papers. (Neither the *Times* nor the *Post* had ever been prohibited from using such second-hand material.) By the time Friday—the day for Julian's scheduled trial in the *Globe* case—came around, the other newspaper cases would be headed for the Supreme Court, so the *Globe*'s hands were tied until they were resolved. The attorneys for the Boston newspaper never bothered trying an urgent appeal on Julian's initial ruling to the U.S. Court of Appeals for the First Circuit, so they had no opportunity to participate in the controversy at the high court.

While the court cases were proceeding in New York, Washington, and Boston, there was a new development in Chicago. In that city, under a local journalistic tradition, the first editions of the morning newspapers are published around dusk the night before, and the first editions of the evening newspapers appear early in the morning. Thus at about 5 P.M. on Tuesday June 22 the first edition of the Chicago *Sun-Times* for Wednesday June 23 hit the streets; it carried a story, based on top-secret documents, detailing the advance knowledge of Kennedy administration officials of the 1963 coup that overthrew the Saigon regime of Ngo Dinh Diem. Among the documents printed was a memorandum from former Assistant Secretary of State Roger Hilsman encouraging strong U.S. support for the South Vietnamese military plot against Diem. Editor James F. Hoge, Jr., declared that the *Sun-Times* story was based on already declassified documents and on "access to sources" who had the Pentagon Papers.

Hoge, like Winship, had never imagined initially that his newspaper would be able to compete effectively with the series of articles in *The New York Times*. For the first week of the disclosures the *Sun-Times* ran summaries of the *Times* and *Post* stories. As events developed, however, Hoge and his Washington bureau embarked on the only true "investigative reporting" of the entire Pentagon Papers controversy. Although they had tried several times, they never established contact with Daniel Ellsberg, who had been providing the Papers, directly or indirectly, to most of the rest of the press. The *Sun-Times* was also in a unique position because it never actually possessed its own copies of the documents but merely had "access" to the partial copies of government officials and private citizens.

Hoge had decided that his tabloid-size newspaper should have some "action to back up all the words on the editorial page" in support of what the other newspapers had done, so he eventually had "six people working around the clock trying to get almost anything to print." Hoge himself had once worked in the *Sun-Times*'s Washington bureau, and he had excellent political and social contacts that were crucial to the newspaper's accomplishment. Washington reporters Thomas Ross and Morton Kondracke, who has impeccable sources in the antiwar movement, came up with the first bits of the Papers, but it was a friend of Hoge on Capitol Hill who eventually permitted the *Sun-Times* staffers to come to his office to look at portions of the study. The initial ground rules included a stipulation that the *Sun-Times* would not quote directly from the Papers, and the first story in the June 23 paper did not (although it did quote from the Hilsman memo, which had already been written about elsewhere). The Capitol Hill source was so pleased with the way the story was handled that he later relaxed his conditions. On Thursday June 24 the *Sun-Times* ran another story based on the Papers dealing with the May 1961 mission of Vice President Lyndon Johnson to Saigon to persuade the South Vietnamese government to request American ground troops, despite the earlier opposition to such a request by Diem. This article did quote directly from the Pentagon Papers but avoided printing the full text of the actual classified documents referred to.

The *Sun-Times* stories took on additional poignancy with the publication of a front-page editorial entitled "Sorry About

This" by its major competitor and Chicago's largest-circulating newspaper, the conservative *Tribune,* on Friday morning, June 25. "We want to play it square with our readers and explain why we have not printed something exclusive about the background of the war in Vietnam that would get us enjoined by a federal court," said the editorial. "The primary reason, we must confess, is that no disaffected ex-government employee has handed us copies of the top-secret purloined Pentagon Papers. . . . We may be vulnerable to a charge of sour grapes. We tried to get copies of the Pentagon Papers last week. . . . When the manager of the present Xerox derby dropped it on the third bounce to the *Boston Globe,* we knew we had struck out." Deploring a "hopelessly confused" situation, the *Tribune* came up with its own proposed solution: "We do not believe that the courts should authorize or permit some news media to publish documents in the official custody of a public agency. If one gets the information thru court order, then all should get it. Therefore, we suggest that the whole matter of further publication be held in abeyance until the entire record is studied by an impartial group of editors and government officials skilled in sorting out the perils that indiscriminate publication of classified documents would entail. These documents have lain in inactive files since 1969. A few more days' delay will cause no harm, either to the government or to the people's right to know."

The Justice Department handled the *Sun-Times* disclosures in a totally different manner from those of the other newspapers. There was an initial phone call from the office of the U.S. Attorney for the Northern District of Illinois at 1:30 A.M. on Wednesday June 23 asking what the *Sun-Times* had and what it would print in the future. The editors on duty, without revealing the nature of the newspaper's access, said that the *Sun-Times* would print whatever was "relevant and responsible." There was no immediate action. Subsequent contacts from the government came, instead, in the form of phone calls to Art Petacque, a crime reporter for the *Sun-Times*—the U.S. Attorney's office in Chicago wanted a copy of the *Sun-Times*'s edition schedule so that it could send each day's installment to the Justice Department in Washington by a telecopier. Petacque received several calls, but there was never an outright threat of civil or criminal prosecution; the final call from the U.S. Attorney's office merely suggested that "when it's all over, why don't we get together and have lunch and talk about it." Hoge kept lawyers for the *Sun-Times* informed of the newspaper's plans at each step along the way, but he never called upon them for advice as the *Times* and the *Post* did. "We never allow our law firm to get into that position," Hoge says. "They will always lay out legal alternatives or legal speculations, but they never render an opinion on what we ought to do or ought not to do."

The *Sun-Times* pushed on. Its issue for Friday June 25 included a story on President Eisenhower's action in 1958 to establish a national policy aimed at eliminating Communist control of North Vietnam and uniting it with the South under a regime that would be favorable to the United States. Even when the Chicago newspaper published a story on Saturday June 26 based on a 1969 CIA memo to the Nixon administration —saying that the United States could withdraw from Vietnam immediately and "all of Southeast Asia would remain just as it is for another generation"—there was no move against it by the Justice Department. Hoge was amazed; his slight disappointment at being left out of the dramatic court confrontation was balanced by sheer elation over the opportunity to continue publishing responsible stories based on secret documents.

One of the great revelations of the entire sequence of events concerning the Pentagon Papers was the way the press covered the press. The battle over First Amendment freedoms was undoubtedly a legitimate story, and it received even greater attention in most newspapers than the disclosures of the documents themselves; but there was another central press story, invariably based on curiosity over how each newspaper did its reporting and on the responses of individual editors and reporters to each legal development. When the crisis subsided, Hoge observed: "I had a much better appreciation of people who talk about being harassed by the press." The reaction of others in the press when the *Sun-Times* first made its disclosures based on the Pentagon Papers was overwhelming. "I've never seen anything in my life like the explosion of phone calls we got," Hoge said. "I was utterly amazed. I felt like a kid witnessing something brand new."

Within half an hour of the appearance of the first *Sun-Times* story "all the local radio and TV stations called, everyone had to have a separate interview. They wanted to come over with their cameras and crews and photograph the presses rolling. . . . Every cliché in the business came out. CBS did a marvelous job—they had the presses rolling with this hot information, they had trucks roaring off into the distance, they had the editors sitting up there, very concerned that the presses keep rolling." But as word spread across the country, there was a further wave of contacts: "We started to get calls all through the night and the next day from radio stations all over the world. These guys would call up from El Paso, Albuquerque, from Canada and say: 'Is this the editor?' Then they'd ask your name, give their own name, and identify the station, and then say: 'Okay, Jim (I didn't know these people), how'd you get these Papers?' And then, without any warning, you were on the air. . . . Now I really know why they say radio is a great informational power in this country."

At every newspaper that published the Pentagon Papers the pattern was the same, until editors shied away from answering the phone at all and prepared stock statements that were read by assistants to curious callers.

After the *Sun-Times* published articles based on the Pentagon Papers, the spreading leak began to resemble a dam bursting. On Thursday June 24 both the Los Angeles *Times* and the Knight chain of newspapers joined in the disclosures. The lead story in the Los Angeles newspaper was by Stuart H. Loory, a member of the paper's Washington bureau who had been on a plane to Boston Monday night with the Boston *Globe*'s Washington bureau chief, Martin F. Nolan (who was en route from the capital to help prepare the *Globe*'s Pentagon Papers stories). Loory's piece also dealt with the Kennedy administration, describing how the National Security Council in August 1963 rejected a State Department Vietnam expert's advice to pull out of the war honorably. Supported by Vice President Johnson and Defense Secretary McNamara, Secretary of State Rusk dismissed as "speculative" a report from Paul M. Kattenburg, then head of the State Department's Vietnam Working Group. A companion story by the newspaper's Washington bureau chief, David Kraslow, gave details of the last conversation between Ambassador Henry Cabot Lodge and South Vietnamese President Diem during the CIA-supported military coup in Saigon. The Los Angeles *Times* stories had a special poignancy because just below them on the front page was another article reporting that "a super-secret federal grand jury investigation into the leak of the Pentagon Papers is under way here and two witnesses have been granted immunity to testify."

Assistant Attorney General Robert Mardian attempted unsuccessfully to reach editors of the Los Angeles *Times* on Wednesday night, after the latest disclosures had hit the street in his home town. Robert L. Meyer, U.S. Attorney for the Central District of California, spoke with executive editor William F. Thomas the next morning, however, and was advised that at that point the newspaper had no plans to run additional articles based on the Papers. Subsequently the Los Angeles paper did obtain another segment of the study and

[187]

based another story on it, but there was never any sign of legal action against the *Times*. Because there was not and because of the specific terms of the standing court order against *The Washington Post*, that newspaper was able to take advantage of its special news-service relationship with the Los Angeles *Times* and run its stories in Washington.

Publication by the eleven newspapers in the Knight chain—in Detroit, Miami, Tallahassee, Akron, Boca Raton, Florida, and two each in Philadelphia, Charlotte, North Carolina, and Macon, Georgia—made the Pentagon Papers leak genuinely nationwide. The Knight story reported that Defense Secretary McNamara had become discouraged with the ground war in Vietnam in 1967 and therefore proposed a coalition government in South Vietnam, and that the Papers depicted McNamara as "a tragic figure who rapidly became disillusioned with the war he had recommended." The release of the study in the Knight papers was accompanied by a statement that they tentatively planned to publish no further stories based on the Papers; at the same time Knight president Lee Hills stressed that "we believe [the Papers] represent no threat to the national security of our country."

The Knight newspapers never heard a word from the Justice Department, although they did subsequently print other stories. On Friday morning June 25 Attorney General Mitchell, talking with reporters after testifying before a Senate appropriations subcommittee, observed that both in the Knight newspapers and in the Los Angeles *Times* the stories either were not based on classified documents—an assertion that surprised the editors in both cases, since the stories clearly had been based on such material—or were written so as not to reveal any secret information. Still no action was taken against the Chicago *Sun-Times* or the Baltimore *Sun*, which had also come up with a story based on a fragment of the Pentagon Papers.

There would be still more. On the afternoon of Friday June 25 the St. Louis *Post-Dispatch* appeared with a banner headline over a front-page story from its Washington bureau revealing that a year and a half after the massive American build-up in Vietnam began, Defense Secretary McNamara told President Johnson that the provincial pacification program was "a bad disappointment." The newspaper said that "the several hundred xeroxed pages [from the Pentagon Papers] obtained by the *Post-Dispatch* bore no security classification"; but it noted that "each xeroxed page had a blank space at the bottom . . . where a strip of paper had been laid over the place where a security label usually is stamped." In Boston, Judge Julian amended his restraining order specifically to permit the *Globe* to run the *Post-Dispatch* story verbatim.

The *Post-Dispatch* got its story into print at almost the last possible moment before the Supreme Court was to hear the cases involving *The New York Times* and *The Washington Post*. The U.S. Attorney in St. Louis, Dan Bartlett, called *Post-Dispatch* managing editor David Lipman at about 9:30 P.M.; he asked about the newspaper's future plans—if there were to be more stories—and told Lipman that if the *Post-Dispatch* wouldn't reveal whether there would be, the newspaper would be taken to court. Lipman replied that there would indeed be more, but not until the Sunday edition of the *Post-Dispatch*, because the Saturday afternoon paper has a small circulation. In Washington the Justice Department put out the word that the St. Louis newspaper was holding off pending resolution of the Supreme Court case. But the *Post-Dispatch* editors were incensed by that mistaken interpretation and told the U.S. Attorney that in order to avoid appearing as if the newspaper was yielding to pressure, they would go ahead with a second story on Saturday after all. "In the interest of our reputation and our responsibility to the public," Lipman said later, "we felt we had to move up publication."

That sent Bartlett directly into U.S. District Court in St. Louis. On Saturday June 26, while the Supreme Court was hearing argument on the *Times* and *Post* cases, U.S. District

Judge James H. Meredith issued a nine-day restraining order against the *Post-Dispatch;* his order came just in time to stop the *Post-Dispatch* presses from rolling with the new installment based on the Pentagon Papers.

On Tuesday morning June 29, while the Supreme Court was considering the Pentagon Papers cases, the *Christian Science Monitor*, based in Boston, published its own story based on the study, billed as the first in a series of three. Around noon that day Herbert F. Travers, Jr., U.S. Attorney for Massachusetts, contacted the *Monitor's* editor, Erwin D. Canham, asking that the articles be suspended. Canham refused. At Travers' request, however, Canham described the two further installments to be published in the newspaper. That was enough to produce a press release from the Justice Department stating that the *Monitor* "had cooperated by disclosing . . . the contents of the two remaining installments they propose to publish," so no court action would be taken. Canham, subjected to criticism by other editors, later insisted that "I was in no sense submitting this or seeking clearance. . . . It was the last thing I would have done."

The next day, along with the second article in the *Christian Science Monitor* series, a story based on the Pentagon Papers appeared in *Newsday*, the afternoon newspaper on Long Island. Any Justice Department reaction that might have been contemplated was rendered moot, however, by a Supreme Court decision the same afternoon.

One of the most puzzling aspects of the controversy over the Pentagon Papers was the irregular pattern of the government's reaction to the newspapers that published articles based on the secret study. Of the approximately twenty papers that disclosed various classified documents, only four were ever taken to court—*The New York Times, The Washington Post,* the Boston *Globe,* and the St. Louis *Post-Dispatch.* According to

Assistant Attorney General Robert Mardian, the Justice Department's criteria for deciding whether to move against a particular newspaper were: "Had the newspaper published information from a classified document, the disclosure of which could cause irreparable harm to the United States and which had not been previously in the public domain?" and "Was [the newspaper] intending to continue publication?"

It is obvious that some newspapers gained by fudging their answers when posed Mardian's second question, saying they were not sure or would have to decide when they received new material from the Pentagon Papers. Even when editors answered candidly, it is obvious that they revealed few details about what they had of the Papers; it may have been the mere knowledge—the avoidance of staying up all night—and the deference of editors which satisfied Mardian. The rationale of decisions made on the basis of his first condition, whether the material was classified, is, an any event, difficult to understand; with the possible exception of the first article in the Chicago *Sun-Times*, every story published in the newspapers was based on secret material of the same basic nature. Only *The New York Times* ever published the full text of classified documents, but others came close to doing so and at one time or another all the papers quoted from them and from the narrative of the Pentagon Papers.

A more plausible explanation, offered privately by some Justice Department officials, is that the crisis managers in the government eventually came to accept the newspapers' own argument: that the leak was spreading so far and wide, it would be utterly impossible to plug it up in the courts; one way or another this information was going to become public. (Ellsberg acknowledged later in a speech to the New Democratic Coalition in New York that "I tried to stay one step ahead of the Justice Department's injunctions.") That theory holds up until Friday June 25, when the St. Louis *Post-Dispatch* published its story based on the Papers. Although it had already looked the other way rather than proceed legally against more than a dozen newspapers, the government went to court in St. Louis.

The decision to move in St. Louis at such a late date—the Chicago *Sun-Times* and Los Angeles *Times* had already published very similar material from the Papers on the two previous days—could perhaps be attributed to the overenthusiasm of the U.S. Attorney in St. Louis or to his conversations with the managing editor of the *Post-Dispatch* about the newspaper's plans for further publication. But at least one editor of a major newspaper suggests another basic motivating factor—"bedrock politics. They were selecting out the newspapers they considered the bad guys and leaving the good guys alone." Whether by conscious choice or by accident, all four of the newspapers against whom the Justice Department took action are strong opponents of the Nixon administration; all have been increasingly skeptical about the American effort in Vietnam. The Chicago *Sun-Times*, the Los Angeles *Times*, the Knight newspaper chain, and others, however, regardless of the trends in their reporting since that time, had all supported Richard M. Nixon for President in 1968. They are all notably absent from the lists of newspapers frequently criticized by the Vice President and other administration officials. Many editors have speculated since whether the litigation might not have evolved quite differently if the first newspapers to break the Pentagon Papers had been closer to the hearts of President Nixon and Attorney General Mitchell.

[CHAPTER X]

By 2 P.M. on Tuesday June 22, 1971, when federal appellate courts were convening in New York and Washington, the confrontation between the American press and the Nixon administration was clearly established as the biggest news in the country and was drawing headline coverage internationally as well. Despite the assertion of the Justice Department that it was merely doing its duty to uphold the law, the inescapable impression at home and abroad was that it was trying to slap the wrist of the "fourth branch of government" and seeking to suppress the ugly history of American intervention in Southeast Asia.

Not so, insisted U.S. Attorney Whitney North Seymour in his brief to the U.S. Court of Appeals for the Second Circuit in *The New York Times* case. The only issues, he said, were "whether a newspaper in possession of stolen Top Secret documents vital to the national defense is free to publish them in its sole discretion" and "whether newspaper publication of military and intelligence secrets may be enjoined for the purpose of protecting national security." The *Times*, he contended, was asserting a First Amendment privilege "above the Congress, above the Executive, and inviolate from the Judiciary." It is historically consistent to enjoin publication of the Pentagon Papers, Seymour argued, because "there have been military secrets since the beginning of the Republic, and a 'secret' exists by virtue of the power of the Executive to instruct subordinates not to reveal information to unauthorized persons." He claimed that Chief Justice Hughes's "troop ship" doctrine in the landmark Near v. Minnesota decision—setting out the potential areas where prior restraints were justified—was merely a symbolic one intended to cover a broad scope of national defense activities. The top-secret classification of the Papers, in and of itself, should be accorded "great deference" by the courts, the government insisted; but if that weren't enough, the witnesses before Judge Gurfein had made a compelling case that "disclosure of the material in the *Times*'s possession would gravely endanger the security of the United States."

In perhaps the most controversial part of his brief, Seymour complained that Gurfein had not made an "intelligent finding of fact" because he failed to read the entirety of "the government's central exhibit"—the forty-seven-volume study. Suggesting that he might have preferred a totally secret trial at the U.S. District Court level, Seymour attacked the circumstances of the proceedings before Gurfein, which he said "all transpired in an atmosphere of extreme pressure generated by the presence of scores of newsmen who jammed the courtroom and overflowed into the corridors"; he complained of "murmurs of approval" from those reporters at certain junctures in the trial. Seymour directed the attention of the appellate court to a "Special Appendix" he submitted that highlighted some of the testimony in the secret portion of the proceedings before Gurfein and listed specific pages of the Pentagon Papers that made the risks seem "particularly grave"; what Seymour did not say directly was that he was drawing in part on material used by the government in the case against the *Post* before Judge Gesell in Washington and that he was asking the appellate court to take on a fact-finding role not ordinarily exercised by a court whose job it is to determine whether the lower court made a mistake as to the law. In that regard he also requested, and received, permission from the court to submit new affidavits from "defense agencies" that buttressed the government's case.

Alexander Bickel and the other attorneys for the *Times* submitted an eighty-three-page brief, as well as a sealed memorandum outlining "the lack of substance" in the testimony of the three witnesses during the secret session before Gurfein. The newspaper charged that the government had made its allegations, from the start of the case, in terms of "amorphous generalities"; the brief pointed out that the key government witnesses had only the scarcest acquaintance with the Papers, probably a good deal less than the *Times* reporters who had combed it for almost three months in preparing their articles. Bickel asserted that the hearing in U.S. District Court had been entirely proper, and he pronounced the newspaper thoroughly satisfied with Gurfein's opinion. One of the precedents cited by the *Times* was drawn from a decision written by Chief Justice Burger during his years as a circuit judge in Washington; in this instance Burger had remarked that "a free, open society elects to take calculated risks to keep expression uninhibited."

Invoking a technical point, the *Times* argued that it did not possess "stolen" government property but rather "xerox copies of the documents . . . obtained from an unidentified source." Historically, the brief said, the Espionage Act had been used only in "an ordinary espionage situation," except in one case involving the mistaken sale of classified radar equipment to a private citizen as surplus; it had never been used with respect to publication of information. Citing the arguments in its affidavits, the *Times* pointed out that "former President Johnson, appearing on a CBS television program, [once] brandished a document of the same vintage and on the same subject as the documents now in the possession of *The New York Times* (and no doubt equally classified) and read from it to the public."

The *Times*'s brief also traced the legislative history of the Espionage Act to its origins in 1917, when Congress deleted a proposed provision that would have authorized the President in wartime to "prohibit the publishing or communicating of, or the attempting to publish or communicate, any information relating to the national defense which, in his judgment, is of such character that it is or might be useful to the enemy." That provision was denounced at the time as a form of "precensorship." Again, in 1953 and 1957, Congress specifically considered extending the Espionage Act to cover newspapers but rejected that course as constitutionally unacceptable. "This prosecution cannot be allowed to do what Congress itself declined to do," said the brief. The *Times* also dealt at length with the government's persistent demands that the newspaper's copy of the Pentagon Papers be produced in court in order to permit an orderly resolution of the issues; such a demand, it was asserted, violated not only the First Amendment and the ruling of the Ninth Circuit Court of Appeals in the Earl Caldwell case but even the Attorney General's own "guidelines" meant to reduce the number of subpoenas to newsmen.

Also before the U.S. Court of Appeals for the Second Circuit were the briefs of several *amici curiae*, all on the side of the *Times*. The American Civil Liberties Union, representing the twenty-seven members of Congress led by Bob Eckhart (D-Tex.), went further than the *Times* and contended that Judge Gurfein had erred in suggesting that the government has "inherent power" to protect its interest through an injunction.

In the absence of a specific congressional statute on the point, said the ACLU, no such "inherent power" could override the absolute protection of freedom of the press in the First Amendment. The National Emergency Civil Liberties Committee, speaking in its own brief for several scholars and writers claiming a particular interest in the Pentagon Papers, urged the appellate court to dismiss the government's suit against the *Times* entirely for lack of jurisdiction; the committee argued that "irreparable injury may . . . already have occurred to the public interest as a result of the temporary restraining order," since members of Congress might have been swayed to vote in favor the McGovern-Hatfield antiwar amendment on June 16 if more information from the Pentagon Papers had been available to them.

The argument before the appellate court went very poorly for *The New York Times*; Seymour was agile, eloquent, and for the most part successful in his interchanges with the eight judges, while Bickel fumbled and was continually harassed by Chief Judge Henry J. Friendly.

Seymour declared that the Pentagon Papers case was of "major national importance . . . to the interests of the United States, which is engaged in combat in Southeast Asia, in delicate peace negotiations in the Mideast, in a war of nerves in Central Europe, and in sensitive discussions on strategic arms limitations. . . . While in the past, courts have mouthed the existence of an exception to the First Amendment in proper circumstances, here for the first time are the circumstances which support the actual implementation of such an exception." Casting the government in the role of the martyr in the case, the U.S. Attorney said he realized that the position he was advocating was "highly unpopular"; he complained of the "veritable cabal of the nation's press" at Gurfein's hearing and of being hissed at as he entered the appellate courtroom that afternoon. Seymour said it was essential for the court to consider that the Papers were "stolen property" that had come into the hands of the *Times* through "a breach of trust by a government employee." He dismissed the *Times*'s affidavits on previous instances of publication of classified material on the grounds that they involved "one-shot disclosures," which were impossible to restrain. (Many of the affidavits actually also cited series of newspaper stories.) In order to preserve the authority of the executive branch, Seymour said, the government was willing to set an interdepartmental task force at work reviewing and declassifying the Papers, with the result promised in forty-five days.

With the encouragement of the court, Seymour embarked on a substantive description of what the *Times* should have done: ask permission from the Defense Department to publish the Papers; use its editorial columns to urge their declassification; or file a suit under the Freedom of Information Act for their release. "If newspapers would follow these procedures and use whatever arguments and noise and editorializing they can muster to expedite the process, I have no doubt that even in this case much of this history, which all of us will concede is fascinating, could be published, and at the same time it could be sanitized so that the dangerous portions which really imperil military operations and diplomatic relations could be excised."

No sooner did Bickel rise to speak than he found himself in an argument with Judge Friendly about whether the *Times* could be said to have obtained "stolen" documents. Friendly went on to accuse the professor of suggesting that "the courts have no power to do anything," and Bickel had to spend much of his time backing down from and denying such characterizations of his position. The *Times* lawyer also went to pains to defend the handling of the case by Judge Gurfein, labeling the government's description of that hearing and of alleged pressures from reporters in the audience "astonishing, a totally unwarranted suggestion"; indeed, argued Bickel, Gurfein had asked the government to "show him where the shoe pinches" and then read those parts of the Pentagon Papers "where the government pointed him to read." Bickel pleaded with the appellate court to reject the shifting analogies made by the government: "This is not a copyright case. The government can't get a copyright for publications anyway. It is not a rivers and harbors case. It is no nuisance case. It is no tort case. It is not a case of a contract that affects publication rights between private parties. And it is not a case . . . of the publication rights of prisoners held in a federal penitentiary. This is a First Amendment case. . . . It is an unprecedented case, but there is no novelty, I think, about the applicable First Amendment doctrine."

Before the court retired to a secret session to consider classified matters, New York University law professor Norman Dorsen, speaking for the ACLU, sounded a somber note by pointing out that "this case already represents a severe defeat for the First Amendment" because of the outstanding restraining order. Things went equally poorly in the closed hearing, however, and the *Times* was pessimistic about the prospects.

In the District of Columbia Circuit, on the other hand, the prognosis appeared to be much better for the *Post*. Although the nine-member court had only a narrow "liberal" majority, there was a greater sense of urgency about the Pentagon Papers case and a long string of precedents from the same court that viewed government secrecy with skepticism. With this in mind, Attorney General Mitchell decided to roll out his heavy artillery for the appellate argument in the *Post* case.

At 11 A.M. on Tuesday June 22 the Solicitor General of the United States, Erwin N. Griswold, received a telephone call from his boss, the Attorney General. Mitchell, who had not consulted Griswold at any point in the development of the Pentagon Papers litigation, shocked the Solicitor General by asking him to argue the government's case only three hours later. Griswold, in his formal, almost nineteenth-century manner, demurred, pointing out that he had never even looked at the Papers (except for the portions published by the *Times* and the *Post*) and had followed the case in the lower courts only distantly because he had been busy with other matters currently pending before the Supreme Court. Solicitors General had argued major cases below the Supreme Court level in the past, to be sure, but generally they had had far greater preparation and were themselves involved in developing and guiding the cases through the federal judiciary; since his appointment in 1967 as the government's chief courtroom advocate, however, Griswold had not done so, and it was forty years since he last appeared before the U.S. Court of Appeals for the District of Columbia Circuit as a junior staffer in the Solicitor General's office before embarking on a long career in teaching law. Griswold had private reservations about the overkill in the way the government had handled the newspaper cases thus far, but when the Attorney General persisted he went along. (Griswold, a Justice Department source explained later, was acting as "a good soldier. When the general says 'Charge!'—well, you charge.") Ever conscious of protocol and propriety, the Solicitor General worried that it might be inappropriate to appear in the appellate courtroom wearing the brown shoes and "loud tie" he had on that day. He phoned his wife and asked her to meet him in the courtyard of the Justice Department at 12:15 P.M. with black shoes, a somber tie, and some sandwiches; meanwhile he had only a short time to educate himself on the Internal Security Division's battle on behalf of national security.

When Griswold arrived at the U.S. Court of Appeals wearing the proper shoes, he was accosted by a deputy clerk who, following the standard procedure for lawyers who did not ordinarily argue there, asked him who would move his special admission to the bar of the appellate court for the purpose of the *Post* case. "If your records go back far enough," the

Solicitor General replied testily, "you'll find that I was admitted to practice here forty years ago."

The briefs submitted on each side followed essentially the same lines as those before the Second Circuit Court of Appeals in New York. Signed by Assistant Attorney General Robert C. Mardian of the Internal Security Division, the government's brief charged Judge Gesell with failing "to comprehend the nature of the power of the Executive with respect to the conduct of foreign affairs" and asserted that "the government does not have the burden of supporting a Top Secret classification." Mardian also pressed for a ruling that would require the *Post* to turn over its copies of the "stolen" documents. The *Post's* brief, in florid language, insisted that "the problems and difficulties—real or imagined—which may accrue to the government from these publications afford no warrant for their unprecedented demand to shackle the press" and said that "an immediate grave threat to national security" would be the only condition justifying a prior restraint. "It may be that some foreign governments which, under different systems employing censorship as a way of life, may not fully comprehend why their repressive measures are here rejected," said the *Post* in confronting the issue of diplomatic problems that might grow out of the disclosures, "but this fact constitutes no valid reason for compromising those principles which have served freedom so long and so well." The newspaper also warned the appellate court that "the government's efforts will ultimately prove futile"; with more and more newspapers breaking the story, "one thing is certain: public revelation of the contents of this controversial report will continue apace, and all of it will soon become available to the American public."

In his oral argument before the nine judges, Griswold contended that "the integrity of the institution of the Presidency" was at stake and asked the court to balance against freedom of the press the "equally fundamental right of the government to

[201]

function." With the courtroom packed to twice its normal capacity, the Solicitor General rattled off a list of legal situations he considered parallel to disclosure of the Pentagon Papers: the theft and unauthorized publication of an Ernest Hemingway manuscript, violations of the "law of literary property," unauthorized publication of photographs of Queen Victoria of England. Judge J. Skelly Wright, incredulous at the examples, cut in and urged Griswold to direct his comments toward the First Amendment. "You know the First Amendment as well as I do," the judge scolded. The Solicitor General pressed on the *Post* and on the court the government's offer to conduct a forty-five-day declassification review of the Papers and then to indicate which sections might be permissibly published; but *Post* attorney William Glendon rejected that proposal as so much "government by handout." "The press must be free to persevere and find the truth the best they can," Glendon said. "It's time that the presses were allowed to roll again." If the *Post* had filed suit under the Freedom of Information Act, as Griswold suggested, "I think it is safe to say that we wouldn't get [the Papers] that way until the war was over," Glendon complained. Turning the newspaper's own arguments against the *Post*, Griswold asserted that the press is as secretive as the government: Is it "such a terrible thing" in government and yet "all right" for the press? he asked. The Solicitor General argued that confidentiality of communication is as essential to the government as is confidentiality of sources to the press.

The judges, unlike their counterparts in New York, were clearly unimpressed with the government's case, and their remarks from the bench seemed to foreshadow another setback for the Justice Department. Chief Judge David L. Bazelon asked Griswold whether he seriously contended that the fact of the Papers being government "property" had a bearing on the outcome. Noting the government's offer to declassify a large portion of the Papers, Judge Harold Leventhal suggested that this was "a refutation of [its own] argument that the classification system is conclusive." The discussion about press disclosures having a bad effect on foreign governments, Leventhal said, reminded him that "many foreign governments were upset to learn after World War I that our treaties have to be approved by the Senate." Judge Roger Robb, who had voted to enjoin publication the first time around, raised the problem of further disclosures in other newspapers (copies of the Boston *Globe*'s articles on the Pentagon Papers were brought into the courtroom during the hearing); he queried whether the government was "asking us to ride herd on a swarm of bees."

After two hours of public argument, the court went into a one-hour secret session, during which the appellate judges inspected the secret exhibits from Gesell's hearing. During the closed session, the *Post* made a significant concession—agreeing not to publish "very limited quotations from two documents which the *Post* did not deem to be of reportorial significance," as executive editor Benjamin Bradlee explained it later; the stipulation not to print those items (which the *Post* never even confirmed publicly were among its portion of the Pentagon Papers) was made on the advice of the *Post*'s lawyers "to avoid needless delay in the court's consideration" of the case. That agreement, like other matters in the closed hearing, was to be kept confidential but was later revealed by Circuit Judge George E. MacKinnon in his dissenting opinion in the *Post* case.

Both appellate courts once again extended their restraining orders overnight while the *Times* and *Post* cases were under submission. On Wednesday June 23 there was an additional unannounced closed afternoon session before Judge Bazelon between the lawyers on both sides of the *Post* case, apparently initiated by the government's attorneys, who were worried by the sentiments expressed by the judges during oral argument and were encouraged by the *Post*'s concession in the closed hearing on Tuesday. The discussions focused on an affidavit that had been submitted before Judge Gesell by Vice Admiral Noel Gayler, director of the National Security Agency at Fort Meade in Maryland. Gayler had contended that disclosure of the Papers threatened to reveal the extent of the American military capacity to intercept secret messages of other countries, but Gesell had found his affidavit, like the others in the government's case, lacking in specifics and thus unconvincing. Now the government was back before Bazelon to supplement Gayler's affidavit by citing a specific radio intercept in the Pentagon Papers that was part of the Defense Department's evidence purportedly proving that North Vietnamese vessels fired on American ships in the Gulf of Tonkin in August 1964.

But the *Post*'s lawyers summoned the newspaper's Pentagon correspondent, George Wilson, who remembered that the exact same message was quoted in the public transcript of an executive session of the Senate Foreign Relations Committee on February 20, 1968. Wilson, surprising lawyers on both sides with his precision, pulled a copy of the transcript from his back pocket and pointed to the quotation of the message. The Justice Department representatives, obviously taken aback, hurriedly sent for their own copy of the transcript and for a further comment from the National Security Agency; NSA responded merely by citing the fact that the "time group" on the cable was included in the Pentagon Papers, whereas it had been omitted in the Foreign Relations Committee transcript; the time group, NSA claimed, would permit other nations to calculate how quickly the United States deciphered coded messages. But that point too was unconvincing as a reason for banning publication of the Pentagon Papers, especially since the *Post* had refrained from printing the time groups or full texts of messages it quoted from the study.

During the approximately thirty hours while the two appellate courts were considering the Pentagon Papers cases, there were several unusual contacts between them. At one point Chief Judge Friendly phoned his counterpart in Washington, Chief Judge Bazelon, and they attempted to assure that both decisions would be released at approximately the same time so that one case would not get substantially ahead of the other in the judicial system. Law clerks for several judges in the two cities also exchanged calls to discuss the issues, and the members of each court were aware in advance that the two circuits would reach conflicting conclusions.

All seventeen circuit judges considering the government appeals expressed a feeling during their deliberations that they were taking on an awesome responsibility in attempting to resolve a major constitutional conflict between the executive branch and the press; the glare of intensive publicity apparently made them feel more pressure than usual. At the Second Circuit Court of Appeals in New York, that translated into a bitter battle among judges who ordinarily agree upon a middle-of-the-road consensus. Four law clerks at that court split up the material in the government's "Special Appendix" and worked almost all night analyzing it, coming in the next day with a nearly unanimous recommendation that Judge Gurfein's decision in favor of the *Times* be upheld. Some of the judges, however, appeared to ignore the recommendation and chose not to examine the material from the Papers themselves, relying instead on their instincts, including their concern that the documents had been "stolen." Chief Judge Friendly and Judge J. Edward Lumbard, the two consistently conservative and most senior members of the court, argued for an outright reversal of Gurfein's decision and the granting of an injunction against the *Times*. They were joined by Judge Paul R. Hays, who was named to the bench by President Kennedy while he was chairman of the Liberal party in New York State but had been a conservative judge. Judge J. Joseph Smith, who often voted a liberal line on other issues, was less certain about how strong the ruling against the *Times* should be, but on the basis of his experience as a member of the House Armed Services Committee when he was a Congressman from Connecticut he was inclined to go along with the conservatives.

The other four judges, however, were opposed to granting an injunction against the *Times*. Judge Irving R. Kaufman, who had been on the bench for twenty-two years and had, as a federal district judge, sentenced Julius and Ethel Rosenberg to death for espionage, led a particularly emotional fight in favor of the *Times*. As a First Amendment scholar, he was disappointed by Bickel's presentation for the newspaper but nonetheless felt the issue was clear. (Ironically, Kaufman had ordered shares of *The Washington Post*'s stock offering through his broker only a few days earlier, but he felt compelled to cancel the order when the *Times* case reached the appellate court, lest he be open to charges of a conflict of interest.) Kaufman was joined by Wilfred Feinberg, another liberal on the court, and by James L. Oakes, a former Republican Attorney General of Vermont who had been named to the court by President Nixon only a week earlier. (The Second Circuit includes the states of New York, Connecticut, and Vermont, and custom dictates that judicial appointments be spread among the three states.) Oakes drafted a strongly worded memorandum on freedom of the press and won praise from his colleagues for his "courage" in displaying such strong independence from the administration that had so recently named him to the court.

That left Walter R. Mansfield, a noted civil libertarian who had been elevated by President Nixon to the appellate court from his position as a federal judge for the Southern District of New York only a few weeks before Oakes. (Were it not for his promotion Mansfield, rather than Judge Murray Gurfein, would have handled the *Times* case in U.S. District Court, as the judge in charge of the motions calendar for the week beginning June 14, 1971.) Mansfield was not persuaded by either side, and his vote became crucial, since a 4–4 tie would have had the automatic effect of affirming Gurfein's ruling. He hammered out a rapid compromise, agreeing to vote with the majority if it would avoid granting an injunction against the *Times* and instead send the case back to Gurfein for new secret hearings on the items in the government's "Special Appendix" and any additional material the Justice Department wished to claim was especially dangerous to national security. Another part of the compromise involved an agreement that the court would not issue written opinions—which were already in preparation—revealing their sharp differences.

Mansfield carried the day, and by a 5–3 vote the Second Circuit Court of Appeals issued an unsigned opinion drafted by Friendly. In one sentence the court remanded the case to Gurfein, giving him ten days to rule on the material specified by the government. There was no reversal of what Gurfein had already ruled, just another opportunity for him to rule otherwise. On Friday June 25, the court said, the *Times* would be free to publish any parts of the Pentagon Papers not specially designated by the government for the new proceedings before Gurfein; and that, the judges in the majority believed, was a very generous interim settlement.

The U.S. Court of Appeals for the District of Columbia is accustomed to angry disputes among its nine judges. Unique in the nation, the court has had jurisdiction not only over the same matters as other federal appellate courts but also over the ruling of several federal regulatory agencies and, until the local court system in the nation's capital was recently reorganized and strengthened by Congress, over most local criminal cases in Washington. For years the court's disparate ideological blocs were led by Chief Judge David L. Bazelon, a liberal named to the court by President Truman in 1948, and Warren E. Burger, an Eisenhower appointee. Burger was a constant dissenter from Bazelon's groundbreaking opinions expanding the scope of the criminal insanity defense, and he also objected strenuously to the court's sweeping pronouncements on administrative law. By the time Burger left the appellate court to become Chief Justice of the United States in 1969, he and Bazelon hardly spoke to each other, and this legacy persisted in 1971 with two well-defined coalitions on the court, the "conservative" one now bolstered by three Nixon appointees, Roger Robb, George E. MacKinnon, and Malcolm R. Wilkey.

The Pentagon Papers case was a rare occasion for general agreement among the judges, however, with seven of the nine indicating their rejection of the government's argument; the only problem was to draft a majority opinion that would be acceptable to all seven. Joining the usual "liberals"—Bazelon, J. Skelly Wright, Carl McGowan, Harold Leventhal, and Spottswood W. Robinson III—were Edward Allen Tamm, a former aide to FBI director J. Edgar Hoover who, as one court source puts it, "knows a secret document when he sees one"; and Robb, a staunch opponent of Bazelon and Wright who, along with Robinson, had instituted the first restraining order against the *Post* and sent the case back to Judge Gesell for a full trial. Robb had a personal history of opposition to government secrecy, having served as an attorney for Otto Otepka, the State Department officer disciplined for turning classified documents over to the Senate Internal Security Subcommittee. Unlike their colleagues on the appellate court in New York, the judges had personally examined much of the government's evidence and simply found it unpersuasive as a basis for prior restraint.

The seven judges fully upheld Gesell's decision for the *Post*, finding that "the government's proof, judged by the standard suggested in Near v. Minnesota . . . does not justify an injunction. Their unsigned ruling cited Chief Justice Burger's opinion in the Chicago leafletting case only a month earlier stressing the "heavy presumption against [the] constitutional validity" of restraining publication. During their deliberations, the judges had been informed of still more news breaks involving the Pentagon Papers, as well as President Nixon's decision to make the study available to Congress; they noted that "our conclusion . . . is fortified by the consideration that the massive character of the 'leak' which has occurred, and the disclosures already made by several newspapers, raise substantial doubt that effective relief of the kind sought by the government can be provided by the Judiciary." Nonetheless, they granted another extension of the restraining order to preserve jurisdiction for the Supreme Court.

Only two judges dissented. Malcolm R. Wilkey, the newest Nixon appointee to the court, often considered a partisan jurist, caused a substantial delay in the release of the decision for the *Post* with the writing and revision of his four-page opinion citing a "small percentage [of the Papers] which . . . could be grievously harmful to this country." "When I say 'harm,'" Wilkey explained, "I mean the death of soldiers, the destruction of alliances, the greatly increased difficulty of negotiation with our enemies, the inability of our diplomats to negotiate as honest brokers between would-be belligerents." He and Judge George E. MacKinnon, in a separate dissent, suggested remanding the case to Judge Gesell for further findings on specific documents, as was done in the Second Circuit.

On Thursday June 24 *The New York Times* appealed to the Supreme Court for a review of the Second Circuit decision in the government's favor; the newspaper asked the high court to consider eight separate legal questions, including the absolute one of "whether, consistent with the First Amendment, a court may restrain a newspaper from publishing articles relating to public affairs." Bickel and his associates urged the court to iron out "the plain inconsistency between the two appellate decisions" and demanded an immediate hearing of the case because "not only has the public's right to know been infringed for over a week but the *Times*, which courageously initiated the publication of the documents, is being pre-empted by other newspapers." The *Times* also asked that all restraint against it be lifted while the Supreme Court considered the case.

The government had been expected to do much the same thing—ask for immediate Supreme Court review—in the *Post* case that it had lost in the District of Columbia Circuit. But it sought at first to avoid the Supreme Court and filed instead for a rehearing of the *Post* case at the appellate court level, seeking a ruling in conformity with the one handed down by the Second Circuit in New York. Solicitor General Griswold's petition included a surprising argument for the government: that unless the Washington case were conformed to the one in New York, "*The New York Times* will be under a restraint which is not applicable to *The Washington Post* [and] this will be unfair to *The New York Times*." Reconsideration, Griswold advised, would also give the appellate court an opportunity to clear up "uncertainty" over exactly what the *Post* had agreed not to print during the first secret appellate court session. At almost the same moment, however, the Solicitor General was filing an opposition to *The New York Times*'s petition at the Supreme Court, stating that a new hearing before Judge Gurfein was appropriate because the government was "unable to prepare as complete a submission" in the *Times* case as it had in the *Post* case. That point was picked up by attorneys for the *Post* who, opposing the request for reconsideration in Washington, argued in a hasty brief that "the government's procedural problems in New York should not be permitted to delay this case here."

The District of Columbia Circuit was of much the same mind. After consulting for several hours on Thursday afternoon ("having the greatest respect for the Solicitor General, we have given his petition careful consideration," the court noted), the seven-man majority that had ruled for the *Post* a day earlier reaffirmed its decision and set out its reasons more fully: "We are satisfied that the government had appropriate opportunity [before Judge Gesell] to make the kind of showing appropriate to justify a prior restraint on the nation's historic free press." Confronting the differences between its own decision and the one in New York, the court said that it could deal with the facts only as adduced in Washington and that "considerations of the comity [the comparative treatment of different cases by different courts] may not be stretched unduly when what is involved is a prior restraint on the press we do not find constitutionally authorized." Most important, the appellate court noted that in addition to the *Times* and the *Post* "newspapers not before either court" would have to be taken into account. Reeling off a list of the latest papers to disclose the Pentagon study, the judges noted again their "concern . . . whether effective relief of the kind sought by the government can be provided by the judiciary." Definitively denying the petition, the appellate court added that "the matter is now ripe for presentation to the Supreme Court." MacKinnon and Wilkey again dissented.

Taking his cue from that, Griswold relented and appealed the *Post* case to the Supreme Court on Thursday night June 24. That move required backing down from his position earlier in the day and agreeing that the *Times* case was also ready for review by the high court. In both instances, the Solicitor General acknowledged, "constitutional issues of great magnitude" were presented.

The Supreme Court lost no time in acting. On June 25, at what was scheduled to be its last regular Friday morning conference for the 1970–1971 term, five justices voted to take the newspaper cases on an emergency expedited basis and to hold an unprecedented Saturday morning session the next day to hear oral argument from the government, the *Times*, and the *Post*. Four justices—Hugo L. Black, William O. Douglas (voting by telephone; he had already left the capital to spend the summer at his home in Goose Prairie, Washington), William J. Brennan, Jr., and Thurgood Marshall—dissented, saying they would have refused the cases, and immediately lifted all restraints against the *Times* and the *Post*. But the majority—Chief Justice Burger, John M. Harlan, Potter Stewart, Byron R. White, and Harry A. Blackmun—imposed on the *Post* the restriction of not publishing items listed in the "Special Appendix" from the *Times* case; the government was also given several hours to specify additional items in the Pentagon Papers considered especially sensitive, publication of which would be provisionally enjoined pending resolution of the dispute by the Supreme Court. Whatever was left of the Papers could be published by the newspapers in the meantime.

[CHAPTER XI]

After the Supreme Court agreed on Friday June 25 to take
the Pentagon Papers cases and relaxed the formal ban on all
but the especially sensitive material to be specified by the government, the editors of *The New York Times* and *The Washington Post* faced an immediate serious decision: Should they
accept the distinctions made by the Departments of Defense
and State and go ahead with publication of the material that
was being indirectly authorized for release? There was a
serious practical problem, of course, since both papers had
already prepared the subsequent installments of their series of
articles; and once the government list was available, these
stories might have to be culled through to ascertain whether
any particular sentence or paragraph violated the restrictions.
It was a dangerous process to attempt under deadline pressure,
but not to print what had been cleared for publication threat-

ened to render less credible the urgency that both newspapers had been impressing upon the federal courts.

Early in the day Rosenthal took a stand on principle, saying that the *Times* could not go along with the notion that government bureaucrats were selecting—even temporarily—what could appear in print. "That would be publishing under conditions. We're not inclined to do that," Rosenthal said. At the *Post* the principles were interpreted as cutting the other way. "We felt that the public right to know demanded that we give serious consideration to printing [another story based on the Papers] if we could print anything of substance without violating the court order," Bradlee said.

The problems of both Bradlee and Rosenthal were made much easier when the complete government list of purportedly extrasensitive matters was submitted to lawyers for the newspapers at 5 P.M. Friday afternoon. The list was enormous in scope, covering a huge percentage of the material in the Pentagon Papers and prohibiting, as Rosenthal put it, "anything but a truncated version" of what had been planned and written. What is more, the list of items was itself classified top secret. That meant that the editors themselves, who did not have the appropriate clearance from the Pentagon, were not permitted to look at even a characterization of what they were banned from publishing; only the lawyers in each case and a few selected reporters, who had special clearance for the purpose of the litigation, were trusted by the government to see the list. Only after receiving the recommendations of three *Post* lawyers and reporter George Wilson could Bradlee declare that "it is so substantial a list as to make it physically impossible for us to decide, in the time allowed, what we could print, even if we chose to print anything."

The Justice Department reacted angrily to what it felt was a self-righteous decision by the two newspapers to refuse to proceed with publication on a limited basis and issued a statement contending that the *Times* and the *Post* had only themselves to blame for being in a bind. "The Department of Justice has repeatedly requested that [they] disclose to the court contents of the documents in their possession," the statement said. "Both newspapers have consistently refused to do so. Had they made that disclosure, it would have been possible for the Department to tell each newspaper which passages and sections in their documents were covered by the [temporary Supreme Court injuction]. The *Times* and the *Post* chose instead to adhere to their position and as a result are unable to print without being in jeopardy of violating the court order."

The top-secret status of the crucial list came as no surprise to those familiar with the inscrutable American government system of classification. It is an area governed and guided almost not at all by congressional legislation or pronouncements from the courts, but rather by executive orders and departmental directives that have produced a great deal of irrational ritual and very little genuine security within the government. The basic guideline for classification policy had been Executive Order 10501, issued by President Eisenhower on November 5, 1953, for the purpose of "Safeguarding Official Information in the Interests of the Defense of the United States." It formally established three basic categories: "Top Secret," for "that information or material the defense aspect of which is paramount, and the unauthorized disclosure of which could result in exceptionally grave damage to the Nation such as leading to a definite break in diplomatic relations affecting the defense of the United States, and armed attack against the United States or its allies, a war, or the compromise of military or defense plans, or intelligence operations, or scientific or technological developments vital to the national defense"; "Secret," for "defense information or material the unauthorized disclosure of which could result in serious damage to the Nation, such as by jeopardizing the international relations of the United States, endangering the effectiveness of a program or policy of vital importance to the national defense, or compromising important military or defense plans, scientific or technological developments important to national defense, or information revealing important intelligence operations"; and "Confidential," for "defense information or material the unauthorized disclosure of which could be prejudicial to the defense interests of the Nation."

As amended over the years by Presidents Eisenhower and Kennedy, the order stressed that "unnecessary classification and overclassification shall be scrupulously avoided," but it virtually guaranteed that it would not be avoided by extending classification authority to a host of agencies from the Atomic Energy Commission to the Panama Canal Company and Tennessee Valley Authority. There were no reliable guidelines for determining when disclosure of information "could" lead to one of the specified evils and no provisions for downgrading a classification upon review without the express consent of the person who had classified it in the first place. Special "groups" of information were subsequently defined that would be excluded from automatic downgrading or declassification, and the executive order was packed with requirements such as "opaque inner and outer covers" for all classified material, a ban on any telephone communications with regard to it, and a direction that "the head of each department and agency . . . take prompt and stringent administrative action against any officer and employee of the United States, at any level of employment, determined to have been knowingly responsible for any release or disclosure of classified defense information or material" contrary to the terms of the order.

Proclamation of Executive Order 10501, which gave permanent status to many emergency and wartime rules, launched what William G. Florence, a long-time security expert for the Air Force, calls a "classification craze." Desks at the Pentagon—and in myriad other agencies—were equipped with trees of rubber stamps that permitted bureaucrats at all levels to qualify minute bits of information for indefinite obscurity and secrecy. Overclassification was tacitly encouraged in training programs for new government employees and military recruits, who were shown anti-Communist films and lectured on the need for faithfully keeping government secrets. Although the executive order did not, and legally could not, specify that divulging classified information was a crime—no law specifically states what information must be kept secret, and only under carefully defined circumstances does disclosure fall under such laws as the Espionage Act—employees of the Post Office Department, the Federal Communications Commission, and the Peace Corps, among others, were constantly warned against "breaking the law" through indiscretion. Quite apart from the fear of punishment, government officials came somehow to believe that their own work might take on more importance if they stamped it with a classification.

Florence, who left government service just before the Pentagon Papers controversy broke, cites long lists of occasions when classification was taken to absurd extremes. One of the most extraordinary was the Defense Department's "Program 949," the system of surveillance satellites that in the 1960s became an extension of the nation's "early warning" apparatus to prevent surprise attacks by foreign powers. In June 1969 an Assistant Secretary of the Air Force made a public comment about "the capability of the 949 satellite system to both detect missile launches off the launch pad and forecast their trajectory and combine those data with long wave-length infrared midcourse tracking." Such information was made widely available to Congress when the Pentagon was seeking appropriations for the system. On the books, however, absolutely everything relating to Program 949 was considered top secret, including the procurement of all supplies, down to desks and paper clips. A particular problem arose when officers at one Air Force base working on the program urgently needed some paint. The rules required that even a purchase order for a can of paint be stamped secret, and such a purchase order could not be shown to any ordinary paint or hardware store. Florence had to step in to help revise the regulations governing Program 949 so that the paint could be purchased without the appearance of a gross violation of security. "You can have your paint or you can have your security, but you can't have both," he advised.

In some instances the rules of "derivative classification," which require that any compilation of documents (such as the Pentagon Papers) receive the highest classification contained in any of its parts, result in putting secret stamps on newspaper clippings, public speeches, and other material that is circulating freely in other parts of the government. Occasionally, defense contractors employ this technique and the extreme extension of it in order to direct more serious attention to their work from the upper echelons of the Defense Department. A recent report entitled "A Test Method for the Verification of the Nuclear Hardness of the Single Degree of the Free-Floated Integrated Gyroscope," prepared by a laboratory at the Massachusetts Institute of Technology, for example, noted on its cover that "overall classification of this report is secret, to protect the compilation of information . . . although the highest classification of any individual page is Confidential." In fact, only one page in the entire report was stamped confidential, and according to one expert the information on that page could have been restated to obviate any necessity for classification. In an assertion that Florence labels blatantly "phony," one government affidavit in the Pentagon Papers case claimed that "it is sometimes necessary to classify a document in which no single piece or part is itself classified."

Occasionally, professional classifiers on the highest level become exasperated with the overreach of the executive order's dictates. Several years ago one of the members of the Joint Chiefs of Staff sent a memo to his colleagues suggesting that the top-secret classification was being used excessively and urging a change of policy; but that memo itself was marked top secret, assuring that few people would see it and that its message would not be taken very seriously by those to whom it was addressed.

Among other problems, overclassification of government materials costs the American taxpayer an enormous amount of money—Florence estimates $50 million annually—for security storage facilities, paper work, and employees' time for keeping classified items properly filed and separated from other data.

In 1970 a Special Task Force on Secrecy set up by the Pentagon's Defense Science Board reported that "the amount of scientific and technical information which is classified could profitably be decreased perhaps by as much as 90 percent by limiting the amount of information classified and the duration of its classification." Florence's estimate, made on the basis of a career in the security business, goes even further. During hearings in the midst of the Pentagon Papers fight he told the House Foreign Operations and Government Information Subcommittee: "I sincerely believe that less than one-half of one percent of the different documents which bear currently assigned classification markings actually contain information qualifying even for the lowest defense classification under Executive Order 10501. In other words, the disclosure of information in at least 99½ percent of those classified documents could not be prejudicial to the defense interests of the nation."

The classification system dogged major figures on all sides throughout the Pentagon Papers litigation. On Sunday night June 20, for example, when *Post* lawyer William Glendon was in Washington to prepare for the Monday hearing before Judge Gesell, despite the rules governing discovery of each other's evidence by adversaries, the Justice Department initially refused to show him the secret affidavits that would be central to the legal case advanced against the newspaper.

Gesell ordered the government to make them available, however, and the Justice Department agreed on the condition that the *Post* lawyers read them at department headquarters. Glendon went to the Justice Department and, under the constant watch of an FBI agent, read the affidavits, showed them to his colleagues, and took a few notes. Suddenly Assistant Attorney General Robert Mardian entered the room and announced that it was forbidden to take notes. They argued bitterly back and forth until Glendon announced that "I'm under a lot of pressure; I'm going to take these notes and I'm going to walk out of the room with them. Now this fellow [the FBI agent] here is a lot younger and bigger than I am, and I'm sure that you are going to try and stop me—if you do, there's going to be a helluva fight and I know I'm going to lose; but when I stand up in court tomorrow and I've got a few bandages on me, I'm going to tell people exactly what happened: that I was beaten up by the Department of Justice." Mardian walked out of the room and eventually returned with his deputy, Kevin Maroney, who worked out a compromise—Glendon would take personal responsibility for the secrecy of his own notes. Those notes are now locked in a vault at the Pentagon. Later, in the Washington office of his law firm, Glendon was under the constant view of security agents while he prepared the newspaper's secret briefs at various stages of the litigation; at one point the agents helped to proofread the *Post*'s brief for the Court of Appeals at 2 A.M. No objection was raised, amazingly enough, that the secretaries who typed the *Post* briefs based on classified material had no clearance.

The Supreme Court's announcement on Friday afternoon June 25 that various government departments could specify what they considered most sensitive in the Pentagon Papers flushed out the overclassification mentality at the State and Defense departments to the point that even the security-conscious lawyers handling the case for the Justice Department were exasperated. The same supplemental statement of items that had dismayed the editors of the *Times* and the *Post* was ultimately disavowed by Solicitor General Griswold before the Supreme Court. "I find it much too broad," Griswold told the justices in an unusual expression of disgust with his own clients within the government. Even after the list had been compiled, Griswold also revealed, the State Department tried to add four more items by telephone at 9 P.M., four hours after the Supreme Court deadline.

Griswold, worried that he might hurt the government's case at the Supreme Court by overstating it, determined on Friday that he would have to step in and compile his own definitive list of items on which the government's national security could rest at the high court. Assistant Attorney General Mardian had a set of the Pentagon Papers delivered to the Solicitor General's inner sanctum on the fifth floor of the Justice Department. After calculating that it would have taken him ten weeks to read all forty-seven volumes at a rate of two hundred words per minute, Griswold called in the government's purported experts to brief him. Griswold sat down on a blue leather sofa in his office with, in turn, William B. Macomber, Jr., Deputy Undersecretary of State for Administration; Lieutenant General Melvin Zais, director of operations for the Joint Chiefs of Staff; and Vice Admiral Noel Gayler, director of the National Security Agency, saying to them: "Look, tell me what are the worst, tell me what are the things that really make trouble." Griswold took handwritten notes on a yellow legal pad as the three men reeled off a total of forty-one items they were most concerned about. After reading each item in the Papers, Griswold found that in his judgment many could lead to a situation of political embarrassment, but they would surely not endanger national security. "It was perfectly plain to him that the Papers were overclassified in places," according to one high-ranking Justice Department official. Attorney General Mitchell was personally opposed to any further narrowing down of the government's case but reluctantly relented in the face of Griswold's judgment. The Solicitor General reduced the forty-one items specified by Macomber, Zais, and Gayler to only eleven (one of them comprised the four "diplomatic" volumes in the Papers, detailing American efforts through other countries to negotiate a Vietnam settlement and obtain the release of prisoners of war).

One reporter close to the case suggested later that the military experts had refrained from telling what they were genuinely most worried about as a potential security threat in the Papers. "The spooks didn't trust even the government lawyers," he said. "The generals probably could have come up with some devastating stuff in the Pentagon Papers if they tried harder and trusted the people they had to tell."

Having delegated the government's main legal brief to an assistant, Griswold set about writing the supplementary secret brief on Friday night, and that was when his own trouble with the Pentagon security men began. They objected, for example, to the fact that Griswold's secretary would be handling classified material while typing his brief, and told him that they would have to find someone else to do the job. Griswold, ordinarily gentlemanly to a fault, told the security agents to "get out" of his office and to tell their supervisor that "the Solicitor General of the United States will not follow your instructions." Griswold stayed until 3:15 A.M., his secretary until 4 A.M., and then the office—where the Pentagon Papers were temporarily stored—was kept under overnight guard by the FBI. On Saturday morning, utterly unaware of court rules and procedure, the security men raised a fuss when Griswold filed his secret brief with the clerk of the Supreme Court, to them just another person without clearance who would get a look at defense secrets. And they were appalled that the Solicitor General actually found it necessary to give copies of the brief to lawyers for the enemy, the *Times* and the *Post*. Indeed, after the Supreme Court argument, as they had done at the U.S. Court of Appeals in Washington, agents scurried to reclaim the secret briefs from the tables where the lawyers sat. Under the special rules of the Pentagon Papers litigation, attorneys for the newspapers were not even authorized to keep a copy of their own secret briefs in their private files.

The Solicitor General's office showed signs of enjoying the supersecretive subculture at the last minute too. Griswold filed a motion for a closed *in camera* argument before the Supreme Court on Saturday morning June 26 without notifying the lawyers for the *Times* and the *Post*. When those lawyers arrived at the Supreme Court later the same morning, the clerk told them that such a motion had been filed and denied by the court, but that this fact was a secret, so they were not permitted to tell their clients, the newspapers. Chief Justice Burger, however, revealed that classified bit of information by announcing as the court convened that the government's motion had been denied by a 6–3 vote.

[CHAPTER XII]

Great cases may make bad law, according to the old aphorism of Justice Oliver Wendell Holmes, but whatever else can be said of them, great cases make great confrontations. And great confrontations, dramatic confrontations between eminent personages over issues of public as well as philosophical concern, are the stuff of historic footnotes to the law. The very uniqueness of the Pentagon Papers controversy—and the coverage it was guaranteed to receive from a press that was itself a litigant—assured that this was one Supreme Court case that would be catapulted into the public consciousness. But as much as anything else, the extraordinary argument before the high court on Saturday June 26 was significant as a clash between two great constitutional scholars, Alexander M. Bickel and Erwin N. Griswold.

There was something inherently theatrical about Bickel's

appearance in *The New York Times* case. He had never argued before the Supreme Court, although he had once clerked there for the late Justice Felix Frankfurter and had built his own academic career as an analyst and a critic of the high court as an institution of the American government. In October 1969 Bickel, Chancellor Kent professor of law and legal history at Yale, had returned to his alma mater, the Harvard Law School, to deliver the Holmes Lectures—by his own designation the high point of his legal life ("That's all I lived for," he said recently). Over the space of three lectures, he took on the "Warren Court," which had under the leadership of Chief Justice Earl Warren wrought a constitutional egalitarian revolution with its decisions in racial cases, legislative reapportionment, and the procedural rights of criminal suspects, among others. Handling the same material that had been the subject of emotional and often irrational political criticism, Bickel used his lectures to argue that the Warren Court had become carried away with itself and overstepped the invisible limits that society had drawn for it, intervening in areas of social policy that would more appropriately have fallen in the jurisdiction of the political process and the more political legislative and executive branches of government. His Holmes Lectures were converted into a well-circulated and widely discussed book called *The Supreme Court and the Idea of Progress*. Because it was phrased primarily in a legalese unreadable by most of the public, Bickel's arguments escaped the attention of many politicians in Congress who would have liked to legislate the Warren Court out of business, but they were noted by judges on all levels of the federal judiciary.

Bickel, now forty-six years of age, looked forward to appearing before the Supreme Court in a case with such profound implications; some of his colleagues suggest that he accepted *The New York Times*'s midnight plea for help only because he knew that the Pentagon Papers case would ultimately have to be resolved on the highest level. "I felt more comfortable there than in any other court," Bickel said later, "because it is so much like home. . . . I live my whole life with the Supreme Court; I know its history, I know the people. . . . It's the institution I worry about." (One professor at another law school suggests that the "worry" is actually just ambition. "Bickel has been strumming the congressional guitar for years," he says, in the hope that he will be named to the high court or a lower-level federal judgeship.) The Pentagon Papers provided him with a vantage point closer than a lectern at Harvard or Yale for telling the court what it should do and how to reach the appropriate ends by moderate rather than absolute means. To the chagrin of what remained of the hard core of the Warren Court—and especially to Justice Hugo L. Black —Bickel simply did not believe that the First Amendment provided sanction for an absolute freedom of the press; besides, he was forced to act now less as a professor than as a lawyer for his client, *The New York Times.* "I think to have argued this case on the basis of an absolute position would have been foolish to the point of being almost unprofessional, so far as safeguarding the interest of my client was concerned," Bickel says. "If you go into these cases with an ideological interest, like the American Civil Liberties Union, you've got nothing to gain but your ideology and nothing to lose but your ideology; then you have the luxury of an absolutist position. . . . I had to win a case." And to win, Bickel calculated, he had to pick up the vote of at least one swing justice, either Potter Stewart or Byron R. White.

In planning the major *amicus curiae* brief for the *Times* and other news organizations in the case of Earl Caldwell, Bickel had charted a moderate position, suggesting that under extraordinary circumstances a reporter could be compelled to testify; the *Times* later praised this position editorially as "reasonable and realistic." (In contrast, attorneys for *The Washington Post* filed a separate *amicus curiae* brief with the Supreme Court in the Caldwell case demanding "an absolute, unqualified privilege" for newsmen from being required to testify in government investigations.) Eloquent, sincere, eminently self-confident, and quick on his feet, Bickel now appeared before the Supreme Court to urge that the very moderateness of his position was one more reason why the newspapers should prevail.

Representing the other side before the Supreme Court was a man who entered Harvard Law School when Alexander Bickel was nine months old, Erwin Nathaniel Griswold. Griswold, in fact, had been one of Bickel's teachers during his two decades as dean of the law school. Now almost sixty-seven, he held twenty-one honorary degrees, had been a member of the U.S. Civil Rights Commission, and was perhaps the country's leading expert on the Fifth Amendment. Griswold—"the Gris" to generations of law students—was an uncontroversial man, an expert on tax law, who kept the Harvard Law School on a staid, consistently unexperimental course over the years, and who earned appointment by President Johnson as Solicitor General in 1967 on the basis of pure professionalism rather than any firm political loyalties or partisan attachment to causes. Less a constitutional scholar than a tough and stubborn advocate, Griswold rode the political tides and was kept on as the government's chief courtroom lawyer by the Nixon administration; his principles were flexible enough to permit him to sign a controversial Justice Department brief in the fall of 1969 asking the Supreme Court to delay the implementation of a desegregation order in Mississippi (allegedly part of an administration deal to obtain the support of Mississippi's Senators on other measures then before Congress). Whatever influence Griswold had in John Mitchell's Justice Department he exercised quietly and behind the scenes or in the subtle way he chose to argue cases before the high court; but occasionally he took the rare public, exhibitionist route of refusing to sign briefs or to argue cases in which he did not agree with the government's position.

Impeccable in his swallow-tailed morning coat, Griswold somehow looked as if he belonged in the Supreme Court's red-draped courtroom. If Bickel saw himself as properly "at home" before the court, Griswold seemed almost part of the furnishings that make up a great institution. Bickel sounded ceremonious, Griswold comfortably sonorous. The Solicitor General's voice rose and fell with natural, precise punctuation. He had never liked the press much; even as dean of the law school he was one of the few high officials at Harvard University who regularly refused to speak with reporters from the student newspaper. Nonetheless, on the basis of rigorous, last-minute preparations he had resisted the temptation to argue an absolute case with regard to the Pentagon Papers. Like Bickel, he was advancing a moderate position that he thought was most likely to carry the day for his "client." Griswold was already secretly pleased that the government had made the point that a prior restraint of publication could exist, at least temporarily while the courts weighed the merits of granting a more permanent one; now he was directing the court's attention to a very limited number of items in the secret Vietnam study, asking for a partial injunction based on the individual or cumulative danger that they might pose to the national security.

In contrast to the two gentlemen scholars representing the *Times* and the government was William R. Glendon, a rough-and-tumble lawyer who had never lost his small-town New England accent while climbing through the ranks of one of New York's most prestigious law firms. His language was gruff and direct (for example, when Chief Justice Burger referred to the *Post* as having "come into court," Glendon said that his client had been "dragged into court kicking and screaming"), something of a relief in juxtaposition to the formalisms and posturing of Bickel and Griswold. Glendon stumbled rather more noticeably over questions from the justices than did the others and certainly seemed much less at home, almost an intruder on the great men's special date with destiny. He too advanced a moderate position on the Pentagon Papers, a cause for substantial concern among some *Post* editors who doubted Glendon's enthusiasm about the case from the start.

The Solicitor General's open brief at the Supreme Court acknowledged that in contrast to the original position taken by the government before Judges Gurfein and Gesell, it now sought a "much narrower injunction." The brief also conceded openly for the first time that the security classification on the material and "however the newspaper[s] may have come into possession of it" were not necessarily crucial to the decision. Back again, however, was the reliance on copyright law and the "common law right of literary property"—which might have had substantial influence in England, where the "crown copyright" protects the government's sole right to publish information that is the property of the people, but which is utterly inapplicable in the United States. Griswold also relied upon the President's power in the conduct of foreign affairs and his authority as commander in chief of the nation's armed forces. "Obviously, in circumstances like those here, the only effective means of protecting the nation against the improper disclosure of military secrets is to enjoin their impending publication," he said. "To limit the President's power in this regard solely to punishment of those who disclose secret information would render the power meaningless: the harm sought to be prevented would have been irreparably accomplished." There was also a trace of an apocalyptic prediction: "Relatively innocuous consequences today may develop into serious and sometimes virtually insolvable problems in the future."

The *Times*'s brief before the Supreme Court dealt once more with the unusually strong presumption against prior restraint built into the First Amendment, as interpreted throughout the nation's legal history; where there had been exceptions, the brief contended, they were in connection with "the redress of individual or private wrongs," as in libel suits. As for the dissemination of classified documents, the *Times* argued, the

President had the power to enforce executive branch regulations—"he can discipline, he can discharge, and he can repossess government property"—but Congress had never passed legislation authorizing prior restraint as a means for dealing with security leaks. If an exception to the ban on prior restraint were to be established, Bickel's brief contended, "it would arise only when publication could be held to lead directly and almost unavoidably to a disastrous event. The probabilities must be very high, near to certainty, and the chain of causation between the publication and the feared event must be direct." Arguing against the remand of the case to Judge Gurfein, which had been imposed by the Second Circuit Court of Appeals, the *Times* pointed out that two district judges and two appellate courts had already reviewed the government's evidence and failed to find anything that could lead to such a disastrous event—and "all these judges could not have been that wrong." Unless the basis for a prior restraint can be spotted "expeditiously," the *Times* added, the litigation itself becomes a form of censorship, inevitably delaying publication just for the sake of preventing the case from becoming moot. This is exactly what had happened in the Pentagon Papers case; on the day of argument before the Supreme Court the *Times* had already been restrained for eleven days and the *Post* for seven days.

"Press and government have a curious, interlocking, both cooperative and adversary relationship," the *Times*'s brief concluded. "This has been the case more or less in this country since the extension of manhood suffrage and the rise of an independent rather than party-connected or faction-connected press. It is not a tidy relationship. It is unruly, or to the extent that it operates under rules, these are unwritten and even tacit ones. Unquestionably, every so often it malfunctions from the point of view of one or the other partner to it. The greater power within it lies with the government. The press wields the countervailing power conferred upon it by the First Amendment. If there is something near a balance, it is an uneasy one. Any redressing of it at the expense of the press, as this case demonstrates, can come only at the cost of incursions into the First Amendment."

The Washington Post's brief, pointing out that the government's position had shifted considerably over time in the lower courts, addressed itself to Griswold's "miscellaneous contentions." It noted, for example, that the government's reliance on the Espionage Act was misplaced, because Congress, in amending that law in 1950, had specifically stated: "Nothing in this Act shall be construed to authorize, require, or establish military or civilian censorship or in any way to limit or infringe upon freedom of the press or of speech as guaranteed by the Constitution of the United States." Even if there were such legislation, the *Post* continued, Congress could not "by legislation, set aside the mandate of the First Amendment." The *Post* also rapped the government for repeatedly suggesting that the newspaper should have tried to obtain the Pentagon Papers through a lawsuit under the Freedom of Information Act, while at the same time contending that the Papers would not be declassifiable under that act; the brief cited another case where a private citizen "waited some three years or more only to learn that he could not obtain access to documents some twenty-four years old."

But the core of the *Post*'s argument lay in the assertion that "despite the continuation of this ill-conceived litigation, the government's efforts to suppress the truth will not prevail. Copies of all or substantial portions of the Vietnam History have already found their way into the hands of an undetermined number of persons outside the government. . . . Thus, one thing is certain: public revelations of this controversial history will continue apace until it will all become available to the American public."

Before 6 A.M. on Saturday June 26 a line was forming at the Supreme Court building on Capitol Hill; by the time the argument began at 11 A.M. there were 1,500 people—concerned law students who had traveled through the night from distant cities, curious private citizens, and tourists—all competing for the scant 174 seats available to the public in the courtroom. By 9:45 A.M. Mary Drake, a postcard vendor at the Supreme Court entrance, gave up on a good business day and tucked her wares into a closet rather than be trampled underfoot. It was an extraordinary display of interest in the proceedings of a government institution that had often been considered esoteric by much of the public, but that had been wrapped in a swirl of contention ever since opposition developed to the social revolution of the Warren Court.

In the view of many court watchers, the institution had been degraded in the public mind by President Nixon's much touted efforts to remake it in a mold that conformed to his own notion of "strict constructionism." In practical effect, that had meant trying to force the Senate to endorse the President's repayment of a 1968 campaign debt by nominating a conservative Southerner to fill the seat of resigned Justice Abe Fortas. But the Senate rejected Clement F. Haynsworth, Jr., of South Carolina after opponents discovered alleged financial improprieties in his record similar to those attributed to Fortas; it subsequently rejected G. Harrold Carswell of Florida, who had a long record of segregationist and anti-civil rights activity on and off the bench. The administration finally succeeded in getting Harry A. Blackmun of Minnesota onto the court in 1970, but there were still open wounds from the bitter fights over Haynsworth and Carswell. For that reason, among others, the Supreme Court was a beleaguered body in the summer of 1971, less trusted and revered than the civics books had taught that it should be.

With the arrival of the Nixon administration's "Minnesota twins"—Blackmun and Chief Justice Warren E. Burger, who had been confirmed in 1969 as the President's choice to replace the retiring Earl Warren—the court was growing more conservative, less audacious, and perhaps less consistent in some areas of the law. Even Justice Hugo Black was beginning to have second thoughts about some of the decisions of the egalitarian era and occasionally voted with the growing conservative bloc in new cases to trim back the effects of the more sweeping earlier decisions. The Supreme Court was not yet by any means a "Burger Court," but rather a "post-Warren Court" that was utterly unpredictable. Burger had poor relations with some of his senior colleagues on the bench and with veteran court employees; he had exercised his prerogatives as Chief Justice in an intensely political manner. The Chief Justice was prone to embark on highly controversial crusades, including a drive for streamlining the nation's courts to protect the presumed interests of society in general, possibly at the expense of the procedural rights of criminal suspects. He spoke out continually against "a small minority of lawyers" for their alleged misconduct in vigorously defending the people charged in so-called political trials. Overzealous trial lawyers, the Chief Justice would complain readily, have "more adrenalin than judgment."

Burger made no secret of his intense dislike for the press; speaking to the American Law Institute in Washington only a month before the Pentagon Papers case reached the Supreme Court, he said that his complaints about "the end of rational thought process" and incivility were "relevant to the news media." He noted that in nineteenth-century Britain "news media were intensely partisan and vicious and it was not uncommon for political leaders to horsewhip newspaper reporters," and he suggested that there had been a "revival" of nineteenth-century "Know-Nothingism" among the news media in contemporary American life: "Editorials tend to become shrill with invective and political cartoons are savagely reminiscent of a century past." Burger then added that his remarks should be noted by "newspapers not too distant from this building where I speak." He was speaking at the Mayflower Hotel, two blocks from the headquarters of *The Washington Post*. Later, in July, at the annual convention of the American Bar Association in New York, the Chief Justice stressed during a television interview that "we can't do anything about the media. This is a matter of self-restraint. . . . We have just got to have a pervasive civility in dealing with all our problems, and it is more important when the problems are difficult than when the problems are easy."

Although no one could have known it at the time, the unusual Saturday session in the Pentagon Papers case was the last argument before the "post-Warren Court" as it was then constituted. Before the next court term began in October 1971, Justice Hugo Black, the court's unrelenting defender of the First Amendment, would resign after falling ill. (Black died at eighty-seven a few days after resigning having served thirty-four years); and Justice John Marshall Harlan, its intellectual conservative, on learning that he had spinal cancer, would also resign suddenly, giving President Nixon and Attorney General Mitchell an opportunity to nominate two more justices. (Harlan died several months later.) In the newspaper cases the post-Warren Court was characteristically divided, with the four sure liberals voting not to take the issue up at all and merely to reverse all outstanding injunctions against the press and with three conservatives—Harlan, Burger, and Blackmun—voting not only to take the cases but also to grant a secret argument. Justices Stewart and White, customarily caught in the middle, wanted to hear the arguments but opposed going behind closed doors.

Bobbing back and forth on their black leather rocking chairs, the nine justices listened impatiently to Solicitor General Griswold, until Justice Stewart cut in to direct him back to the issue at the heart of the case, whether disclosure of any material in the Pentagon Papers would pose "such grave and

[234]

immediate danger" as to permit an exception to the traditional prohibitions against prior restraint. Harlan, clearly troubled by the hasty schedule that had brought the controversy to the Supreme Court in less than two weeks, quizzed Griswold about how much judicial time had been spent on reviewing the Papers. Reacting to Stewart's assertion that the classification markings of the documents were not central to the case (and perhaps to the disagreement within the Justice Department and the Pentagon on this issue, Griswold reminded the court and himself that he "must be careful not to concede away in this Court grounds which some responsible officers of the government think are important." As for the articles that were appearing in other newspapers, the Solicitor General told Justice William J. Brennan, Jr., those had "all kinds of window dressing" but no new disclosures (which was, by the newspapers' own account, not true). Griswold also repeated his promise of a thorough declassification review of the Papers within forty-five days, regardless of the Supreme Court's decision. (The declassification would ultimately take twice that long.)

In a colloquy with Justice White, Griswold observed that the government's chances of winning a criminal case in connection with the Pentagon Papers would be weak if it lost the injunction effort: "I find it exceedingly difficult to think that any jury would convict or that an appellate court would affirm a conviction of a criminal offense for the publication of materials which this Court has said could be published." Falling back on the especially sensitive material specified in his closed brief, the Solicitor General warned gravely that publication of it "will affect lives. It will affect the process of the termination of the war. It will affect the process of recovering prisoners of war."

Bickel made it clear from the start of his presentation that "we concede, and we have all along in this case conceded for purposes of the argument, that the prohibition against prior

[235]

restraint, like so much else in the Constitution, is not an absolute." But he contended that the inherent powers of the President did not include the capacity "to make substantive law," in the absence of action by the Congress, "which can form the basis for a judicially issued injunction." The government was seeking to make its case, Bickel argued, on the basis of "a chain of causation, whose links are surmise and speculation, all going toward some distant event," rather than any immediate consequence of publishing.

The turning point in the argument probably came when Justice Stewart, apparently wavering between the two sides, posed a hypothetical case to Bickel: "Let us assume that when the members of the Court go back and open up this sealed record, we find something there that absolutely convinces us that its disclosure would result in the sentencing to death of a hundred young men whose only offense had been that they were nineteen years old and had low draft numbers. What should we do?" Bickel, groping for an answer to a difficult dilemma, first said that "I am as confident as I can be of anything that your Honor will not find that when you get back to your chambers." Stewart pressed him: "You would say the Constitution requires that it be published, and that these men die, is that it?" Bickel, with no time to consult his clients—who might have felt otherwise—finally said: "No, I am afraid that my inclinations to humanity overcome the somewhat more abstract devotion to the First Amendment in a case of that sort." He went on to concede that the feared event that could justify a prior restraint need not be "of cosmic nature."

Justice William O. Douglas later cut in to express his dismay that Bickel was apparently reading the First Amendment to "mean that Congress could make *some* laws abridging freedom of the press. . . . That is a very strange argument for the *Times* to be making." Chief Justice Burger followed up with a slap at the press, suggesting that the newspapers were claiming for themselves a right—confidentiality of sources and of operations —that they would deny to the government.

No sooner had William Glendon risen to·argue for the *Post* than Justice Stewart pressed upon him the same question about the "simple deaths, say, of a hundred or two hundred young men." Rather than be trapped, Glendon simply insisted that "the government has not yet brought anything like that case to your Honors, nothing like that. What we have heard . . . is much more in the nature of conjecture and surmise." What the case boiled down to, Glendon argued, was one of "broad claims and narrow proof" by the government, which he portrayed as stalling for time to continue its search for a single item that might persuade a court of impending danger to national security. Burger brought up his complaints against the press again: "You say the newspaper has a right to protect its sources, but the government does not?" Glendon said he saw "no conflict" in that position, since the press is fully protected by the First Amendment. When Justice White expressed his surprise that the *Post* was contending that not a single document in the forty-seven-volume study was entitled to a top-secret classification, Glendon stressed that it was up to the government to specify any that were. "Now it may be," he added facetiously, "that the government would feel that the courts should become the Defense Department's security officer, and that the courts should delve into this pile of paper, forty-seven volumes, on its own from time to time, whenever the government is so moved that the courts should work for them."

Before Glendon sat down, he too was castigated by one of the absolutists on the court, Justice Hugo Black, for appearing to suggest "that the First Amendment, freedom of speech, can be abridged by Congress if it desires to do so."

On rebuttal, Griswold ran into trouble with Justice Thurgood Marshall, who warned that if the court decided for the

[237]

government, it might set a precedent requiring injunctions against press disclosures of similar government studies in the future. "Wouldn't we then—the federal courts—be a censorship board?" Marshall asked. "That is a pejorative way to put it," Griswold said. "I do not know what the alternative is." But Marshall shot back that "the First Amendment might be." The Solicitor General went on to argue that the phrase "no law" in the First Amendment "does not mean 'no law,'" but must be interpreted under contemporary conditions and exigencies. He then chastised the *Times* for putting the public's right to know aside for three months while examining the Pentagon Papers and only later becoming "frantic about it" when the case came into court.

The argument concluded at 1:13 P.M., and the justices retired to private deliberations. The newspapers had hoped for an immediate ruling the same day, with full opinions to follow later, so that they would be free to resume full publication of articles based on the Papers in their Sunday editions, but there was no word from the court. On Monday June 28, while announcing decisions in other cases, Chief Justice Burger merely noted that the court's term had been extended indefinitely while the newspaper cases were under submission. As the unprecedented prior restraint reached its two-week anniversary, the *Times* and the *Post* worried that they would have a long wait while other newspapers that the government had not taken action against went on publishing their own stories. It became apparent, however, when Justice Douglas left town to resume his summer vacation in Goose Prairie, that the case had been decided already and that the court simply needed a few days to pull its opinions together.

One of the most important central figures in the Pentagon Papers controversy was sitting out the court cases in hiding, but not in obscurity. Probably no one would have liked to attend the argument at the Supreme Court more than Daniel Ellsberg, but he was still underground, waiting for the proper moment to surface and formally claim the personal responsibility he felt so strongly. Ellsberg was exasperated by the fact that the fight over freedom of the press had so thoroughly supplanted the actual content of the Papers as the biggest story in the country, but he took a certain discreet satisfaction from the efforts of the government to suppress the history of American involvement in Vietnam. He hoped that it would only whet the appetites of the public to read the Papers carefully if all restraints were lifted.

In the meantime, Daniel Ellsberg's name became a household word. He was on the covers of the major newsmagazines, and his disappearance only enhanced the mystery surrounding him. On Wednesday June 23 Ellsberg granted an exclusive interview to Walter Cronkite of CBS, at a secret location in the Boston area. (To get to Ellsberg, Cronkite had to follow an elaborate set of instructions aimed at avoiding any chance that the FBI would pick up his trail.) "It must be painful for the American people now to read these Papers," Ellsberg told Cronkite, "and to discover that the men to whom they gave so much respect and trust, as well as power, regarded them as contemptuously as they regarded our Vietnamese allies." Asked if he could find any heroes in the history of the war, Ellsberg cited only a sergeant who refused to fire at civilians during the massacre in the Vietnamese village of My Lai; he asserted that the American government "bears major responsibility for every death in combat in Vietnam in the last twenty-five years —and that's one to two million people." Reiterating his contention that the Nixon administration was in its own way escalating the war in Vietnam, Ellsberg said the lesson of the Pentagon Papers and current policy was that "the people of this country can't afford to let the President run the country by himself." He avoided, however, directly acknowledging that he had originally leaked the Papers to the press.

[239]

But a lawyer from the Internal Security Division of the Justice Department, Paul Vincent, was already in Los Angeles directing an urgent grand jury investigation of reports that the Papers had been taken out of the Rand Corporation while Ellsberg was on the staff there. On the basis of affidavits from Carol Ellsberg, his former wife, and three other people, U.S. Magistrate Venetta S. Tassopoulos issued a warrant for Ellsberg's arrest on Friday night June 25, just ɛ ˙ the Supreme Court arguments were being prepared. The warrant charged that Ellsberg had illegally possessed large numbers of volumes from the Papers and had made photocopies of them. (The investigation had been aided by the grand jury testimony of Lynda Sinay, the Los Angeles advertising woman who made a Xerox machine available to Ellsberg late in 1969.)

The next day, two attorneys for Ellsberg—Leonard Boudin, a leading civil liberties lawyer from New York who had defended Dr. Benjamin Spock against conspiracy charges and was now a guest lecturer at the Harvard Law School, and Charles Nesson, a young Harvard law professor also involved in representing controversial radical causes—held a press conference in Boston; they said Ellsberg would surrender himself on Monday June 28 at the office of the U.S. Attorney there. The delay was necessary, they explained, because the Justice Department had refused Ellsberg's offer to turn himself in earlier on the condition that he be guaranteed release without bail over the weekend. The lawyers said that in their view Ellsberg had "violated no law, disobeyed no order of any court, and of course will appear in response to any process," such as the arrest warrant.

At 10 A.M. Monday morning Ellsberg appeared as promised at the Post Office Building in downtown Boston, where the federal courts and U.S. Attorney's office are located. Arriving in a taxi, he told the waiting crowd of newsmen and admirers that he had made the Papers available to Senator Fulbright in 1969 and later to the *Times*. "I did this clearly at my own jeopardy," he said, "and I am prepared to answer to all the consequences of these decisions. That includes the personal consequences to me and my family, whatever these may be. Would you not go to prison to help end this war?" He added that his "only regret" was not releasing the Papers to the press much sooner. At the U.S. Attorney's office Ellsberg was formally placed under arrest by FBI agents, photographed and fingerprinted in the U.S. Marshal's office, and then led to a bail hearing before U.S. Magistrate Peter Princi by two marshals who held his arms tightly. The government, suggesting that Ellsberg "has the resources to remain in hiding and frustrate this court," demanded that bail be set at $100,000; Boudin, on the other hand, demanded his client's release on personal bond. Princi agreed to a release on liberal terms only after Ellsberg rose in court to "make myself responsible to appear" at subsequent court proceedings. The magistrate ordered that Ellsberg's passport be turned over to the court and granted a $50,000 personal recognizance bond, which required no cash payment unless Ellsberg should fail to appear at any time he was scheduled to be in court.

Later the same day the Los Angeles grand jury returned an indictment against Ellsberg, charging him with unauthorized possession of "documents and writings related to the national defense," with failing to turn them in to officers of the government, and with converting the documents to his own use; he was not specifically charged at that time, however, with transmitting the Papers to anyone else.

Meanwhile, in Washington amid great pomp Defense Secretary Melvin Laird sent one copy each of the forty-seven-volume study to the House of Representatives and the Senate. Marked top secret in huge letters, the cardboard cartons containing the Papers were immediately locked up in a vault in the office of the Secretary of the Senate and in the rooms of the House Armed Services Committee, pending the establishment of congressional rules concerning access to the Papers.

While Ellsberg was being indicted and arrested, while Congress—hardly an airtight repository—began to have access, and above all while other newspapers continued their disclosures, the Supreme Court was preparing its pronouncements in the *Times* and *Post* cases. Because of the intense time "pressure" in the case, Chief Justice Burger later explained, it was determined not to attempt to consolidate the justices' views in only a few opinions, as is standard practice: "The simplest thing to do in getting it out in a hurry is each justice states what is on his mind." Late Wednesday morning June 30 word was passed to the nervous group that had been keeping a daily vigil in the Supreme Court's basement press room that the court would convene at 2:30 P.M. that day to announce its decision in the Papers case. At precisely 2:34 the full court, minus Douglas, took the bench, and Burger briefly summarized an unsigned order in favor of the newspapers, freeing them immediately to publish material from the Pentagon Papers.

What the court's real "opinion" was would be a difficult thing to discover, for it was expressed in nine separate essays, six of them supporting the newspapers in greater or lesser degree and three of them favoring the government or refusing to state a position on the merits of the case.

The opinion that appeared to state the court's lowest common denominator against prior restraint was that of Potter Stewart. Noting the President's "enormous power in the two related areas of national defense and international relations . . . pressed to the very hilt since the advent of the nuclear missile age," he said that "the only effective restraint upon executive policy and power . . . may lie in an informed and enlightened citizenry—in an informed and critical public opinion which alone can here protect the values of democratic government. For this reason, it is perhaps here that a press that is alert, aware, and free most vitally serves the basic purpose of the First Amendment. For without an informed and free press there cannot be an enlightened people." At the same time,

Stewart observed, "the Executive [Branch] must have the largely unshared duty to determine and preserve the degree of internal security necessary" to exercise its power successfully; but he delivered a stern warning about the effects of overclassification: "I should suppose that moral, political, and practical considerations would dictate that a very first principle of . . . wisdom would be an insistence upon avoiding secrecy for its own sake. For when everything is classified, then nothing is classified, and the system becomes one to be disregarded by the cynical or the careless, and to be manipulated by those intent on self-protection or self-promotion." Congress could enact laws controlling the circumstances of the Pentagon Papers, Stewart said, but it had not; in the newspaper cases, he complained, "we are asked . . . to perform a function that the Constitution gave to the Executive, not the Judiciary. We are asked, quite simply, to prevent the publication by two newspapers of material that the Executive Branch insists should not, in the national interest, be published. I am convinced that the Executive is correct with respect to some of the documents involved. But I cannot say that disclosure of any of them will surely result in direct, immediate, and irreparable damage to our nation or its people."

The absolute First Amendment position was represented in what would be the last opinion written by Hugo Black. "I believe that every moment's continuance of the injunctions against these newspapers amounts to a flagrant, indefensible, and continuing violation of the First Amendment," he said, scolding his fellow justices for suggesting "that the publication of news may sometimes be enjoined. Such a holding would make a shambles of the First Amendment. . . . the Solicitor General argues . . . that the general powers of the government adopted in the original Constitution should be interpreted to limit and restrict the specific and emphatic guarantees of the Bill of Rights adopted later. I can imagine no greater perversion of history."

Much of Black's opinion, in fact, was devoted to a castigation of Griswold and an encomium to the free press, whose role he defined as "to serve the governed, not the governors. . . . Only a free and unrestrained press can effectively expose deception in government." Alluding to his own disgust over the Vietnam war, Black added that "paramount among the responsibilities of a free press is the duty to prevent any part of the government from deceiving the people and sending them off to distant lands to die of foreign fevers and foreign shot and shell. In my view, far from deserving condemnation for their courageous reporting, *The New York Times, The Washington Post,* and other newspapers should be commended for serving the purpose that the Founding Fathers saw so clearly. In revealing the workings of government that led to the Vietnam war, the newspapers nobly did precisely that which the Founders hoped and trusted they would do." He concluded that "the word 'security' is a broad, vague generality whose contours should not be invoked to abrogate the fundamental law embodied in the First Amendment. The guarding of military and diplomatic secrets at the expense of informed representative government provides no real security for our Republic."

Justice Douglas, in the opinion he left behind before returning to the West Coast, agreed. "These disclosures may have a serious impact," he observed. "But that is no basis for sanctioning a previous restraint on the press. . . . The dominant purpose of the First Amendment was to prohibit the widespread practice of governmental suppression of embarrassing information. It is common knowledge that the First Amendment was adopted against the widespread use of the common law of seditious libel to punish the dissemination of material that is embarrassing to the powers-that-be. . . . A debate of large proportions goes on in the nation over our posture in Vietnam. That debate antedated the disclosure of the contents of the present documents. The latter are highly relevant to the debate in progress. Secrecy in government is fundamentally antidemocratic, perpetuating bureaucratic errors. Open debate and discussion of public issues are vital to our national health."

For his own part, Justice Brennan sought to stress "that our judgment in the present cases may not be taken to indicate the propriety, in the future, of issuing temporary stays and restraining orders to block the publication of material sought to be suppressed by the government. . . . there has now been ample time for reflection and judgment; whatever values there may be in the preservation of novel questions for appellate review may not support any restraints in the future." Brennan implied that of all the nineteen lower court judges to deal with the Pentagon Papers furor, only Judge Gesell had acted properly, by refusing even to stay his own rulings briefly. As a guide for the future, he instructed that "only governmental allegation and proof that publication must inevitably, directly, and immediately cause the occurrence of an event kindred to imperiling the safety of a transport already at sea can support even the issuance of an interim restraining order. . . . every restraint issued in this case, whatever its form, has violated the First Amendment—and none the less so because that restraint was justified as necessary to afford the Court an opportunity to examine the claim more thoroughly."

Justice Marshall, picking up Alexander Bickel's tacit invitation to do so, wrote that it would be "utterly inconsistent with the concept of separation of power for this Court to use its power of contempt to prevent behavior that Congress has specifically declined to prohibit. . . . The Solicitor General does not even mention in his brief whether the government considers there to be probable cause to believe a crime has been committed or whether there is a conspiracy to commit future crimes." Reviewing the congressional refusal in 1917 and in the 1950s to extend the Espionage Act to cover newspaper publication, Marshall concluded that "either the government has the power under statutory grant to use traditional criminal law to protect the country or, if there is no basis for arguing that Congress has made the activity a crime, it is plain that Congress has specifically refused to grant the authority the government seeks from this Court. . . . It is not for this Court to fling itself into every breach perceived by some government official nor is it for this Court to take on itself the burden of enacting law, especially law that Congress has refused to pass." Nowhere in his opinion, however, was the First Amendment even mentioned.

In a long opinion that barely straddled the fence between concurring and dissenting (but that attracted the agreement of Justice Stewart), Justice White said he voted with the majority "only because of the concededly extraordinary protection against prior restraints enjoyed by the press under our constitutional system." He said he was quite convinced that disclosure of some material in the Pentagon Papers "will do substantial damage to public interests," but that the government had not effectively carried its burden in court. In a remark that produced great discomfort for the newspapers and substantial glee within the Justice Department, White stressed that "terminating the ban on publication of the relatively few sensitive documents the government now seeks to suppress does not mean that the law either requires or invites newspapers or others to publish them or that they will be immune from criminal action if they do. Prior restraints require an unusually heavy justification under the First Amendment; but failure by the government to justify prior restraints does not measure its constitutional entitlement to a conviction for criminal publication. That the government mistakenly chose to proceed by injunction does not mean that it could not successfully proceed in another way." He then invited the attention of the Justice Department to the statutes that he thought might be applicable and advised that "I would have no difficulty sustaining convictions under these sections," a point that Griswold had already conceded during the oral argument. In a reassuring caveat, White pointed out that "I am not, of course, saying that either of these newspapers has yet committed a crime or that either would commit a crime if they published all the material now in their possession."

In his dissent, Justice Harlan complained that the court had been "almost irresponsibly feverish in dealing with these cases. . . . [A] frenzied train of events took place in the name of the presumption against prior restraints created by the First Amendment. Due regard for the extraordinarily important and difficult questions involved in these litigations should have led the Court to shun such a precipitate timetable." Harlan then listed seven major questions that ought to have been seriously considered in the course of the Pentagon Papers dispute. He noted, however, that "forced as I am to reach" a judgment on the substantive issues in the case, he would have ruled to send the cases back to Judges Gurfein and Gesell for additional hearings on the government's contentions. The executive determination of what should be considered secret deserves preference, Harlan said, in what would also become his last opinion after sixteen years on the court. "Even if there is some room for the Judiciary to override the Executive determination," he added, "it is plain that the scope of review must be exceedingly narrow. I can see no indication in the opinions of either the District Court or the Court of Appeals in the *Post* litigation that the conclusions of the Executive were given even the deference owing to an administrative agency, much less that owing to a co-equal branch of the government operating within the field of its constitutional prerogative."

The court's junior member, Justice Blackmun, said that he agreed with Harlan's opinion as well as with much that White had said "by way of admonition." He also felt that consideration of the newspaper cases had proceeded too quickly: "The country would be none the worse off were the cases tried quickly, to be sure, but in the customary and properly deliberative manner. The most recent of the material, it is said, dates no later than 1968, already about three years ago, and the *Times* itself took three months to formulate its plan of procedure and, thus, deprived its public for that period." He complained that the issues required "court opinions of a quality better than has been seen to this point" (a surprising statement from a justice who had himself been criticized for insufficient and confusing opinions during his brief time on the high court). Blackmun chose to identify himself with the views of the one judge among nineteen in the lower courts, Malcolm R. Wilkey of the U.S. Court of Appeals for the District of Columbia Circuit, who had actually found documents in the Papers that if published might produce "harm" to the nation.

In an extraordinary conclusion, Blackmun said: "I hope that damage already has not been done. If, however, damage has been done . . . then the nation's people will know where the responsibility for these sad consequences rests." Alone on the court, and alone among a total of twenty-eight judges, he suggested that the newspapers might actually become responsible for prolonging the war in Vietnam and further delaying the release of American prisoners of war.

The thrust of Chief Justice Burger's dissent was also on procedure and the "unseemly haste" in which the cases had been conducted. "We do not know the facts," he insisted. Among other things, Burger exaggeratedly characterized the newspapers as making an absolute claim under the First Amendment and mocked the *Times* for asserting "a sole trusteeship" over the public's right to know. In addition to the prior restraint exceptions delineated by Chief Justice Hughes in the Near v. Minnesota opinion, he suggested, "there are no doubt other exceptions no one has had occasion to describe or discuss. Conceivably such exceptions may be lurking in these cases and would have been flushed out had they been properly considered in the trial courts, free from unwarranted deadlines and frenetic pressures."

"Would it have been unreasonable," Burger asked, "since

the newspaper could anticipate the government's objections to release of secret material, to give the government an opportunity to review the entire collection and determine whether agreement could be reached on publication?" He characterized as "hardly believable" the notion that "a newspaper long regarded as a great institution in American life would fail to perform one of the basic and simple duties of every citizen with respect to the discovery or possession of stolen property or secret government documents. That duty, I had thought—perhaps naively—was to report, forthwith, to responsible public officers. This duty rests on taxi drivers, justices, and *The New York Times.*"

Emerging from consideration of what he called "this melancholy series of events," Burger noted that "we all crave speedier judicial processes, but when judges are pressured as in these cases the result is a parody of the judicial process."

Amazingly, a week later, Burger told the American Bar Association that the Supreme Court had been "actually unanimous" in the Pentagon Papers case about "the basic problems of First Amendment rights of newspapers."

[CHAPTER XIII]

The 6–3 decision by the Supreme Court was received jubi-
lantly by newspapers across the United States, which—whether
enjoined or not, whether printing Pentagon Papers or not—had
become immensely involved in the confrontation between government and press. Banner-headlined virtually everywhere, the
high court ruling encouraged even the more timid newspapers
to join in the disclosures, material for which would now be
readily available on wire service tickers from three or four
different sources at once. The litigants, above all, swung into
immediate action to vindicate their original plans.

At *The Washington Post* deputy national editor Mary Lou
Beatty heard the news first on a phone line to the Supreme
Court; she shouted to a quieter than usual news room: "It
looks as though we've won." Almost simultaneously managing
editor Eugene Patterson emerged from the wire room, jumped

onto a desk, and called to his colleagues: "We win, and so does *The New York Times*." Reporters applauded and began paying off bets they had made during the four days of waiting for word from the Supreme Court. Within moments executive editor Ben Bradlee posted a memorandum to his staff: "There is just no way of saying how proud I am of this wonderful newspaper and everyone on it. The guts and energy and responsibility of everyone involved in this fight, and the sense that you all were involved, has impressed me more than anything in my life. You are beautiful." There was an outpouring of official statements, and *Post* publisher Katharine Graham said: "We are extremely gratified, not only from the point of views of newspapers . . . but gratified from the point of view of government, good government, and the public's right to know." Without regard to whether the information had appeared elsewhere, the *Post* printed three articles from its Pentagon Papers series on Thursday morning July 1.

"It's a glorious day," said *New York Times* managing editor A. M. Rosenthal. "We won it. We've all won it. We've won the right to print." Out of their own sense of history Rosenthal, *Times* publisher Arthur Ochs Sulzberger, and general counsel James C. Goodale held a press conference to express their delight. Sulzberger declared it "a landmark case" and described himself as "extremely ecstatic." Like a locker room after a big football victory, the *Times* news room was closed to outsiders a half-hour before the Supreme Court convened, but one reporter said later that at the moment the news was learned "silent disbelief" was immediately followed by "a great deal of hugging, handclapping, and jumping up and down." The *Times* published its edition with two unchanged installments from its original series, both based on the Kennedy administration, and also announced that the entire series and accompanying documents would be published ten days later as a paperback book.

In Boston, the editors of the *Globe* had set up an elaborate procedure to assure that if the Supreme Court decision was favorable to the newspapers, there would be time to retrieve their copy of the Papers from the bank vault before the 4 P.M. bank closing time. As soon as word came over the news wires that the Justices had ruled favorably, John Driscoll, assistant to *Globe* editor Tom Winship, pulled the documents out of the bank; as Driscoll was heading for the *Globe* offices in Dorchester, veteran fire department reporter Frank Mahoney rushed downtown in his special car with a flashing red light to bring the *Globe* lawyers photocopies of the wire stories. The lawyers, who had prepared court papers in advance, attached the wire stories and went immediately before U.S. District Judge Anthony Julian; he rescinded his tough restraining order in conformity with the high court ruling so that, in Winship's words, "we could get back to newspapering." While the *Globe* prepared to run the remainder of its Pentagon Papers in the last edition of its afternoon paper, Winship praised the Supreme Court for having "reaffirmed our constitutional right to put out a newspaper without the government or the courts looking over our shoulder." In St. Louis the *Post-Dispatch* was freed from its restraint after Judge James H. Meredith dictated an order by telephone from Minnesota, where he was attending the Eighth Circuit Judicial Conference. The order was issued in time for the *Post-Dispatch* to resume its stories based on the Papers in its final edition that same afternoon, Wednesday June 30.

From the Justice Department and the White House there was no official comment on the outcome of the unprecedented effort to bridle the newspapers. Presidential press secretary Ronald Ziegler was rankled by reporters' requests for President Nixon's reaction to the Supreme Court decision and provided this unsettling answer: "There is really no need for him to issue a statement on this. The President's view on the First Amendment is well known." The Pentagon sent Congress a message saying that as soon as a declassification review was completed, it would provide a copy of the Papers to every member of each body. Congressional reaction was predictably partisan. Congressman William Moorhead (D-Pa.), chairman of the House Subcommittee on Foreign Operations and Government Information, whose hearings that same week had been given new life by the Pentagon Papers controversy, complained that the high court decision had not been unanimous. Senator Barry Goldwater (R-Ariz.) said he hoped the administration would push ahead with criminal prosecution of Daniel Ellsberg and the management of *The New York Times.*

Virtually obscured in the excitement over the Supreme Court decision was the fact that the night before, a relatively unknown U.S. Senator from Alaska had done what other members of Congress had been refusing to do for more than a year and a half. In an unusual one-man session of the Senate Subcommittee on Buildings and Grounds, of which he was chairman, maverick Democrat Mike Gravel invoked his congressional privilege in distributing large chunks of the Pentagon Papers to anyone in the press who wanted them. Although it stirred little reaction at first, Gravel's decision would become one of the most significant in the saga of the Pentagon Papers, and his name would become almost as important as that of Daniel Ellsberg in the legal whirlpool that followed. It also insured the availability of some sections of the Papers that might otherwise never have reached the public.

Maurice Robert Gravel, the son of French Canadians and a native of Springfield, Massachusetts, moved west to Alaska to seek fame and fortune after his graduation from Columbia University. He found both, first as a real estate developer and then as a young member of the Alaska state legislature. In 1968 Gravel challenged veteran Alaska politician Ernest Gruening, then 81, for the Democratic nomination for the Senate. Gruening, along with Oregon's Wayne Morse, had taken the most radical antiwar stand in the Senate, labeling the United States the aggressor in Vietnam. Gravel won the primary and the general election, and on arrival in Washington he had the image of a moderate Democrat concerned largely with home-state issues. Although Gravel later pointed to the May 1970 American invasion of Cambodia as the moment when he began to consider the war a major issue and agreed to be a co-sponsor of the McGovern-Hatfield amendment, he waited more than six months to speak out about it. An impulsive, unpredictable man, Gravel did not tell his staff in advance when he made his first comments against the war, without preparation, on the Senate floor on December 15, 1970. After that Gravel began casting about for an issue that he might use as a vehicle for his new-found antiwar feeling, and he settled on the draft, which was up for renewal and was an emotion-charged issue back home; Alaska's age profile is lower than that of the nation in general, so the draft hits the state especially hard.

Gravel had anything but a consistent liberal voting record in the Senate. Although he had opposed the antiballistic missile (ABM, the subject of his maiden Senate speech), he supported President Nixon's nomination of Clement Haynsworth to the Supreme Court, voted to fund the supersonic transport (SST) against the advice of environmentalists, and supported the federal guarantee of a loan to keep the Lockheed Aircraft Corporation afloat. One of his most controversial votes was against changing Senate Rule XXII, which guarantees the right of unlimited debate, or the filibuster, in the Senate. Gravel, among others, felt that the filibuster in changing times could be as useful to liberals as it had been for years to Southern conservatives attempting to talk civil rights legislation to death. Without much visible support, except from Senator Alan Cranston (D-Cal.), Gravel announced that he would launch his own filibuster to prevent the draft from being renewed on schedule on June 30, 1971. No match for the old-time parliamentarians of the august Senate, Gravel had lost the floor the previous December—during a dispute over military aid funds for Cambodia—because he was not sufficiently aware of the rules, but this time he had studied up. He was determined to make his mark at least by stopping the draft temporarily.

On Friday June 18, the same day *The Washington Post* first published a story based on the Pentagon Papers, Mike Gravel got a phone call offering him some sensational props for his filibuster—the same Papers that had been turned away by his senior, better-known colleagues as too hot to handle. "We asked him whether he would be willing to use the material in the draft filibuster," Daniel Ellsberg explained, "and he said yes. So I got him a copy. . . . From all evidence known to me, he was simply the only person in the Senate willing to do it. . . . from the beginning of the year, Gravel had been acting very forthright." Ellsberg had never met the Alaska Senator and really didn't know much about him, but he was disgusted with the others he had tried and still felt that his own legal posture might improve if only the Papers could be officially released by someone who enjoyed congressional immunity under Article I, Section 6, Clause 1 of the Constitution, which provides that "for any Speech or Debate in either House [Senators and Congressmen] shall not be questioned in any other Place."

The intermediaries for Ellsberg, following the technique they were developing with newspapers, suggested cloak-and-dagger meetings for discussing and transferring the Papers; but Gravel, who was a military counterintelligence agent in Europe during the early 1950s ("involved in extensive wire-tapping throughout Europe," as he remembers it), insisted that "we should do things very honorably, honestly, very above-board." One meeting, for example, was held in the middle of a summer day on the Capitol steps, and while Gravel was discussing arrangements, the chairman of the Republican National Committee, Senator Robert Dole of Kansas, interrupted with pleasantries. When the Papers were actually ready for him the following Thursday, June 24, Gravel drove up just before midnight to the Mayflower Hotel on Connecticut Avenue in Washington, in a car with license plates clearly indicating that he was a U.S. Senator from Alaska. Arriving a little ahead of schedule, he went into the lobby, only to run into some visiting Alaskan natives whom he knew from Anchorage. Gravel got back outside just in time for the arrival of another car with a cardboard box the size of a large orange crate. With two staff aides watching from another car (so they would not personally have to handle the material until it had been in the Senator's possession), Gravel transferred the box to the trunk of his own car and drove to his office in the New Senate Office Building.

But Gravel was concerned that security would not be good enough in the busy office building, so he took the Papers to his home in suburban Prince George's County, Maryland. "I put them underneath my bed," he recalled later. "We put little stacks under the bed, little stacks all along my side of the bed, and I joked with my wife that I wouldn't put it under her side of the bed so she wouldn't be endangered by it. And so every night when we were done work, we would take the Papers and put them underneath the bed. That way we had constant security." "Work" at that point meant culling through the documents, deciding what to use, and having those portions retyped for release. At first Gravel told only his wife, his administrative assistant, and his press secretary that he had the Papers; but one by one he invited other members of his Senate staff to "pack an overnight bag and come over to the house." As each one arrived—there were about ten people eventually, sleeping on couches and the floor—Gravel would spell out the options: "I would tell them that I don't know the entire legal ramifications and they could be in danger, but this is what I have and this is what I intend to do. . . . If they wanted to stay, they could stay at their own risk; or if they wanted to leave, they could take about a three-day vacation and say nothing." Everyone stayed.

By Monday Gravel's resolve was strengthened, although his staff was skeptical. He was discouraged that the Supreme Court was not ruling more quickly and feared that the case might drag on for weeks; he also felt insulted by the way the Pentagon had sent the Papers to the House and Senate, in a manner that minimized the opportunities to communicate their contents to the public. To his surprise Gravel discovered that Charles L. Fishman, a slick fast-talking, free-lance political activist in the peace movement who "was sort of drifting into my employ," was a lawyer; on Sunday they had flown to New York together for a Democratic fund-raising dinner and Gravel had confided to Fishman what he was planning to do. By the next day Fishman had two experts in congressional immunity from the Temple University and Rutgers University law schools in Washington doing research on the Senator's unique potential legal problems.

On Monday night Gravel held a staff meeting at his home, to which he also invited a few close friends. They recommended nearly unanimously that he abandon his plan to disclose the Pentagon Papers because of the "political danger" to which he was exposing himself. "But I had made up my mind to do it," he recalled later. "I realized it could possibly cost me my Senate seat, and the worst that could happen would be that I would lose my Senate seat and I'd have to go back to real estate, and I'd probably make a lot of money. I've got a very good talent and I work very hard. . . . But this was very bad because I love the Senate, I've always wanted to be a Senator and that's the worst thing that could happen to me. I had made up my mind on Sunday night that I was ready to pay that price, and once I got to that point I felt okay. . . . Everybody but my wife advised me against doing it, and I just argued—the very simple fact that we are killing people in Vietnam, we're engaging in a murderous war that has no purpose, that does not advance our security, and I don't understand the American psyche that tolerates this. Because of this,

[257]

somebody had to do something. That was one part of the logic. The other part was that I admired Ellsberg for what he did. He had gone to the barricades."

Alan Cranston of California, perhaps the only member of the Senate who could have dissuaded Gravel, called on him at his office on Tuesday morning to try just that. The Alaskan listened carefully but refused to relent; later in the day he scrawled a personal note to Cranston on the back of the letter from the Secretary of the Senate announcing the availability of the Papers on a restricted basis:

> Because of some gift you have . . . there does not happen to be a generation gap between us as colleagues. In fact because of my affection for you . . . I count you one of my closest friends in the Senate.
>
> The Pentagon Papers that I have read convince me that the first and foremost reason that our nation is in a mess today and going toward bankruptcy is as a result of our paranoic fear of communism. This is unfounded for the simple reason we have far and away a superior [sic].
>
> What I'm doing today is in the name of helping this great nation we all love.
>
> My frustration is born of the fact that we as leaders and as a nation are party to the killing daily of innocent people for no apparent reason. . . . certainly it does not add to our security.
>
> Allen [sic], the people have not lost trust in the leadership of this nation. The Pentagon Papers show that the American leadership in government had no trust and continue to lack trust in the Am. people. That is wrong in a democracy.
>
> I hope you will appreciate and understand why I have to do what I am as an Am. citizen and a US Senator.
>
> Mike

Gravel was determined to set a record for the longest filibuster in American history by reading from the Pentagon Papers for thirty consecutive hours, beginning Tuesday night

[258]

and going on through Wednesday midnight, when the draft expired. (The U.S. Senate record was held by Strom Thurmond of South Carolina, who conducted a one-man talkathon against the civil rights bill of 1957 by talking for 24 hours and 19 minutes, interrupted only briefly for the swearing-in of a new Senator; but state Senator Kilmer Corbin of Lubbock, Texas, set the all-time record by filibustering against a state tax bill for 26 hours and 15 minutes in 1955.) Gravel visited the Senate doctor to make preparations in case he should have to stay at his desk on the Senate floor the entire time: he had a urinal to strap to his leg, a liquid diet designed to last for thirty hours, support hose for his legs, and a brace for his bad back. On Tuesday afternoon Gravel spent a couple of hours in a hot pool trying to relax (he had not slept well ever since receiving the Papers) and had an enema "so that I would be completely cleaned out before going on the floor. . . . I was geared up like a guy going into battle."

Late Tuesday afternoon Gravel's press secretary received a call from syndicated columnist Jack Anderson's office, seeking to confirm a rumor that Gravel had the Pentagon Papers and asking what he intended to do with them. The rumor was profusely denied, but at that point Gravel began to worry that word had spread—"maybe someone would assault the office and try to grab the records." He contacted the Washington office of Vietnam Veterans Against the War to send over some "troops" to guard his office while final preparations were made. Gravel wrote personal notes to Majority Leader Mike Mansfield of Montana and Majority Whip Robert C. Byrd of West Virginia, much like the one he had written to Cranston, explaining his motives for the filibuster. He entered the Senate at about 5 P.M. with a huge black satchel and gave the notes to the two Democratic leaders but asked them not to open them until about 11 P.M. Gravel explained privately to them that he hoped to talk for thirty hours beginning at 6 P.M., after all normal business had been transacted, and that Cranston

[259]

would serve as presiding officer whenever no one else was available in the Senate chamber to do so. At Mansfield's request, Gravel agreed to pause for a few hours the following morning to permit time for routine matters.

As Gravel arrived with his satchel, he was approached by Democratic presidential hopeful Senator Edmund Muskie of Maine (whose friendship Gravel had been courting ambitiously). Muskie asked: "What are you going to do, Mike?" "Oh, I'm going to read a little bit," Gravel replied. "What the hell you got?" Muskie asked with a laugh. "The Pentagon Papers?" Gravel laughed back as Muskie went on to discuss politics and then left.

At 5:55 P.M. Gravel took the floor and announced that he was going to talk all night; as a courtesy to Senate employees who would have to stay along with him, however, he instituted a pro forma quorum call. While the Senators' names were read off, the employees would have time to call home and make any other necessary arrangements. That was the freshman Senator's fatal mistake. As is customary, Byrd had informed his Republican counterpart, Robert Griffin of Michigan, of Gravel's plans, and Griffin complained that he did not want to stay or to leave Gravel alone in the Senate chamber. Gravel assured Griffin that he would not offer any unanimous consent requests, but the Republican whip was not satisfied and exercised his opportunity to turn the quorum call into a live one—effectively halting all business on the Senate floor until fifty-one Senators personally appeared to answer to their names, a virtual impossibility to achieve on a summer evening without prior arrangement.

Griffin suggested to Gravel that he "talk another time" that was more convenient, but the Alaskan was adamant and irate. At one point during the quorum call, when Griffin attempted a rapprochement, Gravel told him: "You motherfucker, as long as I'm a member of the Senate, I'll never forget this." Although there were only six Senators in the chambers initially,

Gravel would not give up easily. Back in his office, staff members feverishly tried to round up other Senators to answer the quorum call, but by 7 P.M. only twenty-one members had trickled in to respond to their names. Most Senate Democrats were at a fund-raising party at the Washington Hilton; they were hesitant about returning for a mysterious and uncommon nighttime session—Gravel, out of fear that some unexpected action might be taken against him, had still not revealed the actual purpose of the marathon speech he planned. Senators Walter Mondale (D-Minn.) and Vance Hartke (D-Ind.) did return to the floor and advised Gravel that he "didn't have a prayer" of getting a quorum together. Nonetheless, the Alaskan kept the Senate officially in session until 9:28 P.M., while the roll was droned out over and over again. But only thirty Senators ever responded that night.

At 7:45, however, Charles Fishman ordered the preparation of a press release announcing a night session of the Subcommittee on Buildings and Grounds of the Senate Public Works Committee. "Plan B" was swinging into operation. By virtue of the seniority system, when Senator Thomas Eagleton (D-Mo.) had turned it down to take another position, Gravel had become chairman of Buildings and Grounds, one of the least prestigious and desirable subcommittees in the august body. On a desk in Gravel's office that night lay a lawbook marked at two cases —one indicating that congressional immunity was not confined to words actually spoken in debate but extended to committee reports, voting, "and other things generally done in a session of the House by one of its members," and another affirming that under the Constitution "Congressmen were insulated from criminal sanctions and civil liability if they were engaged in legitimate legislative activity such as the conduct of congressional committee hearings." Notices were hurriedly typed up and slipped under the doors of the dark offices of subcommittee members John V. Tunney (D-Cal.), J. Caleb Boggs (R-Del.), and Lowell P. Weicker (R-Conn.), announcing a hearing to inquire into the lack of adequate funds for construction and maintenance of public buildings in the United States. Senators Alan Cranston and Harold E. Hughes (D-Iowa) were invited to be members of the audience—along with about twenty tourists and a growing contingent of newsmen—and Fishman recruited Congressman John Dow (D-N.Y.), in whose district the U.S. military academy at West Point is located, as a "witness." (Gravel had never met Dow before.) In fact, Dow never testified, because Gravel's "introductory remarks," launched at 9:45 P.M., took several hours.

"I have in my possession the Pentagon Papers," Gravel began, after settling into a hearing room down the hall from his office. "I did not seek to acquire them. They were given to me. To not make them public would be a dereliction of duty morally. . . . I do not have them all, but I believe that I possess more than half of the total work." A stenographer was on hand to get down every word, as Gravel read first from the section of the Papers dealing with the Post-World War II era under President Truman and proceeded chronologically. Television cameras arrived shortly after 11 P.M., and the audience swelled with antiwar veterans eager to cheer Gravel on. Pausing occasionally, the Senator remarked caustically at one point that his was "probably the most historic meeting of the Buildings and Grounds Subcommittee in its history."

At 1 A.M., with television cameras whirring as he reached a section of the Papers describing the severing of arms and legs in battle, Gravel burst out crying. A few minutes later, with tears running down his cheeks, Gravel adjourned the hearing, after obtaining the unanimous consent of all subcommittee members present (himself) to insert the rest of the Papers into the subcommittee record and to leave the record open for an additional ten days. Earlier in the evening Gravel's administrative assistant had received a call from Daniel Ellsberg, who extended his encouragement and appreciation for the Senator's action. The call intensified Gravel's desire to get the Papers out despite having been thwarted in his original plan to read them on the Senate floor; upon returning to his office from the hearing room, he resisted anew his staff's cautions against proceeding on the assumption that the classified documents were now fully covered by congressional immunity and ordered that segments of hundreds of pages each be made generally available to the press. Gravel's slow-moving photocopy machine turned out only one copy of each page, but the segments were then rushed by reporters to the news room of *The Washington Post* for duplication in massive quantity. The next morning, the Washington bureau of the Associated Press xeroxed more of the Papers being issued from Gravel's office and put out large chunks of the Pentagon study on its news wire. If there had been any limits at all on dissemination of the Papers up to that point, they were now removed. On the morning the Supreme Court was preparing to rule on the government's suits against the newspapers, virtually every news organization with a Washington bureau, and many without, were preparing stories based on the secret study of American policy in Vietnam.

It was not immediately clear whether Gravel had actually violated the law or Senate regulations, but there could be no doubt that he had transgressed the unwritten, uncodified rules of the Senate club. The Alaskan had promised to return to the Senate floor on Wednesday morning June 30 to read more from the Papers, but he never appeared, instead staying home to rest. "I was tired. I figured I had done my thing," he explained later. The members of the club used the occasion to do theirs, criticizing Gravel publicly and privately from the moment the Senate convened that day. Barry Goldwater urged that Gravel "should have his security clearance removed." Warren Magnuson (D-Wash.) called the night hearing "highly irregular." B. Everett Jordan (D-N.C.), chairman of the Senate Committee on Rules and Administration, suggested that "I may

[263]

have to consider changing the rules on late committee meetings." Buildings and Grounds Subcommittee member Lowell Weicker (R-Conn.) flatly pronounced Gravel's meeting illegal and said that "his handling of this was poor." Chairman Jennings Randolph (D-W.Va.) let it be known that the parent Public Works Committee was not about to pay for the transcription of proceedings, because the meeting covered matters "not germane to our committee's business." If Gravel had come to work that day, he would have found that Democratic Whip Robert C. Byrd had invoked a rule of germaneness and engineered a three-minute limit on speeches not directly relevant to legislation under consideration. Democratic leaders toyed with the idea of putting the entire Senate into executive session if Gravel tried to read from any further classified documents on the floor.

Republican leaders Hugh Scott of Pennsylvania and Robert Griffin of Michigan met with Democratic leader Mike Mansfield that day to express their anger with Gravel and to urge that disciplinary action be taken against him. But Mansfield emerged from the meeting saying that he did not "intend to demean or castigate any Senator without good, sufficient, and overruling cause. Gravel feels this matter deeply and personally and that explains his motive." The personal note had obviously worked. On Saturday of the Fourth of July weekend, while Congress was in recess, Gravel met privately with Mansfield— both had stayed in Washington for the holiday—and it became clear to the Alaskan Senator that he was not in serious trouble; it was agreed, however, that Gravel should make an "explanatory statement" to the Senate and, at the first opportunity, to the Public Works Committee.

When the Senate reconvened after the long weekend, Gravel went to Public Works Committee chairman Jennings Randolph and found him "very angry"; only because the committee had never gotten around to adopting formally a new Senate rule requiring adequate notice to all committee or subcommittee members before any meeting (intended to prevent chairmen from acting arbitrarily and excluding members in disfavor from meetings) did Randolph back off from taking action against Gravel. On the floor, however, the Alaskan was received enthusiastically by many of his colleagues, including James Allen (D-Ala.), John C. Stennis (D-Miss.), and others who thoroughly disagree with his politics. In keeping with his promise to Mansfield, he rose to read a rough-hewn, defiant, but somewhat humble statement:

There are instances in one's public career which bear explanation. For me, the events of last Tuesday evening is such an instance. Often the circumstances surrounding such instances offer sufficient explanation. At times they do not. Let me first say that it was in response to what I sincerely deemed as my duty as a United States Senator, and because I was not able to speak on the floor of the United States Senate, that I convened a hearing before the Subcommittee on Buildings and Grounds which I am proud to chair.

Each of us must act in accordance with the dictates of our conscience. Were it otherwise, we should not serve as Senators. It was within such a framework that last Tuesday I undertook to discharge my obligations. In doing so, perhaps, I did not approach the matter with the same degree of delicacy another would employ. However, I can assure you that I would not place myself below any member in the degree of respect and affection I hold for the Senate. What I did, I did sincerely and patriotically in the best interest of this nation we all love. I did it as a Senator of my State of Alaska, representing the people of Alaska, and as a Senator of the United States working for the interests of all Americans.

What I did, I felt and continue to feel, will bring credit to the United States Senate, not embarrassment. I would never be party to any act that would bring discredit to this august body. In this connection, I have met with the distinguished Majority Leader. I did so seeking his advice and counsel on these matters. For his understanding, I am deeply grateful.

After he had finished, without prior arrangement, Senator Birch Bayh (D-Ind.) also spoke in Gravel's behalf. Things seemed to have been smoothed over successfully. On Thursday July 8, however, the Public Works Committee met in executive session, and the main item of business on the agenda was Gravel's meeting of the week before. Edmund Muskie spoke in support of Gravel. When the issue arose of how the expense of the subcommittee hearing would be met, Senator Weicker, in an apparent attempt to embarrass Gravel, offered to pay half the cost from his own pocket. Several Republican Senators criticized Gravel, but only Robert Dole of Kansas, chairman of the Republican National Committee, appeared eager to press for a declaration that the rump meeting had been "illegal." Gravel, well-primed by his lawyers, reacted by warning that to declare the meeting illegal would be to threaten his congressional immunity and, by extension, that of all Senators. He reread the statement he had previously delivered on the Senate floor, now marked with appropriate references to the committee and with an extra page added:

> I used the Subcommittee as a tool to get vital information to the American people. I did this without consultation with any member of the Committee. I do not regret doing it but do sincerely regret being forced into a situation that jostled the sensibilities of colleagues on the Committee as a result of my holding a hearing in a manner different to the more normal practice.
>
> Because of the unusual nature of the hearing and not over the legality of the hearing, I would like to make my own arrangements for the cost of the transcript in question and any other cost associated with this hearing. I am sure it will not be a personal burden to me because I have already received donations and I have received promises of additional donations.
>
> I will render to the Chairman total accountability of the cost and payment and method of payment which report I presume will be filed with the Committee. I personally hold all members on this Committee in very high esteem and affec-

tion. I hope that all of you will understand my motivation and appreciate my goals regardless of your individual agreement or disagreement on my ideological views on this question.

Eventually, passions cooled and the meeting adjourned without any formal determination of the status of Gravel's hearing or any pronouncement on his conduct. Gravel ultimately had the transcript prepared at his own expense and locked it up in his office safe.

Officially, the matter was concluded. But in interviews later established members of the Senate club acknowledged that Gravel had broken the "rules" in a way that could haunt him throughout his career in the Congress. Some senior Senators merely questioned whether the Alaskan's action had been worth the trouble, especially since the Supreme Court ruling was imminent. But one Democrat running for President complained that Gravel had been "hysterical" and, like Ellsberg, had come off as "a repentant hawk trying to get right on the issue of Vietnam." Gravel's midnight hearing, this Senator added, was "90 percent grandstanding." Later, however, when Gravel was under attack by the Justice Department, one of his staunchest defenders would be Senator Sam J. Ervin, Jr. (D-N.C.), chairman of the Senate Constitutional Rights Subcommittee and one of the leading congressional spokesmen for individual liberties, freedom of speech—and congressional immunity.

Mike Gravel is a man with a great sense of personal history, and on June 29 he felt he had reached a major crossroads with his decision to make the Pentagon Papers generally available, a step that no other member of Congress had been willing to take. Gravel wanted to have his own official chronicler on hand in the Senate to keep track of events and record them for posterity. He called Paul Jacobs, a television commentator in San Francisco with whom he was friendly, to ask for suggestions. Jacobs recommended Leonard S. Rodberg, a fellow at the Institute for Policy Studies in Washington and a Ph.D.

physicist who was formerly chief of science policy research for the U.S. Arms Control and Disarmament Agency. Rodberg had recently co-edited a book entitled *The Pentagon Watchers* and was a well-known figure in the intellectual antiwar movement. He was signed on as a member of Gravel's personal staff only a few hours before the attempted filibuster, although the Senator never met his new aide until after the Buildings and Grounds Subcommittee hearing. Rodberg, who was already familiar with the Pentagon Papers from the institute, followed his new employer's actions throughout the night—recording, for example, the exact moment at which he broke down crying while reading from the Papers—but only talked with him at length for the first time on July 5.

By then Gravel had decided that he would like to publish his copy of the Pentagon Papers—officially, the record of his subcommittee hearing—which was more complete than any other version that would ultimately be generally available to the public. The Senator, relatively unacquainted with the press, was deeply disappointed that the newspapers, after winning their Supreme Court victory, did not publish a new series of stories based on the material he had made available.

On July 8 Gravel flew to New York with Rodberg and David Obst, a young antiestablishment literary agent in Washington, to arrange publication of the Papers by Simon and Schuster in a single eight-hundred-page telephone-book-size volume. After brief discussions, the publishing firm seemed enthusiastic and agreed to an initial printing of 200,000 copies. Gravel was satisfied enough to fly off to Alaska, while Rodberg and Obst handled final details with a lawyer on Simon and Schuster's board of directors, who wanted to read the Papers before approving the agreement. Leaving half the Papers in New York with the board member, Rodberg and Obst returned to Washington on Friday night July 9 to prepare the rest for submission to the publisher. At midnight, however, they received a phone call saying that the deal was off. That same night Bantam

Books had released the paperback edition of *The New York Times* stories on the Pentagon Papers. The Bantam edition sold thousands of copies in the first few hours it was available, and Simon and Schuster felt that book would "eat up the market."

The next week Rodberg and Obst tried several other New York publishers, but none was willing to take a business risk with Gravel's copy of the Papers. Obst was soon diverted to marketing Ellsberg's collected essays on Vietnam in book form, and Rodberg, in desperation, turned to less well-equipped academic publishers. Carrying the Papers in two enormous satchels, he went to Boston to see the MIT Press, which had already discussed the Pentagon Papers on a hypothetical basis and had agreed that it would be a good idea to publish them. Rodberg met with Howard R. Webber, director of the university press, who agreed to recommend publication to his editorial board. The board met on Friday July 16, not in the offices of the MIT Press as was customary, but in the office of the university president. At the meeting a corporate lawyer from Boston warned that to publish the Papers might be "a criminal act," and considerable discussion was focused on the number of people at MIT with security clearances and the extent to which the university is dependent on defense research contracts for income. The board vetoed the project. At the Harvard University Press, the refusal came before the editorial board even had an opportunity to consider publishing Gravel's copy of the Papers.

Rodberg turned finally to Beacon Press, the nonprofit publishing arm of the Unitarian-Universalist Association in Boston, which had offered to step in if other, faster options fell through. Beacon, which is financed by the wealthy, liberal church organization, was not constrained to view Gravel's project from a strictly financial point of view like the New York publishers, nor from a legal or political point of view like the editorial board of the MIT Press. Gobin Stair, the gray-bearded former artist who is director of Beacon, felt that "social responsibility" required that Beacon step in where other publishers would not so that a relatively full edition of the Papers would be available to students and scholars—as originally intended when McNamara commissioned the study. Gravel had originally hoped for substantial royalties from prompt publication of the Papers, which he planned to channel into an antiwar fund, but Beacon could not afford any such commitment and would be much slower to publish; just to put out the "Gravel edition" of the Papers in both hardcover and paperback would mean a risk of almost a quarter of a million dollars. Instead of royalties the publisher agreed to pay a fixed amount toward Gravel's legal expenses incurred in connection with publication.

[CHAPTER XIV]

On Thursday night July 15, 1971, President Nixon went on nationwide television to make a brief and startling announcement: he had accepted an invitation to visit Peking. In an historic departure from one of the basic myths of post-World War II American foreign policy, the United States would apparently no longer contend that Chiang Kai-shek's regime on Taiwan represented all of mainland China, and the President's visit would be the first major step toward "normalization of relations" with the Chinese Communist government that had come to effective power in 1948. Nixon's visit had been arranged during a secret trip to Peking by presidential national security adviser Henry A. Kissinger, who met with Chinese Premier Chou En-lai from July 9 to 11, while the American public was told that Kissinger was suffering from an "indisposition" in Islamabad, Pakistan.

News of Nixon's plans for a new China policy promptly took over the newspaper headlines, the magazine covers, and prime television time, automatically pushing aside any continuing debate over Vietnam and the Pentagon Papers. The administration selectively released additional details and photographs of Kissinger's visit to Peking. "For Most Americans It Was an Event to Cheer" read the headline on Max Frankel's assessment of the China announcement on the front page of *The New York Times*'s week-in-review section the following Sunday, and that view was hardly disputed in the flood of news analyses and commentaries that followed. The President was riding high, and the institution of a wage-and-price freeze in August also seemed to meet with wide popular acceptance.

Many political analysts expected the Pentagon Papers controversy—and the administration's apparent defeat in court—to subside and even disappear in the flush of excitement over new foreign and domestic policy successes. The White House floated a somewhat convincing story that the Justice Department's action against the newspapers had been partially based on a fear that disclosure of the Papers would jeopardize Kissinger's delicate secret mission to Peking; release of such an enormous archive of secret documents, it was theorized, might have led the Chinese to believe that the United States could not be trusted to deal in confidence. If the administration now concentrated on its successes, many Democrats feared and many Republicans hoped, the Pentagon Papers would slip into obscurity and Daniel Ellsberg's goals would be substantially frustrated. But just as it had done before by acting against the newspapers, the Justice Department became the prime mover in keeping the Papers in the forefront of the national consciousness and the news. Attorney General John Mitchell, returning from a convention of the American Bar Association in London, vowed that anyone who had violated the law would be vigorously prosecuted, just as several justices on the Supreme Court had suggested they should be.

In California, although Ellsberg had already been indicted on two counts (for allegedly violating the federal Espionage Act and the general statute covering theft of government property), attorney Paul C. Vincent of the Justice Department's Internal Security Division pressed ahead with a grand jury investigation and continued to insist that Anthony Russo testify about the circumstances surrounding the photocopying of the set of Papers that Ellsberg used at Rand. Against the advice of his lawyer, an influential California politician named Joseph Ball, Russo adamantly refused to testify, despite a grant of immunity from prosecution. Claiming every constitutional privilege he could find, Russo appealed his citation for contempt of court all the way to Justice William O. Douglas, circuit judge for the Ninth Circuit Court of Appeals. When the government denied Russo's claim that he was the subject of government electronic surveillance, Douglas turned down Russo's appeal as frivolous, and Ellsberg's close friend faced an indefinite jail term as the cost of his stand on principle. (The jail sentence for a recalcitrant grand jury witness can last as long as the service of the grand jury itself, and the prosecutors in Los Angeles were casually suggesting that the grand jury investigating the Pentagon Papers case might sit as long as eighteen months.) Russo surrendered himself on August 16. He originally expected his time in prison to be both a rest and an opportunity to establish rapport with people whose rights he had been defending while working for the Los Angeles County Probation Department; instead it turned into a nightmare. When he was first processed, the Los Angeles county jail's computer broke down and Russo was herded with other prisoners into an overcrowded booking area while officers went through a slow manual procedure. Russo later claimed that after protesting loudly that the civil rights of the prisoners were not being respected, he was taken to an isolation cell, handcuffed, shackled, and beaten. Russo was eventually transferred to the federal prison on Terminal Island in Los Angeles harbor, where he had an equally hard time; for almost seven weeks he remained in jail as a symbol of the Justice Department's determination to press the Pentagon Papers investigation.

In the meantime, Daniel Ellsberg was fighting to have the case against him transferred from Los Angeles to Boston, where his lawyers felt a more sympathetic trial jury might be drawn. One maneuver after another was rejected by federal court in Boston, however, and Ellsberg appeared in Los Angeles for arraignment on August 16, the same day that Russo turned himself in at the county jail. Ellsberg pleaded not guilty and made it clear that he would ask any jury to try the Vietnam war as well as him; expressing the view that the jury would have to read the Papers carefully in order to decide the case, Ellsberg posed as the major question in controversy: "Was I right in my thinking that the Papers deal with high crimes by officials of our government?"

According to the textbooks, the law is objective and consistent; but in practical fact its evolution and application are a very random matter, depending largely on those charged with deciding specific issues. Depending on the President who named him, whether his appointment was mostly on merit or as a reward for loyal political activity, whether or not he takes an activist view of his role on the bench, and what his politics are, one judge will invariably see a case differently from another; and both will find ample precedent to justify their views. Thus it was significant when Murray I. Gurfein and Gerhard A. Gesell, entirely by chance, became the judges in the Justice Department's suits against *The New York Times* and *The Washington Post*. Other judges might have decided quite differently. So, in California, the man chosen by random draw to preside over Ellsberg's trial was U.S. District Judge William M. (Matt) Byrne, Jr., like Gurfein a very recent appointee to the bench and like Gesell a well-known civil libertarian. (Byrne had been in Washington for his Senate confirmation hearing at the time the administration was moving against the

Times. He told friends in the capital that he sympathized with Gurfein for having been handed such a controversial case on one of his first days on the bench and observed that he would not want the same thing to happen to him.) A Democrat, Byrne had served as U.S. Attorney for the Central District of California during the Johnson administration and had continued in that capacity for eighteen months under President Nixon, until a Republican replacement was named. But Byrne was distinctly on the outs with the Nixon administration and John Mitchell's Justice Department; he was chief counsel to the President's Commission on Student Unrest, led by former Pennsylvania Governor William W. Scranton, which placed a large share of the blame for university discontent squarely on the President's shoulders. When California Democratic Senator Alan Cranston pushed Byrne for a federal judgeship, Republican George Murphy blocked the appointment; but Murphy was defeated by Democrat John Tunney in 1970, and the two Democrats then combined forces in the Senate to block other judgeship nominees favored by the White House until the Nixon administration agreed to follow through with Byrne's appointment. Byrne was by no means assumed to be automatically favorable to Ellsberg, but he had a reputation for evenhandedness and was not expected to be guided on the bench by his former job as a federal prosecutor. Ellsberg's lawyers were confident, in any event, that Byrne would be fairer than many of the other old-time judges they might have drawn in Los Angeles, and after Byrne was assigned to the case they dropped their effort to have the trial moved to Boston.

The release of the Papers and the indictment had immediate consequences for Ellsberg's personal and professional life. His long-standing and firm ties with the defense and foreign policy establishments were effectively cut (although not without reluctance by Ellsberg; on several occasions he phoned old friends to ask, for example, if they had heard how

Henry Rowen, president of the Rand Corporation, had reacted to the disclosures).

Ellsberg came uneasily to his new role as a champion of what remained of the nonviolent "peace movement." He was not really comfortable in any movement; his had been an individual and very personal act of political defiance. Even when giving a public speech and dealing generally with Vietnam, Ellsberg would discuss presidential candidates in terms of his own relationship to them, rather than in the larger context of which candidate might be likely to get the United States out of Vietnam fastest. He never forgave Senator George McGovern, for example, for declining to move with the Pentagon Papers, and Ellsberg made gratuitous public remarks against McGovern, whose position on Vietnam was probably closer to Ellsberg's than that of any other major presidential candidate.

Moving back and forth between Cambridge, New York and the West Coast, stopping sometimes in Washington, Chicago, and other major cities, Ellsberg emerged as a polished public speaker. "Brothers and sisters, I am really high on you. . . . This is a celebration," he said to a roar of applause at a banquet for the Federal Employees for Peace in Washington in September. He went on to free-associate for almost two hours about everything from his own anxieties about going to jail to the lessons that might be drawn about American society from the violent prisoner revolt in Attica, New York. On October 1, along with some of the grand old veterans of the peace movement—Senator Wayne Morse, Dr. Benjamin Spock, and folk singer Joan Baez, among others—he received an American Peace Award from Business Executives Move for Vietnam Peace. Later in the month, although he didn't quite fit into the radical-chic setting, Ellsberg wowed a luncheon meeting of the New Democratic Coalition in New York. And so it went: after being the featured speaker at the "Winter Soldier" hearings of the Vietnam Veterans Against the War in Boston, Ellsberg stopped in at a

Massachusetts voter registration rally and stole the spotlight from several visiting politicians: his first major public appearance in Los Angeles drew thousands to the Hollywood Bowl. All across the country Daniel Ellsberg's coming was announced in underground newspapers and leaflets, as well as through the normal channels of communication, in a way that few people had been heralded since Martin Luther King, Jr. So unable was Ellsberg to turn down an invitation or opportunity to speak that he completely missed the manuscript deadline for a collection of his essays on Vietnam, to be published by Simon and Schuster (after the publisher had already advertised that it would be available in November). Before switching to Simon and Schuster, Ellsberg had signed a $150,000 contract with the Dell Publishing Company, but the contract was canceled when he failed to meet his deadline there.

As the cult of Ellsberg supporters grew, each piece of writing about him was put under the microscope by his supporters to determine whether it was going to help or hurt the nation's newest *cause célèbre*. Peter Schrag, writing in the *Saturday Review*, may have explained best what the special appeal of Ellsberg was: "It is still difficult fully to describe his act [of disclosing the Papers], or what it means, or to guess where it will lead. ... The fact is that although the war is unpopular, it continues. Ellsberg's challenge to the system that produced it—the system of politics, its endemic amorality, and its accompanying intellectual assumptions—falls beyond the familiar militancy of the streets and the polite partisanship of the parlor pacifists." But Ellsberg also retained a certain aura of mystery and excitement; the public release of the Pentagon Papers became an act that almost everyone wondered about his own capacity to commit.

Above all, the Papers provided a convenient focus for intra-establishment dispute. As Ellsberg's refutation of the "quagmire" theory of American involvement in Vietnam gained currency, Arthur Schlesinger, Jr., the former aide to President Kennedy who still purported to speak as the conscience of the liberal tradition in American politics, took to the pages of the *New York Review of Books* to reassert a modified quagmire thesis that rejected Ellsberg's implications of evil intentions behind American policy. Leslie Gelb followed with a statement of a middle-ground position that was unacceptable to both Ellsberg and Schlesinger, and the somewhat incestuous written debate over who had the proper interpretation of why we were wrong in Vietnam continued through the winter. A panel discussion at the annual meeting of the American Historical Association in New York raised the issues of the quality of the Papers and the appropriateness of their early release, with Harvard history professor Ernest R. May first denouncing the study as poor, "even if judged by relatively low standards," and then being forced by Ellsberg to acknowledge publicly that he too had a hand in preparing the Papers. May defended the proposition that some government records would have to remain closed to public scrutiny for twenty years, lest they be used prematurely for expedient political purposes or lest a fear of disclosure warp the policy-making process. Nonetheless, the majority of the historians at the New York meeting in December seemed to support Ellsberg's action enthusiastically and applauded his assertion that the Pentagon Papers had been "too important to wait."

If there were ever a threat that the Papers might fade from public significance and attention, or that they were becoming the concern primarily of a narrow academic community, the government quickly eliminated the possibility by pressing ahead with an easily noticed and widely publicized investigation of how the Papers were disclosed, accompanied by a threat to prosecute anyone who might have been even marginally involved. More than six months after the Papers were originally released FBI agents had still not correctly pinpointed where Daniel Ellsberg stayed during his twelve days underground, although they had learned a little bit about virtually everything else that might be considered remotely

[278]

connected with the Papers, the papers, and the Ellsbergs. Federal investigators had gone as far as Morocco, where Richard Holbrooke, one of the members of the Vietnam History Task Force, was serving as country director for the Peace Corps, and South Vietnam, where interviews were conducted with every willing person who had known Ellsberg during his tour of duty there. But the most obvious focus of the FBI probe was in Cambridge, Massachusetts, where agents combed the Harvard and MIT communities for clues to Ellsberg's activities and his personality, compiling information of questionable relevance to a criminal prosecution. One close friend and frequent dinner companion of Daniel and Patricia Ellsberg, Sam Popkin, was greeted by two agents at his office at Harvard's Center for International Affairs within a few hours of his return from a trip to a political science convention in Germany. Popkin had the feeling that the agents were trying to elicit negative comments about Ellsberg, and he noted that they stressed words like "emotions," "psychiatric," and "stability." They also urged Popkin to discuss his own views about the war in Vietnam and pressed him to choose between "money" and "glory" as Ellsberg's probable motive for disclosing the Papers. If anyone declined to talk with the agents or insisted upon having a lawyer present, that was usually enough to guarantee that he or she would be subpoenaed before a grand jury; those who did cooperate were sometimes subpoenaed anyway. The investigation became so pervasive that one of Boston's semi-underground newspapers, *Boston After Dark*, printed a practical warning to its readers in midsummer: "IMPORTANT: If you are approached by FBI agents, you do not have to talk with them. Beware of lying to G-men. The Bureau assumes that those who lie are trying to protect someone. If you receive a subpoena to appear before a grand jury, be sure to contact a lawyer for advice."

The FBI investigation also reached into the newspaper offices, where editors came to assume that the government had informers who were providing certain details of how the Pentagon Papers were obtained. Neighbors and friends of Neil and Susan Sheehan were questioned extensively, and the Sheehans' bank account records were subpoenaed and inspected. Curiously, at *The Washington Post* federal agents contacted only people who might be least likely to have relevant information for the investigation—among them Ben Bagdikian's former wife and a photographer named Harry Naltchayan, whose only connection seemed to be that he shared an Armenian surname with Bagdikian and Robert Mardian, head of the Internal Security Division in the Justice Department.

If the FBI met resistance elsewhere, it had no trouble at the heart of the establishment, the Council on Foreign Relations in New York. Without so much as the slightest protest, the council abrogated its own rule requiring absolute secrecy of internal documents and deliberations and turned over to FBI agents a paper entitled "Escalation as a Military Strategy in Limited War," which Ellsberg had delivered at a seminar there in November 1970. Rather than counseling a stand on principle which could have involved the staid group in unsavory, unseemly court proceedings, the council's lawyers merely advised that the Ellsberg report be provided to the FBI. (The action drew a bitter protest from some of the council's best known members.)

Most of the investigating in the Pentagon Papers case was accomplished, however, through the use of federal grand juries in Los Angeles (the same one that indicted Ellsberg in June) and Boston, where the government realized that much of the recopying and transferring of the Papers had taken place. Since Mardian's appointment to direct it in 1970, the Internal Security Division had embarked on a spate of grand jury investigations of alleged subversives around the country. When possible, the investigations were tucked away in cities where they were less likely to be noticed immediately

—for example, Seattle, Washington; Tucson, Arizona; and Harrisburg, Pennsylvania. Historically, under English common law grand juries were used to protect the public from malicious prosecutors; sitting as the peers of those who were charged with crimes, the grand jurors passed on whether there was probable cause to believe that the individuals charged had committed the crimes and whether a "true bill" authorizing prosecution should be returned. In modern American practice, however, especially on the federal level, grand juries are seldom anything but the prosecutor's forum. In only a tiny minority of cases does the grand jury vote against going forward with a case. When pursuing radicals or other political activists for alleged conspiracies to violate the law, the government is in a particularly favorable position: grand jurors are often elderly, solid middle-class citizens with traditional American values. They usually remain silent or chime in with prosecutors' questions about membership in organizations, attendance at demonstrations, and personal friends; they have little patience with or understanding of balky witnesses who force them to spend long hours away from home and work, waiting for courtroom adjudications of whether the witness must indeed testify. And it is easy to imagine that the grand jurors become more suspicious of witnesses who leave the room after each question to consult with a lawyer about the answer, as the witnesses in such political cases invariably do.

There were frequent indications that the Justice Department substantially altered the functions of the grand jury to make it useful in developing viable cases against radicals and others perceived by the Internal Security Division as a threat to the nation. When individuals refused to cooperate with the FBI, for example, a grand jury subpoena became an almost automatic alternative, and the executive branch used the judicial process to perform its investigative work; rather than presenting the clearly established evidence to a grand jury, the government used the compulsory process to produce evidence.

Not surprisingly, in many such investigations a large number of people refused to testify and cited their constitutional rights as protection. Invariably, the government offered them immunity from prosecution—not necessarily total immunity but "use immunity," a product of the 1970 Crime Control Act, which guarantees only that one's own testimony will not be used against him in a criminal prosecution; but that person can still be prosecuted for activities he has discussed if the government can obtain independent corroborating evidence. For some prospective witnesses that is obviously not enough protection; thus political grand jury investigations usually produce a number of contempt-of-court citations for refusals to testify in secret no matter what kind of immunity is guaranteed them by the court; freedom from personal prosecution is not enough to justify going behind closed doors and providing details of what a friend has done—especially if the witness does not happen to agree with the government that his friend has committed a crime by, for example, disclosing secret documents concerning American foreign policy.

There was some question too of whether it was proper to continue with grand jury investigations after Ellsberg had already been indicted in Los Angeles. The clear precedent in law is that the government may not use the grand jury after indictment to gather evidence for presentation at trial; seldom is there any way of enforcing that prohibition, however, except merely by taking government lawyers at their word. It was almost impossible, in fact, to police any aspect of the government's use of the grand jury, because of the built-in secrecy of the institution. Many of these questions concerning the role of the grand jury are in an area of law that is still evolving and developing—for example, early in 1972, the Supreme Court took up the constitutionality of "use immunity"—but the Justice Department nonetheless used the grand jury as a primary tool in responding to the release of the Pentagon Papers.

The Boston grand jury investigation began quietly early in the summer of 1971; on July 7, exactly one week after the Supreme Court ruling in favor of the newspapers, attorney Paul Vincent of the Internal Security Division arrived in Boston and filed an "oath of office" with Russell H. Peck, clerk of U.S. District Court in Massachusetts, indicating that he would present to the grand jury cases involving violation of "the laws relating to the retention of public property or records with intent to convert, the gathering and transmitting of national defense information [the Espionage Act], the concealment or removal of public records or documents, and conspiracy to commit such offenses and to defraud the United States." It might have remained a quiet investigation for some time—looking into the Cambridge photocopy business, the visits to Boston of the Sheehans, and matters involving the *Times*, the *Post*, and the *Globe*—if a member of the grand jury had not been a relative of an executive at one of the newspapers. When some details of the probe leaked out through that conduit, the government treated this as a major breach of grand jury secrecy and transferred the case to a new grand jury. Only after the government subpoenaed the Ellsbergs' bank records did it become clear that the investigation was aimed at tracing Daniel Ellsberg's contacts with the people who received the Papers for each newspaper and publisher.

In August, however, the grand jury began casting a broader net. Subpoenas were issued to Sam Popkin and to Ralph Stavins and Richard Falk, who had worked with the Pentagon Papers at the Institute for Policy Studies. (Falk contributed a chapter to the second volume of the IPS study based on the Papers, *Washington Plans an Aggressive War*, and it had become widely known among his academic colleagues that he saw the secret study long before its publication in the press.) After it became clear that Senator Mike Gravel had arranged for private republication of his copy of the Pentagon Papers, a subpoena was also issued to Leonard Rodberg, the IPS researcher who had been signed on as Gravel's "chronicler" just before the extraordinary session of the Senate Subcommittee on Buildings and Grounds.

Subpoenaing Rodberg was probably, from the government's point of view, one of the major mistakes of the entire Pentagon Papers case. Rodberg enlisted the help of the Center for Constitutional Rights in New York, which was launching a major attack on alleged abuses of the grand jury system, and Senator Gravel moved immediately—through Charles Fishman and the special team of law professor consultants—to intervene on Rodberg's behalf. Although Gravel and Rodberg never met personally until after the controversial subcommittee hearing, for posterity and the lawbooks Rodberg became a trusted aide to the Alaska Senator, required to protect the confidentiality of his employer's business and personal dealings. Rodberg moved to quash his subpoena on First Amendment grounds, but Gravel raised the substantial issue of congressional immunity, arguing that the subcommittee hearing was part of legislative business and that his staff member's activities in connection with legislative business—especially trips to visit publishers with the manuscript that was the official record of the hearing —were protected from inquiry, along with a Senator's, under the "speech or debate" clause in Article I of the Constitution. The scope of immunity under that clause has never been precisely defined, but the Justice Department responded to Gravel's move by seeking to limit it substantially. The actions of the Senator himself "cannot be above scrutiny by those charged to enforce the criminal statutes," the Justice Department argued in its formal answer to Gravel's intervention, since he was not "engaged in official subcommittee business" when he read aloud from the Pentagon Papers. That position was escalated substantially during a subsequent court hearing in Boston, when attorney Paul Vincent asserted that the Justice Department could call any member of Congress before a grand jury and compel him to testify; Vincent pressed for a court finding on whether Gravel's hearing had been "lawful" or "unauthorized" as the touchstone for further inquiry. However, U.S. District Judge W. Arthur Garrity, Jr., noted from the moment that the case came before him that under the doctrine of the separation of powers the judiciary had traditionally been reluctant to intervene in the determination of such matters, which were more properly considered the internal business of each house of Congress. Curiously, in other cases in the federal courts only a year or so earlier the Justice Department's Internal Security Division had taken a position directly opposite to the one it was now pressing upon Garrity, arguing that immunity did extend to staff members not only of individual Congressmen but also of committees and insisting that it was not for the courts to decide what is and what is not the proper business of a duly constituted congressional committee.

At the same time, Falk and Stavins were resisting their subpoenas on First Amendment grounds, arguing that as "scholar communicators" who wrote on matters of urgent public interest they were entitled to the same protection from revealing their sources that Earl Caldwell of *The New York Times* was claiming in his case on the West Coast. The government responded in a similarly strong manner to those claims.

Perhaps because of the overreach of some of his arguments in court and his failure to get the grand jury in Boston moving forward, Vincent was quietly removed from the Pentagon Papers case in September, and a three-man team of special prosecutors—Assistant U.S. Attorney David R. Nissen of Los Angeles, an experienced trial lawyer and an acknowledged expert on perjury; Warren P. Reese of San Diego, a long-time engineering administrator who became a lawyer only at age thirty-five and served for a time as a public defender; and Richard J. Barry of Des Moines, a young lawyer who had been commended for excellence by Attorney General Mitchell—was named to handle all criminal and civil litigation concerning the Pentagon Papers. Their efforts to expedite the investigation, however, were inextricably caught up in an ever more intricate web of legal complications. Each person subpoenaed as a witness raised new objections or found innovative ways to argue claims that had already been rejected.

Ruling in October on the First Amendment claim of Falk and the other academics who did not want to testify, U.S. District Judge Garrity found "crucially distinguishable" differences between the situation of Earl Caldwell and that of the scholar writers. "Reporter Caldwell's sources were members of the Black Panther Party, persons often lacking in education and sophistication whose distrust of government, especially of police and prosecutors, is well known," Garrity wrote. "No persuasive analogy can be drawn between a Black Panther's fear of harassment and prosecution and the anxieties of [Falk's] sources, who likely are highly trained and sophisticated individuals. Such persons, highly placed in the councils of government, education, and industry, undoubtedly will continue to 'leak' confidential but otherwise lawful information to [Falk] and indeed to other scholars, journalists, and consultants too." The judge seemed to be saying that only if his sources were "unsophisticated" was a writer entitled to a constitutional privilege against revealing them.

Later, however, the witnesses came back to court with a new reason for refusing to testify: a concern that their names as potential witnesses had come up in the course of government wiretaps, directed against either their own telephones or those of people with whom they spoke frequently. Falk and Noam Chomsky, an MIT linguistics professor and leading antiwar spokesman who had worked with Beacon Press on preparing Gravel's copy of the Pentagon Papers for publication, said in affidavits that they had had telephone contact with the defendants in the Harrisburg conspiracy trial, where the government had acknowledged wiretapping already. Stavins, for his part, described electronic tests done on his home telephone and his office phone at the Institute for Policy Studies by Rodberg and the owner of "The Spy Shop," a bugging and debugging equipment headquarters in Washington. The tests turned up some rather unusual "radio frequency signals" on the lines.

Although the issue had not been settled by the Supreme Court, several lower federal courts had ruled that a prospective grand jury witness could be defined as "a party aggrieved" entitled to challenge the admissibility of wiretap evidence under the provisions of Section 3504, Title 18, of the United States Code. Following the wording of the statute, Garrity ruled that the witnesses had shown reason enough to believe wiretapping had taken place to require that the government "affirm or deny." Garrity gave the government seven days, but the Justice Department took two months to come up with an answer—a vague affidavit from A. William Olson, Deputy Assistant Attorney General of the Internal Security Division, swearing that inquiries with "the appropriate agencies of the federal government" had turned up no evidence of electronic surveillance of any of the three witnesses or their "premises." When the affidavits came up for review in January 1972 by U.S. District Court in Boston, Chief Judge Anthony Julian (who had ruled against the *Globe* seven months earlier), then handling emergency matters, declared them "insufficient" and again excused the three witnesses from testifying. (There was evidence, among other matters, that an identical affidavit submitted by Olson in the Harrisburg case was demonstrably false.)

Other witnesses kept up running battles on other grounds. Sam Popkin, who felt he could not establish the wiretap claim as firmly as the others, stuck to his First Amendment claim, submitting dozens of affidavits from other distinguished scholars on his behalf and eventually getting the Harvard faculty council to inject itself into the controversy with a resolution urging that the government "demonstrate a strong need for having the questions answered" before being entitled to bring a scholar before the grand jury. David Halberstam, the former *Times* reporter who had talked with Ellsberg while writing his own book about the development of American policy in Vietnam, got an indefinite postponement of his own appearance while he prepared a First Amendment challenge to the subpoena. K. Dun Gifford, a former legislative assistant to Senator Edward M. Kennedy (D-Mass.) and a friend of the Ellsbergs in Cambridge, entered the grand jury room but refused to answer questions; he too asserted a First Amendment privilege on the basis of his position as chairman of the board of the *Morning News*, an experimental newspaper scheduled for publication simultaneously in several cities that did not already have strong daily morning papers. (Neil Sheehan, as well as Gifford, had done some anonymous articles for the first few pilot issues of the *Morning News*.) One witness who lost her battle against testifying was Idella Marx, stepmother of Patricia Marx Ellsberg; after her claim to have been wiretapped was declared spurious, Garrity held Mrs. Marx in contempt of court for refusing to testify. Rather than go to jail, she eventually appeared before the grand jury and answered two days' worth of questions relating mostly to helping her son Spencer, who also lived in Cambridge, change apartments.

In California the Justice Department infuriated Judge Byrne by circumventing his ruling that the government could not have access to personal possessions that Ellsberg had placed in storage in Los Angeles. After Byrne had ruled, the FBI merely executed a warrant it had already obtained from a U.S. magistrate authorizing seizure of a footlocker and several metal cases and cardboard cartons. When it was discovered that they contained little more than Ellsberg's old books and Marine uniforms, they were returned to storage. The grand jury on the West Coast was also frustrated in its attempts to gather testimony. In the middle of October at least seven people refused to appear, including Albert Appleby, the antiwar business executive who had guided Ellsberg on lecture tours in Southern California; Melvin Gurtov, the University of California professor who had worked at Rand with Ellsberg, contributed to the Pentagon Papers, and signed the antiwar letter to *The New York Times* and *The Washington Post*; and Sally Binford, an anthropologist friend of Anthony Russo. Lynda Sinay, the advertising woman who lent Ellsberg her Xerox machine for photocopying the Papers, testified again at length under a grant of immunity; and Ellsberg's fifteen-year-old son Robert spent almost a full day in the grand jury room, with the approval of his mother, after being served with a subpoena at 7:30 in the morning and ordered to appear two hours later.

The most crippling development for the government in the West Coast investigation came in its continuing effort to compel testimony from Anthony Russo. U.S. District Judge Warren J. Ferguson, who took over duty as motions judge of the Los Angeles court on October 1, released Russo from jail that same day on his promise to testify so long as the government provided him with a transcript of what he said in the grand jury room. Seventeen days later, when Russo was subpoenaed to appear again, prosecutor David Nissen flatly refused to comply with Judge Ferguson's order, declaring it "unlawful." Since the government would not promise the transcript, Russo still refused to enter the grand jury room, and Ferguson agreed to consider his ruling further. A month later Judge Ferguson issued an eighteen-page decision strengthening and expanding his earlier one; he noted that a witness was already entitled to talk publicly about what went on before the grand jury, and a transcript would merely guarantee his accuracy. To provide such transcripts, Ferguson said, "will not diminish the effectiveness of the grand jury system or interfere with governmental efforts to investigate crime." The ruling broke with all precedents, however, and the government apparently regarded it as a chink in the grand jury's armor of secrecy. Russo was never recalled to testify, and Ferguson's decision was never appealed, apparently because the Justice Department preferred to have it remain a single district court opinion with limited precedential value, rather than take the risk of having it affirmed by the Ninth Circuit Court of Appeals.

Senator Gravel did more than anyone else, however, to tie the government's investigative hands. Ruling on the Senator's challenge to the subpoena issued to Leonard Rodberg, Judge Garrity of U.S. District Court in Boston dealt a fatal blow to the Justice Department's assertion that it could call Senator Gravel himself if it cared to do so, and the judge rejected the notion that it was any of his business to pass on the propriety of Gravel's emergency subcommittee meeting. He refused to quash the subpoena served on Rodberg, however, saying that the witness could be questioned about anything he did before coming to work for Gravel and about his arrangements for republication of the Papers. Gravel's lawyers, pronouncing Garrity's decision unworkable, escalated their demands; they asked that the government also be prevented from quizzing Howard Webber, director of the MIT Press, who had originally agreed to publish the Senator's copy of the Papers, or anyone else who might have information the disclosure of which threatened Gravel's congressional immunity. When Garrity refused to go along, Gravel's lawyers appealed, and on October 29 two judges of the U.S. Court of Appeals for the First Circuit completely stopped a grand jury investigation, albeit temporarily, for the first time in the nation's history.

A month later the Justice Department was permitted to resume the grand jury investigation on a limited basis, but in January 1972 the appellate court in Boston distinctly extended congressional immunity to cover aides in Rodberg's situation. "It is not only accepted practice, but, we would think indispensable, for a legislator to have personal aides in whom he reposes total confidence," said the opinion by Chief

Judge Bailey Aldrich. "This relationship could not exist unless, during the course of his employment, the aide and the legislator were treated as one." Still, however, the court said that republication was not protected and that Beacon Press officials could be called and even asked about the Senator's actions. In an order denying reconsideration of the ruling on that point, Aldrich let slip that he did not personally feel the Pentagon Papers were germane to the business of Gravel's subcommittee.

Late in January Gravel went to the Supreme Court, asking that congressional immunity be extended to cover the Beacon Press edition and that Aldrich be rebuked for unwarranted interference in the affairs of the legislative branch of government. The Supreme Court accepted the case and scheduled it for expedited consideration in the spring of 1972. Meanwhile, the Unitarian-Universalist Association in Boston, which operates Beacon as its nonprofit publishing arm, filed a lawsuit against the Justice Department for allegedly violating the association's First Amendment guarantee of religious freedom by poking through its bank records in search of checks that would reveal its dealings with Gravel. (The government's answer to that suit, filed by Warren Reese, acknowledged interest in where Beacon's copy of the Papers originally came from.)

But the most dramatic government action with regard to the Beacon Press edition of the Pentagon Papers had come almost four months earlier. In September 1971, just a few weeks before the edition was scheduled for publication, two men who said they were from the office of J. Fred Buzhardt, general legal counsel to Defense Secretary Laird, paid an unannounced visit to the Boston offices of Beacon, seeking the publisher's cooperation with the government. Saying the Pentagon was concerned that material dangerous to national security might appear in the "Gravel edition," and that the Defense Department wanted to prepare for the international "repercussions," they scheduled a later meeting between Beacon and three military officers with "intimate knowledge"

[291]

of the Papers. At the same time, it was learned that Howard Webber of the MIT Press had already met with officials at the Pentagon to discuss the copy of the Papers that Rodberg had shown him while arranging for publication. (Webber later expressed surprise at being subpoenaed.) The special meeting with Beacon was canceled only fifteen minutes before schedule because, Buzhardt explained, Beacon was refusing to show its manuscript to the government, a condition that the Pentagon considered essential to any discussions.

In the meantime, the government was quietly rushing into print with its own expurgated edition of the Pentagon Papers, apparently trying to establish its publication as the "official" and most reliable one, thus hoping to head off any substantial sale of the four-volume set planned by Beacon, which was actually more complete. The day after Buzhardt canceled the meeting in Boston the Pentagon delivered its declassified version of the Papers—without any warning whatsoever—to the House and Senate Armed Services committees. The Government Printing Office was not caught by surprise, however. No sooner did Congressman F. Edward Hebert (D-La.), chairman of the House committee, turn them over to the GPO than public printer Adolphus N. Spence II set his own printers and several private contractors to work producing a twelve-volume photo-offset edition. It took five and a half hours to get them into production, Spence said at the time, only because, as delivered, the Papers were "an ungodly mess." The authorized, declassified version omitted the four "diplomatic" volumes of the study, many of the documents from the Johnson administration, some of the narrative covering American support for the coup that overthrew Ngo Dinh Diem in 1963, and portions covering the "education of the American public" about the bombing of North Vietnam; but almost all the rest was there. In a letter accompanying the submission of the expurgated study to Congress, Rady A. Johnson, legislative affairs assistant to Defense Secretary Laird, said that the declassification review, made by a team of one hundred people drawn from various government agencies, "has been a difficult task, complicated by the pattern of prior unauthorized disclosures and pending and potential actions in the courts. Of course, some of the material has been declassified solely on the basis of prior disclosures. . . . Because of the time constraint imposed on the review, it is possible, even probable, that errors of omission and commission have been made during the review. This, however, represents the best possible effort, taking into consideration the time available and the numerous complicating factors which influenced the review." On Monday morning September 27 the twelve-volume GPO edition of the Pentagon Papers went on sale for $50 a set. It was hard to read, but it had the authenticity of the original documents, since each page was merely a photograph of the original. Among the fewer than fifty buyers on the first day were a number of news organizations and a Washington visitor named Daniel Ellsberg.

Outside the legal arena there were a host of events and new policies that seemed to be triggered by the original unauthorized disclosure of the Pentagon Papers.

As soon as the Defense Department perceived that the copy of the Papers leaked to the press had come from the Rand Corporation, Defense Secretary Melvin Laird sent in Air Force security men to take over the security system at the California think tank. Employees at Rand with top-secret clearance were no longer permitted to use documents in their offices, but rather had to go to a central library where access was much more tightly controlled; an Air Force officer was stationed in the basement of the Santa Monica headquarters of Rand to keep account of the inflow and outflow of all classified government material. "It was not exactly a vote of confidence," observed Rand president Henry S. Rowen wryly. Nor was the whole affair taken as a basis for confidence in Rowen himself, who had been personally responsible for much of the freedom and flexibility that Daniel Ellsberg enjoyed while working at Rand. A few months later it was announced that Rowen would be phased out of his job over a period of eighteen months, and that day-to-day supervision of Rand's work would be taken out of his hands immediately; Rand insiders acknowledged that the shift could be traced directly to the Pentagon Papers controversy.

On August 3 President Nixon, giving the impression that he too was persuaded of the ills of overclassification, asked Congress to appropriate $636,000 to "begin an immediate and systematic effort to declassify documents of World War II"; over five years his program of review was expected to cost approximately $6 million. But as retired Air Force security expert William G. Florence later pointed out, the program was doomed to be a worthless effort; most of the Pentagon's World War II records had already been declassified or downgraded in classification in 1958, under the terms of a directive written by Florence himself. The newly proclaimed Nixon policy would have little effect on the continuing, current abuses of the security regulations by the thousands of bureaucrats with authority to withhold material from the public. Far more significant was a lower-key White House directive ordering that access to classified data be significantly narrowed whenever possible in order to avoid a repetition of the massive leak by Ellsberg. The administration's gut response was not to make information more freely available but to restrict its availability.

In January 1972 the National Security Council came up with its proposed revisions of the security classification system, based in part on the recommendations of an interdepartmental committee. On his return from China, President Nixon approved a new executive order, which insured that some information would be declassified sooner but doomed other material to perpetual secrecy. He temporarily overlooked an NSC proposal that he consider asking Congress for legislation comparable to the British Official Secrets Act.

Less dramatic, and quite amusing to some people, was the fact that after disclosure of the Pentagon Papers, Robert MacNamara also tightened security at the World Bank, warning discreetly that internal memoranda and documents were not to be made available to the press. (Despite the furor over the Papers, MacNamara was named to a second four-year term as president of the bank.)

There were other troubling developments in the direction of greater secrecy. G. Warren Nutter, Assistant Secretary of Defense for International Security Affairs, instituted a "monitor" system in ISA so that someone was always present to keep track of what was said to the press by officials in his division of the Defense Department. The Justice Department extended its ban on the discussion of pending criminal cases to cover dissemination of information on civil cases as well. At the State Department the FBI was brought in to administer lie detector tests in an effort to locate the source of a leak to *New York Times* reporter William Beecher on progress being made at the strategic arms limitation talks between the United States and the Soviet Union. Confidential information inevitably continued to leak out, but the claims of White House communications director Herb Klein that President Nixon was running an "open administration" had less and less substance as time went on.

So pervasive was the impact of the Pentagon Papers that conservative columnist and gadfly William F. Buckley, Jr., made his own foray into the secret documents business in midsummer of 1971, devoting almost an entire issue of his magazine, the *National Review*, to "The Secret Papers They Didn't Publish: Top-Secret Memoranda—1962–1965." The magazine contended that President Johnson had named a special committee called "OVERLOOK" late in 1964 to review the record of American policy in Indochina and make recommendations for the future to the National Security Council; among other things, the *National Review* documents quoted from a purported Joint Chiefs of Staff memorandum to Defense Secretary McNamara early in 1962, which said that "the U.S. must abandon the strategy of graduated response and shift to the 'sharp knock' [quantum escalation] strategy" in relation to North Vietnam, including "demonstration drop of nuclear devices, . . . followed by use of nuclear bombs and devices where militarily suitable. . . ." The Buckley disclosures, touted to Washington reporters as "a journalistic coup" by the press secretary to his brother, Senator James L. Buckley (Con-N.Y.), caused an immediate sensation; the *Times*, the *Post*, and other major newspapers quoted substantially from them. A short time later Buckley called a press conference to admit that his own secret papers had been a hoax, composed entirely in the *National Review* offices. It was a revealing commentary on the confusion of American policy in Southeast Asia, however, that several former high government officials were unable to tell in the interim whether or not the Buckley Papers were genuine.

Much of the press subsequently attacked Buckley for playing with fire and being irresponsible—he lost several clients of his syndicated newspaper column, "On the Right"—but there was no question that he had scored a number of significant points against foreign policy makers and his journalistic colleagues.

Almost from the moment the Supreme Court ruled in favor of the newspapers on June 30, 1971, officials within the Nixon administration made it clear privately that they were bitter over their defeat. They were, for the most part, too clever to be indiscreet or to go public with their anger in the way that Vice President Agnew had done for so long. There was at least one notable exception, however, barely twenty-four hours after the high court decision: *Washington Post* reporter Ken W. Claw-

[296]

son, who was assigned to cover the Justice Department, attended the grand opening of the outdoor concert center at Wolf Trap Farm in the Virginia countryside near Washington with then Deputy Attorney General Richard G. Kleindienst. Clawson had accomplished the unusual task of reporting frankly on the political maneuverings of the Justice Department and at the same time becoming a friend of some of the department's highest officials. (In January 1972 he would leave the *Post* to take up a position as deputy to White House communications chief Herb Klein.) After the concert, over drinks at Kleindienst's home, the Deputy Attorney General chose him as the conduit for a "private message" to Katharine Graham, publisher of the *Post*.

According to a memorandum Clawson later submitted to Mrs. Graham, Kleindienst urged that she contact him, Attorney General Mitchell, or "the public official of her choice" to express her interest "in informally discussing the parts of the documents that pertain to damaging national security." If she did so, the Deputy Attorney General advised, Mrs. Graham would be told that only two sections of the Pentagon Papers must not be published: "information about Communist governments that have acted on behalf of the U.S. concerning the Vietnam situation" and "information showing that the U.S. has the ability to intercept communications between foreign governments." According to Clawson's memo, Kleindienst hinted that "publishers would go a long way toward avoiding criminal prosecution" if they turned over to the government the sections of the Papers containing such information. "Kleindienst emphasized that above action needed 'to avoid situation getting out of control,'" the memo added. "He said it was only matter of time before government obtain[ed] evidence of a type in which it could not avoid proceeding with a criminal prosecution against the newspapers. . . . He conceded that the fallout from a criminal prosecution of the nation's major publications might be ruinous for Mr. Nixon's 1972 candidacy. But he said this should not lead us to believe the government won't go after 'an arrogant press' anyway."

Kleindienst went on to warn, according to Clawson, that both Nixon and Mitchell would not shy away from a fight against the press; the reporter's memo quoted the Deputy Attorney General as saying: "The President is going to pick up a stick and start fighting back. I know he would go to the people on this. If he does, the big issue of the 1972 campaign may not be Vietnam or the economic situation, but whether an arrogant press is free to undermine the security of this country without check." Kleindienst also revealed to Clawson that the Justice Department had given "serious consideration . . . to alleging that Judge Gesell was biased in favor of the *Post*. The idea was dropped, he said, because it was felt such a motion would reflect on the entire federal judiciary."

Katharine Graham was rather alarmed when Clawson passed along Kleindienst's "message," which she regarded as a clear threat. After internal conferences at the *Post*, it was determined that Mrs. Graham's "public official of her choice" would be Secretary of State William P. Rogers (former general counsel to the *Post*) and that Ben Bradlee would call him. Bradlee told Rogers that the *Post* had no intention of printing material in either of the two areas listed by Kleindienst, but that the newspaper also had no intention of turning in its copies of the Papers. Rogers said he thought that sounded fine but that he would have to check with William B. Macomber, Jr., who had coordinated the State Department's policy on the Pentagon Papers. Macomber later called the *Post* to say that he thought there would be no problems, but then called Bradlee back to report that Kleindienst still expected the documents to be turned over.

The *Post* made no further attempts to answer Kleindienst, but about six weeks later, after he had returned from the American Bar Association meetings in London and a vacation,

Attorney General Mitchell called Katharine Graham and said: "I hear you say you have been threatened." (Mrs. Graham had mentioned the incident to several friendly administration officials.) Mitchell said that was "impossible" and suggested that perhaps Kleindienst and Clawson had been drinking too much on the night the "message" was passed. When the Attorney General asked Mrs. Graham if she had "taken it seriously," she replied that she had not, "because I just thought it was ludicrous." Mitchell said: "Well good, because of course nothing like that could have happened. Kleindienst couldn't have done a thing like that."

Pretrial hearings on the indictment against Daniel Ellsberg had been scheduled in Los Angeles by Judge Byrne for January 6. On December 29, 1971, however, after flushing out much of the defense strategy in pretrial motions, the Los Angeles grand jury returned a superseding indictment that substantially escalated the charges against Ellsberg and also named Anthony Russo as a defendant in the criminal case. The indictment included eleven substantive charges against Ellsberg—for stealing, concealing, obtaining, retaining, and conveying the secret documents—and three against Russo—for receiving them. Both men were also charged with conspiracy against the United States, and Lynda Sinay and former South Vietnamese Ambassador Vu Van Thai were named as unindicted co-conspirators. If convicted of all the charges, Ellsberg could face a maximum penalty of 115 years in prison and a $120,000 fine; Russo a maximum of thirty-five years in prison and a $40,000 fine. The significance of the conspiracy indictment was that it would be easier to convict Ellsberg without proving every act with which he was charged. The mention of Vu Van Thai's name in the indictment appeared to be a vehicle for attempting to prove Ellsberg's intent to harm the United States and help a foreign power, as specified in the

Espionage Act, which he was alleged to have violated. The new indictment claimed that, while they were both working at the Rand Corporation, Ellsberg had made available to Thai a volume from the Pentagon Papers—one of the four "diplomatic" volumes which he later acknowledged were too sensitive to be given to the press along with the others.

One factor that strengthened the government's case was that a Pentagon investigation showed conclusively that the stories in *The New York Times* and elsewhere had to come from Ellsberg, because they were all based on the unique copy of the Papers that he transported from Washington to the Rand office in Santa Monica. That material included early drafts of several sections of the study; thus, some documents edited out of the final secret edition of the Papers as transmitted to the Defense Department by Leslie Gelb appeared in the *Times*.

In the meantime, the special team of government prosecutors attempted to push ahead with the investigation in Boston, presumably with the intention of indicting others who "received" the Papers. Joining Senator Gravel in his efforts to restrict the grand jury, Ellsberg's lawyers contended that the government was actually trying to use the Boston investigation to collect evidence for presentation at trial in Los Angeles, a procedure that would violate standing law on the use of grand juries. The entire Boston investigation was stalled again, while the courts adjudicated that contention. It was resolved in the government's favor, but the First Circuit Court of Appeals ordered that Boston grand jury transcripts be preserved, in case that question arose at Ellsberg's trial in Los Angeles. But because of the secrecy of the grand jury, there was no way for anyone—not even the judges adjudicating the conflicts—to know for sure just what the Justice Department was doing.

[CHAPTER XV]

Disclosure of the Pentagon Papers did not end the war in Vietnam. It could not even be stated with certainty, as Daniel Ellsberg and others had hoped, that the revelations of duplicity and deceit in American policy had stimulated any new and militant popular outcry for setting a fixed date for complete withdrawal of American land and air forces from Southeast Asia. Despite the secret U.S. negotiations with the North Vietnamese and President Nixon's journeys to Peking and Moscow, the prospect was for an indefinite, though less visible and offensive, American presence in Indochina. If anything, the Papers and their historical lessons seemed to reinforce the likelihood of that prospect.

Relatively few Americans, in fact, read the Pentagon Papers in any detail. The Bantam edition based on the extensive ten-part series of articles in *The New York Times* sold well over a million copies but resulted in little public reaction. The four-volume "Gravel edition" published by Beacon Press attracted few people beyond university scholars and libraries, and its early sale barely surpassed 10 percent of the original 20,000-copy printing. The expurgated but realistic-looking Government Printing Office version—cumbersome in size, difficult to use without page numbers, and costly beyond the reach of average citizens—barely sold out after three months the five hundred copies allocated for public distribution.

None of the three editions was complete, and none would be for some time. Federal Judge Gerhard A. Gesell, who had been firmest in his stand in favor of the newspapers during the government's effort to suppress publication, ruled in December 1971 against lawsuits brought under the Freedom of Information Act by two Congressmen, John E. Moss (D-Cal.) and Ogden R. Reid (R-N.Y.), and Paul Fisher, a journalism professor at the University of Missouri, seeking release of those parts of the study that remained classified—the four "diplomatic" volumes and other items deleted during Defense Secretary Laird's declassification review. "The public's right to be informed cannot be transposed into a legal requirement that all governmental papers will be automatically revealed," wrote Gesell, affirming his acceptance of the Defense Department's assertion that the still classified material "could, if disclosed, result in serious damage to the nation by jeopardizing the international relations of the United States." In rejecting the Congressmen's contention that they had a right of access to the full Papers, Gesell said that "government, like individuals, must have some degree of privacy or it will be stifled in its legitimate pursuits." He also declined to inspect the disputed sections of the Papers privately in order to assess the reasonableness of the Defense Department's classification decision.

Despite the enthusiasm of Congressmen Moss and Reid, it was apparent that members of Congress were among the worst readers of the Pentagon Papers; even staunch opponents of

American involvement in Vietnam, like Senator J. W. Fulbright, who had a copy long before anyone else, had little time for the Papers and found that they only reinforced their worst suspicions about the evolution of U.S. policy in Southeast Asia. However, Congressman Paul N. ("Pete") McCloskey (R-Cal.) and a few other legislators who had built recent reputations on a disgust for the war felt that the Papers, showing as they did the contempt of a succession of administrations for the legislative branch, might help to recruit new antiwar votes in both houses of Congress. Indeed, late in 1971 the House of Representatives came close to a majority vote against the war, and on several occasions the Senate passed amendments offered by Majority Leader Mike Mansfield (D-Mont.) tying complete withdrawal simply to the release of American prisoners of war by the Communist forces. But the antiwar vote in Congress was still far behind the 73 percent of the American people expressing their disgust with the war in public opinion polls, and most members of Congress were still unwilling to go as far as cutting off appropriations for U.S. military operations in the war zone. The passage of the Mansfield amendments also became an exercise in futility when they were weakened in House-Senate conferences and when President Nixon announced cavalierly that he would ignore them in any event.

As months went by, legal scholars and journalists alike began to realize that the 6–3 Supreme Court decision in the cases of *New York Times* v. United States and United States v. *Washington Post* had been a rather hollow victory for the press. The unsigned opinion of the court said only that the government had failed to carry its heavy burden of proof to obtain a prior restraint, and the individual justices' opinions had as many nasty words for the press as for the government. Many editors felt strongly that the newspapers were worse off after the Pentagon Papers case than they had been before it; and in private conversations high Justice Department officials concurred in that assessment. "We proved one thing emphatically," said one Justice policy maker, "that there *can* be prior restraint of publication while a case is being reviewed in the courts." Nonetheless, the administration seemed to be reluctant to try again soon. If it did try, the prognosis seemed considerably worse for the press, with the conservative wing of the Supreme Court substantially strengthened by President Nixon's replacements for Justices Black and Harlan—Virginia lawyer Lewis F. Powell and William Rehnquist, the man who helped formulate the Justice Department's suits against the press as an Assistant Attorney General.

The tension between government and press continued unabated, to be sure. Late in 1971 *The Washington Post,* with cautious support from *The New York Times* and a few other major newspapers, bolted from the long-standing practice of agreeing not to print the source of information in White House "background briefings" on major foreign policy issues. Under the background system, which flourished and was abused in the hands of President Nixon's national security adviser, Henry A. Kissinger, the news media had been expected to print and broadcast as gospel truth the "official" version of events, using such phrases as "it was understood that . . . ." In the future, executive editor Ben Bradlee ordered, attribution by name would be used whenever possible and the greatest shield that Kissinger and other officials on his level could expect was the citation of "White House officials" or other accurate labels.

As the affidavits of Max Frankel and others had clearly predicted, the Washington press corps continued to operate on the basis of substantial leaks of classified information. A most dramatic demonstration of this fact came late in December 1971 and early in January 1972, when syndicated columnist Jack Anderson obtained from high-ranking government officials a virtual archive of secret documents demonstrating that the Nixon administration had been intensely pro-Pakistani in private while publicly claiming to be neutral during the Indo-

Pakistani war that turned East Pakistan into the independent nation of Bangladesh. Anderson wrote several columns based on the documents, mostly describing secret sessions of the National Security Council's Washington Special Action Group, where Kissinger ordered government agencies to "tilt" against India whenever possible; when Kissinger claimed that Anderson had taken some of his remarks at the sessions "out of context," the columnist released the full texts of some of the documents, first to *The Washington Post* and then to other newspapers. The FBI launched an intensive investigation into how Anderson obtained his material, and President Nixon characteristically announced that access to such material would be further narrowed; the Justice Department, whether because it did not want to get into another court case that became bigger news than the news itself, because Anderson's sources were so high-ranking as to be embarrassing, or because it was concerned that Anderson would turn his phenomenal investigative resources against it, took no action against the columnist.

The administration was hardly reluctant to act against the press in other ways, however. Late in 1971 the White House ordered an investigation into the personal life and work of Dan Schorr, a CBS news correspondent who was frequently hostile to the administration on television. When the FBI was caught in the act, White House officials contended that Schorr was being investigated only because he was under consideration for a "high position" in the Environmental Protection Administration or another government agency—an explanation so preposterous as to be laughable. But the Schorr investigation was a frightening example of the prospects for potential intimidation of newsmen, and many members of the press wondered whether they might not be in the same situation but unaware of it.

Whatever else had come out of the confrontation over the Pentagon Papers, the nation had learned that its classification system was being absurdly abused on all levels of government and that existing regulations and statutes—such as Executive Order 10501 and the federal Espionage Act—offered meaningless and inappropriate guidelines for the protection of "national security."

The press had also learned that, if anything, it should be more bold and outspoken in digging behind official policy, both domestic and foreign; the Pentagon Papers showed how little the public really knew about the origins of the war in Vietnam. Newspapers were painfully aware, after the crisis was over, that they had been too cautious about printing government secrets, and the papers now seemed ready to reject the advice of conservative lawyers whose uncritical acceptance of government arguments was often not in the public interest. *The New York Times* shifted most of its legal business away from Lord, Day, and Lord, the firm that had refused to represent the newspaper in the government's initial injunctive suit turning instead to Cahill, Gordon, the firm that worked with Bickel on the Papers case. In January 1972 *The Washington Post* fired Royall, Koegel, and Wells, out of dissatisfaction with the performance of its lawyers in the Papers case and with their original efforts to persuade the *Post* editors not to print stories about the war history at all. Instead, the *Post* hired the Washington law firm headed by noted criminal lawyer Edward Bennett Williams, Paul Connolly, and former Kennedy and Johnson administration aide Joseph A. Califano, Jr. That their advice would be different became immediately clear when Williams urged the *Post* to go ahead with printing the Jack Anderson documents before even seeing them.

The lessons and the exciting confrontation with the government over the Pentagon Papers were expensive. The *Post* paid over $70,000 for legal services during the two-week crisis in June 1971. At the *Times* legal fees to Alexander Bickel and the firm that worked with him ran up to $150,000—plus another $50,000 in the fall and winter for preparatory legal work in case the newspaper or Neil Sheehan should be indicted on criminal charges in connection with disclosure of the Papers. Attorneys for Daniel Ellsberg estimated that his defense could cost as much as $250,000, and they launched an urgent national fund-raising campaign.

Contrary to the popular belief, the newspapers gained very little of a material nature in return for the costs. The differences in circulation were insignificant. As Chicago *Sun-Times* editor James Hoge puts it: "Most people don't really understand about circulation at all. When the President announced his trip to China, I think we sold an extra 13,000 papers, and when Cassius Clay fought his last fight, which was against some unknown, we sold an extra 35,000 papers." What the newspapers did gain was a new knowledge of and faith in the First Amendment as a fundamental principle of freedom that sets the United States apart from other countries.

[EPILOGUE]

The legacy of the Pentagon Papers case, not surprisingly, has been fought over almost since the moment the Supreme Court ruled in the newspapers' favor at the end of June 1971. It would be comforting to be able to say that the crisis had solidified freedom of the press in the United States to the point where challenges to this fundamental principle are rare and, when raised, easily beaten back. But that is not the way things have worked out.

To be sure, the national media emerged from the Watergate period with new confidence in their power and with substantial, if grudging, popularity among the American public. The film version of *All the President's Men*, Bob Woodward and Carl Bernstein's story of how they penetrated Richard Nixon's Watergate coverup as reporters for *The Washington Post*, made journalists into folk heroes—the true guardians of democratic values against the narrower self-interest of people elected or appointed to public office. Enrollments in schools of journalism and communication skyrocketed.

Along with Watergate, the Pentagon Papers affair seemed to demonstrate the public-spirited virtue of the great institutions of the American press. They were willing, albeit belatedly, to expose the deception of the United States government in Southeast Asia, even at substantial risk to their own financial security. In retrospect, publication of the Pentagon Papers probably was something of a watershed in American foreign policy, helping certain people (especially in the U.S. Congress) overcome their initial reluctance to believe the worst about the war in Vietnam. As a result, the media were thanked for their role in hastening an end to the war, just as they were for their role in getting Nixon to resign the presidency.

But the pendulum swings quickly. The media have not in fact remained so terribly popular,* and in the field of foreign policy and national security they are frequently accused of interfering improperly and compromising the government's secrets. The instinct of bureaucrats has remained the same: to attempt to blame, and punish, the messenger for any bad news about the American role in the world, even as they leak information to make themselves look good. And the instinct of judges is often to give the benefit of the doubt to government agencies rather than to reporters and editors, who often seem arrogant, self-righteous, and obnoxious and appear to want to take matters of state into their own hands. Even when the clashes never get

---

* In a survey conducted by the Gallup Organization for the Times Mirror Company in 1988, 48 percent of the respondents said they think that press reports are "often inaccurate" and 59 percent that the press "tends to favor one side" when reporting on political and social issues. Only 18 percent rated network television news "very favorably," and 21 percent gave that rating to their daily newspapers; 78 percent said they believe the press "often invades people's privacy." In every area the media were rated less favorably than in a similar survey in 1985.

into court, there is a powerful intimidating effect whenever officials accuse writers or broadcasters of doing harm to the national interest.

The first setback after the Supreme Court decision to allow the newspapers to go ahead with their Pentagon Papers stories came the next year, on a closely related matter: maverick Senator Mike Gravel of Alaska lost his effort to have the unabridged version of the Papers published (complete with the four "diplomatic volumes") by Beacon Press in Boston. The high court decided to trust the government classifiers after all, and as a result, the sections of the Papers which are potentially the most revealing remain secret to this day. (Beacon did publish a "Gravel Edition," but without the diplomatic material.)

Also in 1972, the federal courts ruled in favor of the government's attempt to prevent Victor Marchetti, who had worked for the Central Intelligence Agency for fourteen years, from writing and publishing freely about his experiences. On the strength of affidavits submitted by CIA officials, U.S. District Court Judge Albert V. Bryan, Jr., in Alexandria, Virginia, enjoined Marchetti from disclosing information about the agency and, on the basis of "secrecy agreements" the former intelligence operative had signed, ordered him to submit anything he wrote on the subject to the CIA for clearance.

When Marchetti and his co-author, former State Department official John D. Marks, completed *The CIA and the Cult of Intelligence* in August 1973, they did hand it over to the CIA. A month later, the agency designated 339 portions of the book that it wanted deleted; by the time Marchetti, Marks, and the American Civil Liberties Union had sued, objecting to the censorship, the number was down to 168. At first the work was actually published with black spaces corresponding to those deletions, but later Bryan ruled that in all but 27 cases, the information the CIA wanted to suppress had not been properly classified. The book (which received substantial publicity and sales as a result of the CIA's assault on it) eventually appeared almost as written, but not until after a prior restraint had been in effect for a significant period of time.

The CIA struck again in 1980, moving against another former agent, Frank Snepp, who had published a book about the agency's activities in Vietnam without first submitting it for clearance as specified in his employment agreement with the agency. Pressing its case despite its acknowledgment that the book contained no classified material, the CIA eventually won a 6-3 Supreme Court decision that the terms in Snepp's contract were reasonable and that all profits from his book would have to be turned over to the government.

Among the other notorious cases of recent years was one in which the Carter administration obtained an injunction in 1979 from a federal judge in Wisconsin, ordering *The Progressive* magazine not to publish an article describing how to build a hydrogen bomb. The Arms Control and Disarmament Agency claimed at the time that the article, by Howard Morland, was "a flagrant example of deliberate dissemination of sensitive weapons design information . . . likely to damage U.S. interest in preventing the spread of nuclear weapons." Morland and his editor, Erwin Knoll, pointed out, however, that no access to secret material had been necesssary; the writer had relied entirely on published materials and on interviews, many of them arranged for him by the Department of Energy.

While the *Progressive* case was being appealed in the courts, others published the same information in other forms, and so the argument became moot. The government withdrew its objections, and the magazine printed the article as originally intended. Meanwhile, more mainstream news organizations made it clear that they were uncomfortable defending their more outrageous brethren (even those with a long tradition of populism like *The Progressive*). *The Washington Post*, in an editorial, urged the magazine to withdraw the H-bomb article, or at least to delete parts of it, and editor Benjamin Bradlee said he had supported *The Progressive* "with about as much enthusiasm as I would Larry Flynt and *Hustler,*" one of the most brazen pornographic magazines of the period.

Other recent examples of efforts to restrain the press, formally or informally, are legion:

* When the Reagan administration invaded the Caribbean island state of Grenada in 1983 to overthrow a Cuban-supported Marxist regime and to "rescue" American medical students there, reporters were first misled about troop movements in the area and then—breaking an old tradition—prevented from accompanying or observing the U.S. military action.

* When the first exclusively military space shuttle was launched in 1985, the Pentagon ordered that all details of the mission, including the nature of its payload and its strategic objectives, be kept secret. This constituted a major departure from the way the National Aeronautics and Space Administration (NASA), a civilian agency, had always done business. Typically, many details of the mission had already been published in various newspapers and in the authoritative magazine *Aviation Week and Space Technology;* nonetheless, then Defense Secretary Casper Weinberger denounced the press for "giving aid and comfort to the enemy."

* In 1986, as Ronald Pelton, a former employee of the National Security Agency, was going on trial for selling intelligence information to the Soviet Union, both NBC News and *The Washington Post* revealed that Pelton had compromised a top-secret underwater eavesdropping operation by American submarines inside Soviet harbors. This detailed reporting so enraged William Casey, then director of central intelligence, that he threatened to prosecute both news organizations for damaging national security. As is often the case, the threat proved to be an idle one, but along the way the *Post* delayed publication of its story and withheld some details, because it felt unable to judge the validity of the national security objections.

* Samuel Loring Morison, a civilian intelligence analyst for the Defense Department (and the grandson of the famous naval

historian Samuel Eliot Morison), was convicted of espionage in 1985 after he sold *Jane's Defence Weekly* in London photographs taken by an American spy satellite of a Soviet nuclear aircraft carrier under construction. Morison, who had previously been paid as an American "editor" of the British magazine, argued that he was merely discharging a journalistic function, but U.S. District Court Judge Joseph H. Young ruled that "the danger to the United States is just as great when this information is released to the press as when it is released to an agent of a foreign government." Morison's was a rare case, in that he actually went to prison.

The issue of the press's role in national security matters seems never to get very far from the center of public debate. When the CIA station chief in Athens, Richard Welch, was assassinated in 1975 after his identity was revealed in an anti-establishment magazine called *Counter-Spy*, there were calls for restrictions. (It turned out, of course, that Welch's role was well known in Athens and at previous posts where he had served, and the magazine's responsibility for the attack on him was very difficult to establish.)

When William Westmoreland, the former American military commander in Vietnam, sued CBS for libel, there was no claim of a threat to the national defense, but the case was certainly an attempt to force the media to be more cautious and respectful. (CBS had claimed that Westmoreland deliberately understated enemy strength in Vietnam in an effort to demonstrate military success.) The case was settled without a formal verdict; but taken together with Israeli General Ariel Sharon's libel suit against *Time* magazine for its coverage of his role in Lebanon, which was tried in the same courthouse at the same time, it created a climate of intimidation over accusations of recklessness.

Investigations of the media were once again demanded by federal prosecutors in 1988, after a leak of transcripts of wiretapped conversations related to an investigation of corruption in defense contracts. (The conversations implied that illegal payments had been made by defense contractors to members of Congress.) And in that same year, the Justice Department denied the media any opportunity to speak with Anne Henderson Pollard, who was serving a five-year prison term for helping her husband, Jonathan Pollard, sell classified documents to Israel. The government, claiming the restrictions were necessary for national security reasons, would not even permit reporters to interview her about her deteriorating health and the medical treatment she was receiving.

In the end, many of the arguments revolve around the old issues of whether information about national security and foreign policy questions belongs to the government or to the public—and whether concerns in this area can be invoked to limit the behavior of the media, or indeed of government officials who are inclined to blow the whistle on wrongdoing. It is clear that many years after resolution of the dispute over the Pentagon Papers, far too much information is still being classified by the government; at the same time, intelligence officials, possibly with growing support from the public, argue that the press too often uses the excuse of the public's "right to know" to pursue its own agenda of inquiry.

Yet another case testing the limits was working its way through the federal courts as this edition was going to press. Unions of federal workers filed a lawsuit attempting to prevent the Reagan administration from requiring some two million government employees to sign new nondisclosure agreements covering not only classified, but also "classifiable," information. With an eye on that lawsuit, Congress, invoking the First Amendment rights of the employees and its own need for information about waste and fraud in the executive branch, sided with the federal workers and passed a law prohibiting implementation of these new secrecy agreements. But Judge Oliver Gasch, a member of the U.S. District Court in Washington, threw out the law and ruled in favor of the president's right to control access to sensitive information. Quoting the late Justice Potter Stewart, Gasch cited "the constitutional duty of the Executive—as a matter of sovereign prerogative" to protect government secrets. A few months later, however, Gasch chastised the government for failing to define the "classifiable" information that the federal employees were forbidden to reveal.

In the context of the ongoing disputes, it seems useful to recall the eloquent words of the late Judge Murray Gurfein, as he ruled on Saturday afternoon, June 19, 1971, that the Nixon administration had failed to establish its case for restraining *The New York Times* from publishing articles based on the Pentagon Papers:

"The security of the nation is not at the ramparts alone. Security also lies in the value of our free institutions. A cantankerous press, an obstinate press, a ubiquitous press must be suffered by those in authority in order to preserve the even greater values of freedom of expression and the right of the people to know. . . . It is not merely the opinion of the editorial writer or of the columnist which is protected by the First Amendment. It is the free flow of information so that the public will be informed about the government and its actions. These are troubled times. There is no greater safety valve for discontent and cynicism about the affairs of government than freedom of expression in any form. This has been the genius of our institutions throughout our history. It is one of the marked traits of our national life that distinguish us from other nations under different forms of government."

[APPENDIX:
WHERE ARE THEY NOW?]

Abrams, Floyd. Lawyer representing *New York Times*, former student of Alexander Bickel. Private practice, New York City, 1970–present.

Agnew, Spiro T. Former governor of Maryland, vice president of the United States during Pentagon Papers case. Frequent critic of news media. Resigned Oct. 10, 1973, under agreement with Justice Department to admit evasion of federal income taxes and avoid imprisonment. Author of *The Canfield Decision* (1976) and *Go Quietly . . . Or Else* (1980). Since 1974 has run Pathlite, Inc., international trade consulting business based in Crofton, Maryland. Lives in Rancho Mirage, California.

Bagdikian, Ben. Picked up Pentagon Papers in Boston, carried them back to Washington on airplane. Assistant managing editor for national news, *Washington Post*, 1970–1971, ombudsman, 1971–1972. National correspondent, *Columbia Journalism Review*, 1972–1974. Professor, Graduate School of Journalism, University of California, Berkeley, 1977–present; dean, 1985–1988.

Bazelon, David L. Judge, U.S. Court of Appeals for District of Columbia Circuit, 1949–1985, chief judge, 1962–1978; appointed by Truman. Took senior status in 1979, retired in 1985.

Bickel, Alexander M. Lawyer representing *New York Times* before Supreme Court in Pentagon Papers case. Faculty, Yale Law School, 1956–1974. Died Nov. 7, 1974, at age 49.

Black, Hugo L. Associate Justice of U.S. Supreme Court, 1937–

1971; appointed by Franklin D. Roosevelt. Absolute advocate of First Amendment rights, voted in favor of press in Pentagon Papers case, in which he wrote his last opinion. Died Sept. 25, 1971, at age 85; replaced by Nixon appointee Lewis F. Powell, Jr.

Blackmun, Harry A. Associate Justice of U.S. Supreme Court, 1970–present; appointed by Nixon. Voted in favor of Nixon administration's effort to block publication of the Pentagon Papers, later wrote decision legalizing abortion.

Bradlee, Benjamin C. Executive editor of *Washington Post*, 1968–present. Close friend of President John F. Kennedy, author of *Conversations with Kennedy* (1975). Encouraged Watergate coverage that led to Nixon's resignation.

Brennan, William J., Jr. Associate Justice of U.S. Supreme Court, 1957–present; appointed by Eisenhower. Voted in favor of press in Pentagon Papers case.

Bundy, William P. Assistant Secretary of State for East Asian and Pacific Affairs, 1964–1969. Visiting professor and research associate, Center for International Studies, Massachusetts Institute of Technology, 1969–1971. Editor, *Foreign Affairs*, 1972–1984. Retired, teaches occasionally at Princeton University.

Burger, Warren E. Chief Justice of the United States, 1969–1986; appointed by Nixon. Voted in favor of Nixon administration's effort to stop publication of Pentagon Papers. On leaving the Supreme Court, became chairman of the Commission on the Bicentennial of the Constitution, 1987.

Buzhardt, J. Fred. Served in Pentagon as general counsel to Melvin Laird. Brought into White House by Nixon in May 1973, as special counsel on Watergate problems. Called "keeper of the tapes," confirmed to Watergate committee that Nixon had tape-recorded talks since spring of 1971. Twice interrogated by Senate Watergate investigators about Nixon campaign contributions from Howard Hughes. Died December 16, 1978, at age 54.

[318]

Byrne, William Matthew, Jr. Judge, U.S. District Court, Los Angeles, 1971–present; appointed by Nixon. Presided over Ellsberg's trial on espionage and theft charges. Considered for FBI directorship in 1973, but name was dropped after discovery that he met secretly with Nixon and Ehrlichman during Ellsberg trial.

Clark, Roger A. Washington representative of *Washington Post's* New York law firm during Pentagon Papers case. General counsel to Ronald Reagan's Presidential Inaugural Committee, 1980–1981. Practices law in Washington.

Clifford, Clark. President Johnson's Secretary of Defense during completion of the Pentagon Papers study. From the time he came to Washington in 1945 from St. Louis, was involved in major foreign policy decisions in Truman, Kennedy, and Johnson administrations. Practices law in Washington and remains a senior Democratic Party statesman.

Douglas, William O. Associate Justice of U.S. Supreme Court, 1939–1975; appointed by Franklin D. Roosevelt. Voted in favor of publication of Pentagon Papers. Had stroke and retired in 1975, replaced by Ford appointee John Paul Stevens. Died Jan. 19, 1980, at age 81.

Ehrlichman, John. Chief domestic adviser to President Nixon, claimed newspapers were sharing the Pentagon Papers to frustrate the administration's legal maneuvers. Convicted of conspiracy and perjury in connection with break-in at Ellsberg's psychiatrist's office. Served 18 months of 2½- to 5-year sentence before being released in April 1978. Divorced his first wife, grew a beard, and moved to Santa Fe, New Mexico, to write. Remarried in 1978. Now a novelist, whose first book, *The Company*, sold more than a million copies and became a TV series.

Ellsberg, Daniel. Leaked Pentagon Papers. Now a peace activist, has been arrested several times near nuclear installations and government offices, as well as during protests against U.S. policy in Central America. Remains an expert in field of nuclear strategy, serves on strategy task force of Nuclear Weapons Freeze Campaign. Lives in Kensington, California. Son Robert is editor-in-chief of Maryknoll Missions' Orbis Press; daughter Mary, married to Sandinista official, does public health work for Nicaraguan government. Son Michael, from second marriage, is 11 years old.

Ferguson, Warren. Handled government contempt case against Anthony Russo and released him from jail. U.S. District Judge, Los Angeles, 1966–1979; judge, U.S. Court of Appeals for Ninth Circuit, 1979–present; appointed by Johnson, elevated by Carter. Took senior status in 1986.

Frankel, Max. Washington Bureau Chief for *New York Times* during Pentagon Papers case. Editorial page editor, 1977–1986, when he replaced Rosenthal as executive editor.

Fulbright, J. William. Democratic senator from Arkansas, 1945–1975, chairman of the Senate Foreign Relations Committee during Pentagon Papers case. Became committed to American withdrawal from Vietnam, tried to get official copy of the Pentagon Papers, Laird refused request. Defeated in 1974 Arkansas Democratic Senate primary by Governor Dale L. Bumpers. Practices law in Washington, D.C.

Gelb, Leslie H. Supervisor of the team that wrote the Pentagon Papers. Went to work for *New York Times* in 1973, returned to government during Carter administration. *Times* national security correspondent, 1981–1986; deputy editorial page editor since 1986.

Gesell, Gerhard A. Judge in Justice Department's suit against *Washington Post.* Ruled in favor of publication of Pentagon Papers and declined even temporary stay. Judge, U.S. District Court, Washington, D.C., 1967–present; appointed by Johnson. Presided over Fielding break-in conspiracy trial and other Watergate-related cases. Judge in 1988 criminal case arising out of illegal U.S. arms sales to Iran and diversion of funds to Nicaraguan rebels.

Glendon, William R. Argued for *Washington Post* before Supreme Court, as senior New York partner in Clark's law firm. Practiced law until 1985, when he became mayor of Scarsdale, New York.

Goodale, James C. Head of *New York Times* legal department during Pentagon Papers case. Moved through ranks to become New York Times Company vice chariman in 1979. In private law practice since 1980.

Graham, Katherine. Publisher of *Washington Post* during Pentagon Papers case. Now Chairman of the Board, Washington Post Company.

Gravel, Maurice R. ("Mike") Tearfully read parts of the Pentagon Papers during Senate hearing. Democratic senator from Alaska, 1969–1981. Defeated in 1980 democratic Senate primary by Clark Gruening. Involved in real estate in Washington, D.C., 1981–1987. Private consultant in government affairs, Pebble Beach, California, 1987–present.

Greenfield, James L. New York Times foreign editor during Pentagon Papers case. Became assistant managing editor in 1977, now editor of *New York Times Magazine.*

Griswold, Erwin N. Represented government before Supreme Court in Pentagon Papers case. Former dean, Harvard Law School. Solicitor General of the United States, 1967–1973. Practices law in Washington.

Gurfein, Murray I. As a new U.S. District Judge, issued unprecedented restraining order on publication of Pentagon Papers in *New York Times.* Judge, U.S. District Court, New York, 1971–1974; judge, U.S. Court of Appeals for Second Circuit, 1974–1979; appointed by Nixon, elevated by Ford. Died Dec. 16, 1979, at age 72.

Hannon, Joseph M. As chief of the Civil Division in U.S. Attorney's office for the District of Columbia, started government attack on *Washington Post* in Pentagon Papers case. D.C. Superior Court Judge, appointed by Nixon July 1972; reappointed in 1987, despite having been publicly reprimanded by Judicial Tenure Commission for joining in "March for

[321]

Life" demonstration protesting 1973 Supreme Court decision legalizing abortion.

Harlan, John M. Associate Justice of U.S. Supreme Court, 1954–1971; appointed by Eisenhower. Voted in favor of Nixon administration's effort to block publication of the Pentagon Papers. Resigned 1971, died Dec. 29, 1971, at age 72. Replaced by Nixon appointee William Rehnquist.

Helms, Richard M. Director of Central Intelligence, 1965–1973; Ambassador to Iran, 1973–1976. President of Saffer Company, Washington, D.C., international consultants, 1977–present.

Humphrey, Hubert H., Jr. Vice president of the United States, 1965–1969. Elected to Senate in 1948, made unsuccessful bid for 1960 Democratic presidential nomination. Taught briefly at University of Minnesota after being defeated by Nixon in 1968 presidential election. Returned to Senate, 1970–1978. Died Jan. 13, 1978, at age 66.

Johnson, Lyndon B. President of the United States, 1963–1969. Author of *The Choices We Face* (1968) and *The Vantage Point* (1971). Died January 22, 1973, at age 61.

Kaufman, Irving R. Judge, U.S. District Court, New York, 1949–1961; judge, U.S. Court of Appeals for Second Circuit, 1961–present; appointed by Truman, elevated by Kennedy. Chief judge, 1973–1980; took senior status in 1987. Presided over 1951 espionage trial of Julius and Ethel Rosenberg in which defendants were sentenced to death.

Kleindienst, Richard G. Sent private message to *Washington Post* publisher Katherine Graham urging her not to publish certain parts of the Pentagon Papers. Arizona conservative who ran Barry Goldwater's unsuccessful 1964 campaign for president. Deputy Attorney General, 1969–1972; Attorney General, 1972–1973; resigned April 30, 1973. First cabinet-level officer convicted on Watergate-related matters—on a misdemeanor charge of refusing to testify before Congress; given $100 fine and 32-day sentence, suspended, June 1974.

Suspended for one year from law practice in Arizona for unethical conduct in 1976 insurance company fraud. Reinstated July 1983; now practices in Tucson. Author of *Justice: The Memoirs of Attorney General Richard Kleindienst* (1985).

Kissinger, Henry A. Assistant to President for National Security Affairs, 1969–1975; Secretary of State, 1973–1977. Consultant and commentator on international issues, 1977–present. Recent books include *For the Record* (1981) and *Years of Upheaval* (1982).

Laird, Melvin. Refused to release Pentagon Papers to Fulbright. Secretary of Defense, 1969–1972; domestic adviser to President Nixon, 1973–1974; senior counsellor, national and international affairs, Reader's Digest Association, 1974–present.

McCloskey, Paul N. ("Pete"). Republican House member from California, 1967–1983. Lost 1982 bid for Senate to San Diego Mayor Pete Wilson in Republican primary. Practices law in California's Silicon Valley.

McNamara, Robert S. Ordered study of U.S. involvement in Vietnam in 1967. Secretary of Defense, 1961–1968; president of World Bank, 1968–1981. Retired, lives in Washington.

Mansfield, Mike. Democratic senator from Montana, 1953–1977; Senate majority leader, 1961–1977. After assassination of Ngo Dinh Diem in 1963, became an outspoken critic of American involvement in Vietnam. U.S. ambassador to Japan, 1977–1988.

Marder, Murrey. Washington Post diplomatic correspondent, wrote on Pentagon Papers. Chief diplomatic correspondent, 1971–1985. Retired, lives in Washington.

Mardian, Robert C. Chief of Justice Department's Internal Security Division, sent telegram with John Mitchell asking *New York Times* to cease publication of the Pentagon Papers voluntarily. Convicted on basic Watergate conspiracy charge of obstructing justice; conviction reversed, case never retried. Suspended from D.C. and Supreme Court bar in 1975. Reinstated to California bar in 1976, practices law in Phoenix, Arizona.

Marshall, Thurgood. Associate Justice of U.S. Supreme Court, 1967–present; appointed by Johnson. Voted in favor of publication of Pentagon Papers.

Mitchell, John N. U.S. Attorney General, 1969–1972. Sentenced by Judge John Sirica to 2½ to 8 years for Watergate involvement. Served 19 months without ever criticizing Nixon publicly. Disbarred from New York and Supreme Court practice. Civil suit filed in 1976 by former National Security Council aide Morton H. Halperin alleging Mitchell's involvement in illegal wiretapping remains unresolved. In 1981 repaid $50,000 advance from Simon and Schuster for his projected memoirs, which he never completed. Private consultant for domestic and international trade, Washington, D.C., 1979–1988. Died November 9, 1988, at age 75.

Nixon, Richard M. President of the United States, 1969–1974. Resigned during impeachment proceedings related to Watergate scandal, August 8, 1974. Has since written many books, including *RN* (1978), *The Real War* (1980), *Leaders* (1982), *Real Peace* (1984), and *No More Vietnams* (1985).

Patterson, Eugene C. Editor, Atlanta *Constitution*, 1960–1968. Managing editor, *Washington Post*, 1968–1971. Professor of political science, Duke University, 1971–1972. Editor and president, *St. Petersburg* (Florida) *Times, Congressional Quarterly*, 1971–1984; chairman and chief executive officer, 1978–1988. Retired.

Rehnquist, William H. Assistant Attorney General in charge of Justice Department's Office of Legal Counsel during Nixon administration. Associate Justice of the Supreme Court, 1971–1986; appointed by Nixon. Chief Justice, 1986–present; appointed by Reagan to replace Burger.

Reston, James. *New York Times* columnist, received medal of honor in 1986, wrote his last regular op-ed page column August 2, 1987, but continues to contribute.

Robb, Roger. Judge on U.S. Court of Appeals (Washington, D.C.); appointed by Nixon. Voted to prohibit *Washington Post* from publishing Pentagon Papers. Died Dec. 19, 1985, at age 78.

Roberts, Chalmers M. Staff writer, *Washington Post*, 1949–1971. Columnist, *San Diego Union*, 1977–1986. Author of *First Rough Draft: A Journalist's Journal of Our Times* (1973) and *The Washington Post: The First 100 Years* (1977). Retired, lives in Washington.

Robinson, Spottswood W. III. Judge, U.S. District Court for the District of Columbia, 1964–1966; judge, U.S. Court of Appeals for D.C. Circuit, 1966–present; Chief Judge, 1981–1986; appointed by Johnson.

Rodberg, Leonard S. Fellow at Institute for Policy Studies in Washington, D.C., became member of Gravel's staff before Gravel's attempted filibuster to put Pentagon Papers into public record. Professor of Urban Studies, Queens College, City University of New York, 1981–present.

Rosenthal, Abraham M. Managing editor, *New York Times*, 1969–1977; executive editor, 1977–1986. Columnist, 1986–present.

Rowen, Henry S. President of Rand Corporation during Pentagon Papers case. Chair, National Intelligence Council, Central Intelligence Agency, 1981–1983. Currently professor at Stanford University's Graduate School of Business, Senior Fellow at Hoover Institution.

Rusk, Dean. Secretary of State, 1961–1969; Sibley Professor, International Law, University of Georgia, 1970–present.

Russo, Anthony J., Jr. Former Rand Corporation employee, friend of Ellsberg from Vietnam. Urged his girlfriend, Lynda Sinay, to rent her advertising agency's copy machine to Ellsberg to photocopy the Pentagon Papers. Began work as consultant in Los Angeles County Health Department's alcoholism program in 1975. Peace activist involved in antiwar organizing, speaking, and writing since retirement in 1983.

Lives in Santa Monica, California.

Seymour, Whitney North, Jr. U.S. Attorney, Southern District of New York, 1970–1973. Practices law in New York City. Author of *Why Justice Fails* (1973), *United States Attorney* (1975), *Making a Difference* (1984). Served as special prosecutor in perjury case against former Reagan aide Michael Deaver, 1988.

Sheehan, Neil. His "investigative reporting" was credited as basis for obtaining Pentagon Papers. Reporter for *New York Times*, 1964–1972. Winner of numerous awards for excellence in reporting. Author of *A Bright Shining Lie: John Paul Vann and America in Vietnam* (1988), which took sixteen years to write.

Sinay, Lynda. Russo's girlfriend who rented her advertising agency's copy machine to Ellsberg to duplicate parts of the Pentagon Papers. In 1972 married Stewart Resnick, owner and chairman of American Protection Industries, a network of luxury products and services based in Los Angeles, whose subsidiaries include The Franklin Mint and Teleflora. Lynda Resnick co-owns API and became executive vice-president of The Franklin Mint in March 1985.

Sirica, John J. U.S. District Judge, 1957–1986. Chief Judge, 1971–1974; appointed by Eisenhower. Sentenced John Mitchell to prison term for his role in Watergate cover-up. *Time* magazine Man of the Year, 1973. Took senior status in 1977, retired in 1986. Author of *To Set the Record Straight* (1979).

Stewart, Potter. Associate Justice of U.S. Supreme Court, 1959–1981; appointed by Eisenhower. Voted in favor of publication of the Pentagon Papers. Retired in 1981, died Dec. 8, 1985, at age 70. Replaced by Reagan appointee Sandra Day O'Connor.

Sulzberger, Arthur Ochs. *New York Times* publisher, 1963–present.

Warnke, Paul C. Assistant Secretary of Defense for International Security Affairs, 1967–1969; director, Arms Control and Disarmament Agency, 1977–1978; Chief Arms Control Negotiator, 1977–1978. Special counsel to Secretary of State, 1978–1981. Partner, Clifford and Warnke, Washington, D.C., 1978–present.

White, Byron R. Associate Justice of U.S. Supreme Court, 1962–present; appointed by Kennedy. Voted in favor of publication of the Pentagon Papers.

Wright, J. Skelly. Judge, U.S. District Court, New Orleans, 1949–1962. Judge, U.S. Court of Appeals for the D.C. Circuit, 1962–1968; Chief Judge, 1978–1981; appointed by Truman, elevated by Kennedy. Called it "a sad day for America" when publication of Pentagon Papers was temporarily restrained. Died Aug. 6, 1988, at age 77.

Ziegler, Ronald L. Press Secretary to Richard Nixon, 1969–1974; assistant to President, 1973–1974. Stayed with Nixon after his resignation until 1975. President, National Association of Truck Stop Operators, 1980–present.

[INDEX]

Bangladesh, 305
Bantam Books, 268-269, 301-302
Barnet, Richard J., 131
Barry, Richard J., 285
Bartlett, Dan, 189
Battle of Midway, 112
Bay of Pigs invasion, 99
Bayh, Birch, 266
Bazelon, David L., 202, 204, 205, 207-208
Beacon Press, 269-270, 286, 291-292, 311
Beatty, Mary Lou, 250
Beebe, Frederick R., 138, 140, 141, 144-146, 157, 160
Beecher, William, 126-127, 295
Bernstein, Carl, 309
Best, Richard, 57
Bickel, Alexander, 123-124, 125, 137, 164, 166, 169, 195, 197, 198-199, 206, 209, 306; appearance before Supreme Court, 224-227, 228, 235-236, 245. *See also* prior restraint
Bien Hoa airfield, Viet Cong attack on, 34
Bill of Rights, 243, 244. *See also* First Amendment
Binford, Sally, 289
Bingham, Dana, and Gould, 181
Black, Hugo L., 211-212, 226, 234, 237, 243-244, 247-248, 304
Black Panther Party, 86, 117, 286
Blackmun, Harry A., 212, 232, 234
Blouin, Francis J., 166
Boggs, J. Caleb, 261
Bohlen, Charles, 11
"Bosbin," 177-178, 180
Boston grand jury investigation at, 280-291, 300
Boston After Dark, 279
Boston *Globe*, 84, 95, 175-182, 184, 189, 203, 251-252; Ellsberg and, 175-180
Boudin, Leonard, 240
Bradlee, Benjamin, 131, 134, 138, 142, 163, 172, 203, 214, 251, 298, 304, 312; and legal questions on PP, 143, 145, 146-147, 150, 152-153
Brennan, William J., Jr., 212, 235, 245
broadcasting: "chilling effect" on, 117; reaction to PP, 186
Brookings Institution, 22, 31, 54
Browne, Malcolm, 87
Brownell, Herbert, 97, 98, 123
Bryan, Albert V., Jr., 311
Buckley, James L., 71, 165, 296
Buckley, William F., Jr., 295-296

Bundy, McGeorge, 21, 132, 172
Bundy, William P., 21, 34, 35-36, 37, 40, 41, 62
Burch, Dean, 129
Burger, Warren E., 113, 118, 162-163, 170, 195, 207-208, 212, 223, 232-234, 238, 242, 248-249; dislike of press, 233-234, 236-237. *See also* prior restraint
Business Executives Move for Vietnam Peace (BEM), 60-61, 276
busing, constitutionality of, 162
Butler, Jan, 57
Butterfield, Fox, 95
Buzhardt, J. Fred, 109-110, 291, 292
Byrd, Robert C., 259, 260, 264
Byrne, William M. (Matt), 7-10, 274-275, 288, 299

Cahill, Gordon, Sonnett, Reindel and Ohl, 123, 124, 306
Cairncross, Frances, 27
Caldwell, Earl, 86, 123, 196, 226, 285, 286
Califano, Joseph A., Jr., 306
Cambodia, invasion of, 73-74, 119, 254, 255
Canham, Erwin D., 190
Carnegie Endowment for International Peace, 54, 57
Carswell, G. Harrold, 232
Carter, Jimmy, administration of, 312
Carter, Stan, 15
Casey, William, 313
Castro, Fidel, 6
CBS, *see* Columbia Broadcasting Company
casualties, *see* Vietnam War
censorship, prior restraint as, 125, 230, 231, 238
Center for Constitutional Rights, 284
Center magazine, 129
Central Intelligence Agency (CIA), 21, 34-35, 99, 151, 165, 314; advice on U.S. policy, 56, 185; contribution to PP, 29-30; and Ellsberg profile, 5; and Fielding burglary, 6; secrecy agreements, 311, 312; study of bombing, 25
Chicago *Sun-Times*, 183-185, 191, 192
Chicago *Tribune*, 17, 111-112, 140, 159, 184
Chiles, Lawton, 128
"chilling effect," *see* broadcasting
China, 34, 110-111, 271-272, 307

209; Justice Department and, 170, 195, 201, 298; response to ruling by, 160, 161; and suit by Congressmen, 302

Geyelin, Philip L., 132, 138, 143, 145

Gifford, K. Dun, 288

Gladstein, Harry, 139, 145

Glendon, William R., 146, 171, 172, 202, 219-220, 228-229, 237

Gold, Gerald, 90, 91, 95

Goldwater, Barry, 129, 253, 263

Goodale, James C., 98-99, 101-103, 120-121, 122-123, 169-170, 251

Goodell, Charles, 67, 71-72

Goodman, Julian, 129

Gorman, Paul F., 22

Graham, Fred P., 127

Graham, Katharine, 11-12, 15, 115, 138, 140, 145-156, 147, 153, 157, 251, 297-299

grand jury investigations, *see* Pentagon Papers

Gravel, Maurice Robert (Mike), 37, 253-270, 283-284, 311; Ellsberg and, 255-256, 258, 262, 300

Greenfield, James L., 90, 93, 96, 97, 102, 105

Greenfield, Meg, 138, 143

Grenada, 313

Griffin, Robert, 260

Griswold, Erwin N., 118, 119, 199-202, 210-212, 221-223, 224, 234-235, 237

Gruening, Ernest, 253-254

Gruson, Sydney, 90, 95, 121

Gulf of Tonkin incidents, 13, 46, 75, 87-88, 204

Gulf of Tonkin resolution, 33, 68, 76

Gurfein, Murray I., 124-125, 127, 137, 151-152, 157, 164, 165-166, 170, 171, 172, 194-195, 196, 197, 198, 205, 207, 210, 230, 247, 274; on freedom of press, 168-169, 316

Gurtov, Melvin, 22, 58, 60, 289

Hagen, Everett E., 62

Hagerty, James, 129

Halberstam, David, 77, 87, 88, 288

Halperin, Morton H., 16, 22, 29, 56, 84, 175

Hamill, Pete, 137

Hannon, Joseph M., 153, 155

Harlan, John M., 212, 234, 235, 247, 304

Harper's magazine, 77

Harriman, W. Averell, 22

Harrisburg conspiracy trial, 286, 287

Hart, George L., Jr., 118-119

Hartke, Vance, 91, 261

Harvard *Crimson*, 43-44, 176

Harvard Law School, 227

Harvard University, 22, 23, 42n, 279; Ellsberg and, 43-45, 47-48, 52, 53; Kennedy Institute of Politics, 24

Harvard University Press, 269

Hatfield, Mark, 61, 71

Haydock, Robert, 181

Haynsworth, Clement F., Jr., 232, 254

Hays, Paul R., 205

Hebert, F. Edward, 292

Helms, Richard, 25

Hess, Michael D., 124-125, 164

Heymann, Hans, 22

Hills, Lee, 188

Hilsman, Roger, 94, 182, 183

Hinckle, Warren III, 137

Ho Chi Minh, 32

Hoeffding, Oleg, 58

Hoge, James F., Jr., 182-183, 186, 307

Holbrooke, Richard, 22, 279

Holmes, Oliver Wendell, 224

Holum, John, 82

Horelick, Arnold L., 58

Hoover, J. Edgar, 4, 9, 208

House of Representatives, 36; Armed Services Committee, 59, 206, 240, 292; Foreign Operations and Government Information Subcommittee, 92, 219, 253; Interstate and Foreign Commerce Committee, 117; PP delivered to, 241

Hughes, Charles Evans, 112-113, 158, 194, 248

Hughes, Harold E., 262

Humphrey, Hubert H., 18

Hunt, E. Howard, Jr., 5

Hustler, 313

Ignatius, Paul, 145

immunity: congressional, 257, 263, 266, 267, 284-285, 290-291; in grand jury proceedings, 282

infiltration, *see* North Vietnam

Institute for Defense Analyses, 22, 68, 75

Institute for Policy Studies, 76, 89, 131, 267, 283

Israel, 315

"Issues and Answers," 18

[333]

[335]

tion revealed by, 35; shortcomings of, 38; slow initial reaction to, 16-18, 108. *See also* Boston *Globe;* Ellsberg, Daniel; Gelb, Leslie; *New York Times;* policymaking; Sheehan, Neil; Sulzberger; Supreme Court; *Washington Post*

Pentagon Watchers (Rodberg), 268

Petacque, Art, 185

plumbers, 3-6, 8

policymaking, U.S., 46-47, 65-66; Ellsberg and, 55-56, 75-76, 80-81, 135-138, 301; Gravel on, 37; Orwellian vocabulary of, 36-37; media and, 310, 315; PP and, 39-40, 70, 310; and withdrawal option, 55-56

Pollard, Anne Henderson, 315

Pollard, Jonathan, 315

Popkin, Sam, 279, 283-284, 287

Porter, William, 49

Portland *Oregonian*, 17

Powell, Lewis F., 304

Powers, Francis Gary, 99

Powledge, Fred, 116-117

"presidential papers," as perspective on history, 39

press, 310*n*, 315; confrontation with government, 3, 4, 193, 250, 304-307, 310, 313, 314; freedom of, 149, 206, 230-231, 244, 316; harassment by, 186; significance of Supreme Court decision for, 303-304. *See also* First Amendment; prior restraint

Princeton University, 91

Princi, Peter, 241

prior restraint, question of, 102, 161, 174, 238, 246-247; Bickel on, 125, 209-210, 229-230, 235-236; Burger on, 113, 248-249; Douglas on, 244; Gesell on, 158; government arguments on, 166, 193-195, 228; Gurfein on, 168-169; Justice Department spokesman on, 304; Marchetti case, 312

prisoners of war, 4; PP and, 248, 303

Progressive, 312

Public Policy, 79

Radio broadcasting, 186

Rand Corporation, 15, 54, 63-64, 66, 133; Ellsberg and, 4, 29, 45-46, 53, 55, 56-57, 61, 240, 276, 293-294, 300; dissidents within, 57-58, 289; as DOD repository, 40; security regu-

lations, 63-65, 293-294; staff members and PP, 22, 133

Randolph, Jennings, 264-265

Raskin, Marcus G., 131

Reagan, Ronald, administration of, 313, 315

Reese, Warren P., 285, 291

Rehnquist, William H., 108-109, 152-153, 304

Reid, Ogden R., 302

religious freedom, First Amendment guarantee of, 291

Reporter, 48

Republican party, 11, 62, 72, 91, 107, 114, 126, 255, 266; and PP, 110, 272

Reston, James, 15, 89-90, 93, 99-100, 104

Rich, Frank, 45

Rich, Spencer, 162-163

Richardson, Elliot, 41

Robb, Roger, 159, 160, 203, 208

Roberts, Chalmers M., 15, 131-132, 138, 141, 142, 144-145, 146, 147, 150, 155, 172

Robinson, Spottswood W., III, 159, 160, 208

Rockefeller, Nelson, 22

Rodberg, Leonard S., 267-269, 283-284, 287, 290, 292

Rogers, Richard, 105

Rogers, William P., 138, 155, 298

Rosenthal, A. M., 88-89, 93-94, 96, 102, 104-105, 106, 121, 122, 148, 149, 150, 214, 251

Ross, Thomas, 183

Rowen, Henry, 15, 53, 58, 276, 293-294

Royall, Koegell, and Wells, 138, 171, 306

Rusk, Dean, 25, 29, 130, 187

Russo, Anthony, 6-10, 48, 53, 66-67, 107, 108, 273-274, 289-290, 299

sabotage, U.S., against North Vietnam, 32

Saigon, U.S. Embassy in, 39, 56

St. Louis *Post-Dispatch*, 136, 188-190, 191-192, 252

Salant, Richard, 117

Saturday Review, 277

Schlesinger, Arthur, Jr., 79, 94, 277

Schorr, Dan, 305

Schrag, Peter, 9*n*, 277

Schwarz, Daniel, 103

Schwarz, John, 105

Scott, Hugh, 152, 264

Scranton, William, 275

[ABOUT THE AUTHOR]

34
48

Sanford J. Ungar is Dean of the School of Communication at American University in Washington, D.C. From 1971 to 1973 he covered the court cases involving the Pentagon Papers for *The Washington Post*. He is the author of *FBI: An Uncensored Look Behind the Walls, Africa: The People and Politics of an Emerging Continent,* and articles appearing in *The Atlantic, The New York Times Magazine, Esquire, The Economist,* and many other publications. For several years Sanford Ungar was the host of "All Things Considered" and other programs on National Public Radio. He has also been the guest host of "The CBS Night Watch" and has appeared on numerous public, commercial, and cable television programs.